ARTHUR WELLARD

No mere slogger

ARTHUR WELLARD

No mere slogger

BARRY PHILLIPS

LEISURESOLVE LIMITED:OXFORD

Leisuresolve Limited
13 Hawthorn Avenue,Headington,Oxford OX3 9JQ
Tel/Fax 01865-60139

First Published 1996

ISBN 0 9528775 0 3

Printed and bound in Great Britain by
Mayfield Press (Oxford) Ltd
Ferry Hinksey Road, Oxford OX2 0DP

To Mum, sadly missed; Wendy, Gayle, Lucy and Matthew with much love

Contents

List of illustrations

Photographic credits: The author and publisher would like to thank Betty Thurston-Moon and Ennyd Andrews for providing the majority of photographs used in this book. Copyright photographs are from the Hulton Getty Picture Collection Ltd., Sport & General Press Agency, Bath & Wilts Chronicle, Weston and Somerset Mercury, Eastbourne Gazette, Bristol Evening Post and Albert Wilkes & Son.

Foreword
by Harold Pinter

IN JULY 1974 GAIETIES C.C. was engaged in an excruciatingly
tense contest with Banstead. We had bowled Banstead out for
175 and had not regarded the task ahead as particularly
daunting. However, we had made a terrible mess of it and
when our ninth wicket fell still needed five runs to win.
That we were so close was entirely due to our opening
batsman, Robert East, who at that point was ninety-six not
out. The light was appalling. our last man was Arthur
Wellard, then aged seventy-two. He wasn't at all happy
about the reigning state of affairs. He had castigated us
throughout the innings for our wretched performance and now
objected strongly to the fact that he was compelled to bat.
'I can't see the bloody wicket from here, how do you expect
me to see the bloody ball?' As a rider, his rheumatism was
killing him (He had bowled eighteen overs for twenty-nine
runs in the Banstead innings). He lumbered out to the
wicket, cursing.

Banstead were never a sentimental crowd. The sight of
an old man taking guard in no way softened their intent.
Their quickie had two balls left to complete the over. He
bowled them, they were pretty quick, and Arthur let both go
by outside the off-stump, his bat raised high. Whether he
let them go, or whether he didn't see them, was a question
of some debate, but something told us that he had seen
them, clearly, and allowed them to pass.

East drove the first ball of the next over straight
for four, bringing up his hundred and leaving us with one
run to win. The next five balls were clear singles for the
asking but Arthur in each case declined the invitation,
with an uplifted hand. He was past the age, his hand
asserted when running singles was anything else but a mug's
game.

So Arthur prepared to face what we knew had to be the last over, with one run to win. The Gaieties side, to a man, stood, smoked, walked in circles outside the pavilion, peering out at the pitch through the gloom. It appeared to be night, but we could discern Arthur standing erect, waiting for the ball. The quickie raced in and bowled. We saw Arthur's left leg go down the wicket, the bat sweep, and were suddenly aware that the ball had gone miles, in the long-on area, over the boundary for four. We had won.

In the bar he pronounce himself well pleased. 'No trouble,' he said. 'He tried to get me with a yorker. Where's the boy who made the ton? He did well. Tell him he can buy me a pint.'

It was an honour to know Arthur and I shall always remember with some amazement that I actually played cricket with him. We became quite close. I think he decided I wasn't such a bad bloke - for a writer - and for a man of modest cricketing abilities. One day he said to me: 'I've brought something for you.' It was his England cap. 'It's yours,' he said. 'Keep it.' It's on my shelf now.

HAROLD PINTER

Introduction and acknowledgements

The title of this book *No Mere Slogger* is taken from E.W.Swanton's introduction to Arthur Wellard's obituary notice published in *The Daily Telegraph*. Arthur could not have wished for a finer epitaph and it is not hard to imagine his reaction. He was laconic by nature and seldom demonstrative but he would have allowed himself a small expression of approval. It would have been accompanied by that familiar wry grin, which would spread slowly across the rugged features of his suntanned face. He was labelled a slogger because of the immense power of his hitting but, as Swanton astutely observed, there was so much more to Arthur's cricket.

Arthur was a little under six feet two inches tall, a powerfully built man with broad shoulders, huge forearms and enormous hands. Everything about Arthur was larger than life; the same could be said for his cricket. With Wellard batting, bowling or even fielding there could be no dullness and it was his sheer unpredictability that kept supporters on the edge of their seats. When Arthur came to the crease there was always a buzz of anticipation and a sense that something extraordinary was about to happen. The bars would empty and the fielders would scatter to all parts of the boundary. At Taunton, once he had played the first few balls with customary respect, nothing close to the ground was safe. His hits at Taunton are legendary. From the river end, he deposited countless balls into St. James' churchyard and would regularly despatch the ball over the old pavilion and into the car park behind. One such blow dropped by the main gates, a carry of 170 yards, where it bounced and clattered the roof tiles of the brewery on the opposite side of St. James' Street. He was equally as threatening from the pavilion end and loved to hear the splashing sound of the ball entering the river. If there was no splash it usually meant that the ball had soared over the river to the far bank or even further into Colthurst's timber yard, a minimum carry of 150 yards, never to be seen again.

He was essentially a front-foot player and rarely cut or hooked. One of his favourite shots was a pull-drive in the direction of long-on, the delivery being on or outside the off-stump. However, his sixes were more often than not driven straight with seemingly little effort and only a token backlift. Bill Edrich called him the ideal model for a hitter because he always aimed the bat straight down the line of the ball. Anything pitched up was driven in the certain knowledge that it would carry the boundary. He was very partial to slow left-armers but he treated the bowlers alike and even the great Harold Larwood had to suffer the indignity of being carted out of the ground. He was particularly effective on the small Somerset grounds but it is worth noting that all his best scores were made on grounds away from the West Country. His favourite was the Oval where the fielders had a hopeless task of covering the boundary arc between long-off and long-on.

Arthur hit 561 sixes in his first-class career, a truly incredible number. No other cricketer in the history of the first-class game has hit so many, with the probable exception of Gilbert Jessop who played at a time when a six was awarded only if the ball left the ground. A good proportion of Arthur's sixes went out of the ground and this biography will prove that no-one has consistently hit the distances that Arthur achieved. Most of the Wellard legendary blows have been traced and it is pleasing to confirm that the spectacular distances attributed to some of his hits have not increased in the telling and are not the products of fertile minds.

Arthur was a naturally gifted fielder with great courage, lightning reactions and an eagle eye. He would field in any position close to the bat but was especially effective at silly point and silly mid-off particularly to J.C.White's bowling. It was a common sight to see him threatening to run out the batsman who would often need to leave his crease to play White's well-flighted deliveries. Arthur, with his huge safe hands, regularly took breathtaking catches in such positions and there were 375 catches in total during his first-class career.

To dwell too long on his batting and fielding exploits

would do a great injustice to his bowling. It was this part of his game that provided the most valuable contribution to Somerset cricket. He had the natural attributes of a fast bowler and boundless reserves of stamina. He bowled off about thirteen paces and his action was both fluent and economical so that he never appeared to tire. The characteristic leap in the air during the delivery stride and his massive upper-body strength enabled him to bowl with deceptive pace. He would get considerable movement off the pitch and his outswinger would keep the slip cordon constantly on their toes. It was a pity that most of the Somerset close fielders were not up to the job. His simple wish was to bowl all day. Even when conditions clearly did not suit, he would persuade his skipper otherwise. Later in his career, when he was able to alternate between pace and off-spin, the task of getting the ball off him became even more difficult. Arthur took over 1500 wickets for his adopted county in a career that spanned four decades. The total is second only to J.C.White in Somerset history.

Arthur was often a lone combatant for Somerset, which usually inspired him into more belligerent and spectacular all-round performances. It was this tenacious spirit that endeared him most to the Somerset public and made him every schoolboy's hero. He was worshipped by two generations of supporters and his influence prevailed long after he had returned to the South East as tales of his cricketing deeds were passed on to a third generation by fathers, uncles and friends. It is fifty-six years since he played his last game for Somerset yet his name is still revered - more so than our latter-day heroes - and the mere mention of his name is guaranteed to bring a wistful smile to the faces of those fortunate to have known him or seen him play.

In the course of researching Arthur's life it was impossible to find anyone who was less than fulsome in their praises. He was universally liked and had very few critics. In several interviews he was referred to as a 'man's man'; a quaint but fitting description. If there were to be any criticism, it would be for his total lack of ambition and drive. He had no goals in life except to play cricket for as long as possible, which is precisely what he did, still playing well into his seventies. His pleasures were simple and he was rarely troubled by the normal cares and woes of life. He never drove a car in his life and never had a permanent job which didn't involve playing cricket. His simple lifestyle hardly provides the raw material for a biography of great intrigue. However, his story is told lest the Somerset public forget his immense contribution to the history and character of Somerset County Cricket.

The biography makes no apologies for over-estimating his importance. He may have been a large fish in a small pond but who can tell what he might have achieved had he played for a 'fashionable' county. It is clear that Arthur did not fully capitalise on his considerable talents. He did not always have luck on his side but human fallibility was as much to blame for limiting his achievements. It says much about Arthur, an inveterate gambler, that he had no regrets about the cards dealt him in life.

I would like to thank the staff of the Somerset and Oxfordshire Library Services and I am especially grateful to Betty and Fred Thurston-Moon without whom this book would have been impossible to complete. Others who have generously given their time and shared their recollections are acknowledged in alphabetical order as follows: Ennyd Andrews, Leslie Angell, Peter Atkins, Brian Austin, Jim Beard, Alec Bedser, Don Bennett, Ray Brock, Gerald Brodribb, Jack Burrell, D.G.Burridge, John Cameron, Ray Clavey, Len Creed, Robert East, Derek Fenner, David Frith, Huw George, Alf Gover, Lawrence Hawkins, Eric Hill, Michael Hill, Roger Hill, Mr G.Jessop, Clifford Jiggens, Nigel Johns, Trevor Jones, George Langdale, Charlie Moore, Ken Ohlson, Harold Pinter, Peggy Sayers, Alan Scadding, Sir Harry Secombe CBE, Jim Sewter, Tony Sibley, Den Smith, Ernie Smith, Tony Stedall, Harold Stephenson, Jim Swanton, David Sydenham, Kenneth Thomas, Peter Thwaites, Joyce Treasure, Gerry Wells-Cole, Mike White, Arthur Young.

BJP
Oxford, October 1996.

1

Arthur's early years

THE VILLAGE OF SOUTHFLEET lies a couple of miles south of Gravesend in Kent. It is an old and historic village, mentioned in the Domesday Book as held by the Bishop of Rochester and having 25 villagers. It was built around a crossroads that links the small hamlets of Hook Green and Redstreet, providing wider access to Gravesend, Dartford and the Thames Estuary. Southfleet is less than a mile from the A2, which in earlier times had been the route of the Roman road Watling Street, linking the South East of England with London. The road provided access to large centres of population, which ensured prosperity for the village. The industrial and commercial areas of Gravesend have now encroached as far as the busy A2. Fortunately for Southfleet, the land to the south of the road is in the rural extremes of the District of Dartford. The village has consequently preserved its character and remains in sharp contrast to its urban neighbours.

At the heart of the village and clustered around the crossroads is the church, the village school and the local public house. St. Nicholas Church, constructed from stone and flint, was built in the 14th century and the public house, *The Ship Inn*, dates from about the same time. The village school, though not as old, has been educating children for almost four centuries. Despite the modern housing in the village, it is easy to picture how it would have looked when agriculture provided its main source of revenue. Farming is still much in evidence but few of today's villagers have to rely on the industry for their livelihood.

It was a different story a hundred years ago when about a thousand people lived in the village. Most of these people were connected with the cultivation of the surrounding countryside. Over the previous forty years the number of agricultural labourers in Kent had declined by a third as a result of improved farming techniques. Despite the decline, there was plenty of work on the farms and an agricultural labourer could expect earnings of at least seventeen shillings *[85p]* a week!

The guaranteed availability of work was the reason that Ernest Arthur Wellard found himself in Southfleet. Ernest was a native of nearby Farningham where he worked at various times as a gardener, a groom and a farm labourer. At one stage, he had been a gardener to Sir William Hart Dyke at nearby Lullingstone Castle. He moved to Southfleet in 1884, found work and met his future wife, a local girl named Amy Lydia Palmer. They married on Christmas Day 1886 at St. Nicholas Church, Southfleet. Ernest was thirty-two years old, Amy was ten years younger. They set up home in Southfleet and two years later Amy gave birth to their first child, Charles Ernest Wellard. Some six years later, on the 9th September 1895, they had a daughter, Dorothy Amy Wellard.

By the turn of the century, Amy and Ernest were living at 4 Thomas' Cottages, Southfleet, which is one of a tiny row of six identical terraced cottages situated about a mile from the village crossroads. The cottages were built in 1886 to house the agricultural workers who were employed at French's farm nearby. They were brick built with two rooms upstairs, two downstairs and a small scullery at the rear of the cottage. The accommodation was modern by the standards of the day and was ideal for the couple and their growing family.

Amy and Ernest had neither planned nor could afford another child. However, in the late summer of 1901, with Ernest Wellard now approaching his fiftieth birthday, Amy discovered that she was pregnant for a third time. ARTHUR WILLIAM WELLARD was born in the back bedroom of 4 Thomas' Cottages on the 8th April 1902. The mid-wife had no problem delivering Arthur, despite his size. Amy, although only a tiny woman, not five feet tall, had already given birth to two thirteen-pound babies and Arthur came into the world on the same mark.

Three years after Arthur was born, the Wellard family moved to 6 Brakefield Road, another small terraced cottage but closer to the centre of the village. The terrace is still known as the Black Lion Cottages, having been converted from an old barn that belonged to *The Black Lion* public house in neighbouring Red Street. The village with its surrounding countryside was an idyllic' setting for a young boy and Arthur's early childhood produced nothing but happy memories despite the family's poor circumstances.

Arthur attended the village school in Church Street named after its founder, Sir John Sedley and built in 1637. The school now educates children of primary school age but in Arthur's day it catered for children of all age groups. The school's Headmaster, Mr Stokes, would have had good cause to remember Arthur for he was not the easiest of children to handle. Arthur Young, started school the same time as Arthur and has lived all his ninety-four years in Southfleet. He remembers Arthur as a 'bit of a devil and a tearaway' who was constantly playing up the teachers. Even at this young age, he was described as swarthy, thick set and very strong for his tender years. The school had a hard job containing this boisterous, hyperactive child and Mr Stokes was probably relieved when the Wellard family left the village.

The school did offer one thing that would have appealed to Arthur had he remained in Southfleet. It ran a school cricket team that used a meadow at Court Lodge Farm, close to the school. The meadow is now planted with cherry trees but at that time was well appointed and had its own pavilion. Arthur's brother, Charles, had been a promising fast bowler and a key member of the school team but had left by the time Arthur joined the village school. Arthur would most likely have watched his brother play but had no recollection of these times when later questioned about his earliest encounters with cricket. They might, however, have subconsciously influenced his passion for the game that would later dominate his life.

Arthur would have undoubtedly progressed to the school team had the family remained in the village but in 1910, when Arthur was eight years old, the family moved to Bexley. The move was forced on the family because Ernest Wellard could no longer manage the physical demands of his job. Ernest was now sixty years old and the years of hard outdoor labour had taken their toll and left him struggling with the early symptoms of chronic rheumatoid arthritis. The family moved to Bexley, where Ernest took over the tenancy of a public house, *The Black Horse* in Albert Road, owned by Kidd's brewery of Dartford. The job of a publican hardly seems less demanding in a physical sense but Ernest could count on the support of his wife, Amy, who despite her small frame was a formidably strong woman. Ernest also had the support of Arthur's elder brother and sister, who were now past school age.

Arthur very quickly adapted to his new surroundings. Albert Road is only a short distance from Bexley High Street but in these days it was also close to woodlands and open countryside. His parents were busily engaged in running the public house so Arthur was left to his own devices for much of the time. Arthur loved the woods where he could run wild, shelter from adult attention and indulge a very young smoking habit. The habit was never broken and he remained an addicted heavy smoker all his life. His childhood nickname of 'Spider' was also acquired from playing in the woods; a reference to his prowess at climbing trees.

Arthur went to Old Bexley School and continued to regard school as an inconvenience. The teachers considered him a disruptive influence so were not disheartened by his sporadic attendance. The school could not offer Arthur anything to hold his attention although it might have been different if cricket had been on the curriculum. With his father's health declining and the increased pressures on the household, Arthur escaped parental discipline. His father's failing health was partly the cause of his truancy as he was increasingly needed to help run the public house. He left school at fourteen, like many of his generation, with no academic achievement and no idea of what he wanted to do in life. At this stage, it would not have occurred to him that he could earn a living as a sportsman. Although it was clear that he had exceptional sporting ability there had been no opportunity to take part in organised games.

Arthur left school in 1916 with the country in the grip of the First World War. Most young men were fighting in France so there would have been plenty of work opportunities for a strapping six-footer in obvious rude health. Arthur, however, was a naturally lazy person and throughout his working life would never have what might be described as a 'proper job'. He was content to drift along, helping his parents run *The Black Horse* and occasionally taking work as a casual labourer when the need arose. One of these jobs was in a factory where he was required to wield a 26lb hammer all day. It certainly helped to develop the already impressive physique, which would later make light work of wielding a heavy cricket bat. *[Arthur had his bats specially made at Surridge's factory near London Bridge. His bats weighed 2lb, 11 or 12 ounces, not heavy by modern standards, but appreciably heavier than the average for the day].*

With his elder brother away at the War and his father's health deteriorating rapidly, Arthur gradually took on responsibility for running the public house. His involvement with *The Black Horse* at this impressionable age would provide the foundation for his lifelong affinity with public houses and gambling. He loved nothing better than to sit with the regulars and was soon drawn to the card schools where he honed his skills as a cardplayer.

He also showed a preference for male company and had no apparent interest in the opposite sex. He was already well acquainted with his future wife, Jack Trengove, but the pair were not romantically linked at this stage in their lives. Jack had two brothers and Arthur spent much of his spare time with them, especially Cecil Trengove who had similar interests in sport, gambling and shooting. Cecil's uncle owned the nearby farm that specialised in grouse and pheasant shoots and it was here that Arthur first learnt to shoot. Arthur had exceptional hand-to-eye coordination and he quickly became an excellent marksman.

Arthur first became involved in organised sport when in his late teens and immediately showed himself to be a natural sportsman. He took up soccer and was encouraged to play in goal where his physique could be put to good advantage. Goalkeepers of Arthur's day did not receive the protection afforded to their modern counterparts but Arthur was more than capable of holding his own in the goalmouth mêlées. He used to dominate the penalty area and had all the necessary attributes needed of a goalkeeper. He had safe hands, was totally fearless and very agile, considering his size. Arthur played soccer for Kent and became Bexley's regular keeper throughout the Twenties, until cricket finally demanded all his attention. He was good enough to attract the interest of several league clubs, including West Ham United Football Club.

At about the same time as his interest in soccer began to blossom, Arthur became involved with the local cricket club. He joined Bexley Cricket Club at the age of nineteen, after being encouraged to come to pre-season nets by some of the regular players who frequented *The Black Horse*. He also received encouragement from Percy Waistell, the first X1 captain and later chairman of the club. Percy who was head of Reffells' brewery knew the Wellard family through the trade and suspected that Arthur might have some latent potential for cricket. Another Bexley first X1 cricketer paid Arthur's first year subscriptions such was the interest shown in him.

Arthur attended the practice evenings at Bexley's ground just off the Bexley High Street where his bowling in the nets quickly drew notice. After a few games in the second X1 - in which he went in at eleven and took a few wickets - he was promoted to the first X1. He made an instant impression and by June 1921, in his very first season of competitive cricket, he was picked to play for Bexley and District against Kent Club and Ground. Kent's team scored 198 but Arthur excelled himself when asked to bowl, finishing with six wickets for 21 runs against a side that included eight players with first-class experience. It seems incredible that, after such a fine performance, Kent failed to show any interest in this impressive teenager who was literally living on their doorstep. It would be several years before Kent County Cricket Club made a belated move in his direction.

It was not as if Arthur's bowling in the match against Kent Club and Ground had been a fluke. There were a number of outstanding performances during this first season, which should have indicated to the authorities that here was a player of exceptional promise. He took seven wickets in a match on two occasions and headed the Bexley bowling averages for 1921 with 59 wickets, taken at 8.9 runs apiece. Arthur's instant success was no less of a surprise to him than it had been to the club. Arthur had found something in which to excel and his enthusiasm for the game once kindled would never diminish.

During the next few seasons with Bexley he continued to take wickets. In 1923 he again topped the bowling averages with 74 wickets at 12 runs apiece. His batting technique also improved immeasurably, which gained him promotion in the batting order. His first major score came in 1924 in a remarkable match during Bexley Cricket Week. Bexley batted first and started badly. The first four batsmen were out for 56 runs and Arthur very soon found himself at the crease. In the next hour and a half he scored an undefeated 156 that including six sixes and fourteen fours and allowed Bexley to declare at 315 for eight wickets. The opposition's reply of 255 for nine wickets included a century from L.G.Crawley, the talented Cambridge Blue who played cricket for Worcestershire and Essex. Arthur's innings marked a very important step in his development as an all-rounder for Bexley. It also enabled him to head the Bexley batting averages in 1924 with an average of over 31 runs per innings.

Arthur maintained his progress as a batsman in 1925 and again topped the batting averages with 494 runs from 19 innings, averaging just under 30 runs per innings. He was by this stage, one of the best all-round club cricketers in Kent and his reputation as a hard-hitting batsman was growing. He would reserve his best performances for the next season but meanwhile there was still the family business to run.

Charles Wellard had returned to live at *The Black Horse*, having left the Army. Arthur's sister, Dorothy, also lived above the public house with her husband, Cecil Mitchell and their baby son, Peter. Charles was working long hours as a stevedore at Tilbury and Dorothy had her hands full with the baby so neither of them were of much help around the public house. By 1925, both Charles and Dorothy had moved out, the latter to live with her husband and child in Sidcup. This left Arthur and his mother to cope with running the public house as Ernest was now so riddled with arthritis that he was incapable of even the simplest task. Arthur had to spend a lot of time behind the bar as well as dealing with the heavy cellar work. The barrels and crates of beer were not the only things he had to lift; his father was too frail to manage the stairs so Arthur would have to carry him, piggyback style, up and down each day. Arthur's father died on the 24th August 1925 at the age of seventy-three. Unfortunately, he did not live to see his son play professional cricket or experience the sight of Arthur playing for England. It was a matter a great regret to Arthur who had been very close to his father in his final years.

Arthur's life, which had until now been unremarkable, reached its turning-point the following year. From a total of twenty-three innings played for Bexley in 1926, he scored 1006 runs at an average of 52.9 runs per innings. He had incredible success during the July Cricket Week and in the five consecutive days of cricket produced the following performances:

Tuesday	v Mr Platt's X1	145 n.o. and 5-43
Wednesday	v Kent Club & Ground	3 and 5-36
Thursday	v Mr Bowring's X1	41 and 2 wickets
Friday	v Mr Gunton's X1	50 n.o.
Saturday	v Old Charlton	6 wickets

The Kent Club and Ground fixture was closely fought despite the opposition fielding eight professionals. One of these was the brilliant young wicket-keeper Leslie Ames, soon to begin his illustrious first-class career with Kent and England. The game was close because Arthur bowled brilliantly, taking most of the early wickets. The Kent innings is worth recording:

Hearn, lbw, b Wellard	22
Ames, b Wellard	17
F.B. Eastwood, c Crowhurst, b Wheeley	10
Hubble, lbw, b Wellard	0
Todd, c Simpson, b Wheeley	7
H.E.Boyall, b Wellard	0
Norman, c Freemantle, b Wellard	23
Fairservice, b Wheeley	7
Beslee, run out	1
S.Cuckow, c Vine, b Wheeley	3
Brown, not out	0
Extras	15
Total	105

Bexley managed only 83 runs in reply. Arthur, going in at number three, was bowled for 3 runs by the slow left-arm professional Sidney Hearn. The fixture with Kent Club and Ground had been specifically arranged so that the County could take a proper look at Arthur. It was the main reason why the Kent Club and Ground X1 were so strongly represented. Quite why it had taken so long to arrange a trial will remain a mystery. Bexley Cricket Club were one of the top sides in the area and since Arthur's first encounter with Kent in 1921, he had been Bexley's leading player. Arthur was not the only local player to be ignored by the Kent authorities. A few years previously, they let Wally Hammond, born in Dover, slip away to Gloucestershire. The most plausible reason for Kent's tendency to ignore local talent is that, as a predominantly amateur county, they had their quota of professionals and were simply not able to afford anyone else who would clearly need to make a living out of the game.

His performance in the trial match did not seem to impress the Kent County Cricket authorities. The popular and much repeated story was that Kent showed no interest in his future and advised him to consider a career as a policeman. There may have been something in this story but it is more likely a fabrication that suited Arthur and saved him from the necessity of explaining the full and more elaborate story. In truth, Kent were interested in Arthur and his performance in the trial would have been sufficient to generate an offer but for one incident during the game. The real story is recorded in the *History of Bexley Cricket Club*, written by Roger Hill, which recounts the following version of the day's events:

The reasons why Arthur did not play for Kent have been the subject of debate among Bexley members for many years. Recently, George Lovegrove, who knew Arthur well, gave a rather different version to Wisden's. He recalled that, as we have seen, in 1926 the club played the Kent C & G. The Club and Ground X1 was managed by G.J.V.Weigall, a noted autocrat. The match was to be used as a trial for Wellard. The C & G X1 batted first and Arthur took three wickets before lunch. It was Arthur's practice in whole-day games to cycle home in the lunch interval to make sure everything was in order at *The Black Horse*. He went home as usual this day, but unfortunately his mother was having some trouble with rough customers and by the time Arthur had sorted it out and cycled back, lunchless, the game had restarted. His absence was noted and without any enquiry being made as to the reason he was written off as being unreliable. He was not offered an engagement by Kent, despite taking 5 wickets for 36 in the match.

It is a sobering thought that, had fate not intervened in the shape of a few drunken ruffians, Arthur Wellard would have been lost to Somerset cricket. There was one further twist of fate, which occurred a month or so later while Arthur was playing for Bexley. He was introduced to Archie Haywood, a former Kent Club and Ground player, who was just back from coaching at Taunton School. Archie Haywood was so impressed with Arthur's play that he wrote to the Somerset secretary, Mr A.F.Davey suggesting that the County should consider him. Somerset wrote and asked Arthur down for a three-day trial at the end of the season.

Arthur's trial went splendidly and the Somerset captain, John Daniell, was greatly impressed with the young man. It is not hard to see why. He had the perfect physique for a fast-medium bowler and could bowl all day without seeming to reduce in pace. It was exactly what Somerset were seeking in a professional and the administration must have found their good fortune hard to believe. He was immediately engaged for the 1927 season. A contract was produced, which he signed without hesitation and with only a cursory glance at the terms and conditions. He would probably have played for nothing such was his desire to play county cricket.

Kent objected in strong terms, which suggests they had not completely ruled him out of contention and were miffed at having Arthur taken from under their noses. The protest came from Lord Harris, an influential and dictatorial figure in English cricket, who ran Kent virtually single-handedly. It was Lord Harris that forced the MCC to withdraw Wally Hammond's eligibility for Gloucestershire shortly after the start of the 1922 season. This action effectively deprived Hammond of a year's first-class cricket. By 1926, Hammond had done enough to make Lord Harris regret Kent's missed opportunity and this may have been in his mind when protesting so strongly about Arthur. The protest fell on stony ground for, as one contemporary put it, no-one ever got any change out of John Daniell. His Lordship was told in no uncertain terms what he could do with his objections!

Arthur lied about his age when asked by the Somerset authorities. He had assumed that Somerset might not be interested in someone in their mid-twenties with a two-year qualification requirement so he took a year off his age. This was not such an unusual thing to do; the Lee brothers had removed two years from their ages. In Arthur's case, the lie remained undetected and was later to cause considerable confusion. Even as late as 1951, Bill Andrews was perpetuating the lie in Arthur's testimonial brochure. He wrote:

Arthur's age has always been a bit of a debatable point. Actually he was born on April 8th 1903, but whenever he is questioned on the point Arthur is puckishly elastic about it. Not that a year or two matters with him.

It obviously had mattered at one stage although it now seems such a trivial piece of deception. He actually admitted his real age to his Weston team-mates soon after joining Somerset. Lawrence Hawkins, the Weston and Somerset amateur, remembers Arthur explaining that 'fast bowlers age quickly enough!' *Wisden* eventually corrected Arthur's entry in the Births and Deaths record, but not until 1971.

The Wellard family managed *The Black Horse* as best they could following the death of Arthur's father. Amy is remembered for being a strong and uncompromising landlady who was able to call on her two strapping sons if any customer was silly enough to step out of line. Charles returned to live at *The Black Horse*, which at least allowed Arthur time off at weekends to pursue his sporting interests. Arthur's contract with Somerset and the requirement to live in the County finally forced the family to decide their individual futures. Amy Wellard went to stay with her sister Ada in Gravesend and lived there until her death in 1945. She was buried in St. Mary's Churchyard, Bexley alongside her husband. Charles moved to Bexleyheath and remained in the area for the rest of his life. He had no family until marrying very late in life.

Arthur visited his mother occasionally but there was little contact between her three siblings from this time onwards, despite them living in close proximity to each other. Arthur's sister stayed in Sidcup for the rest of her ninety years but made no effort to keep in contact. Arthur used to say that Dorothy was 'too posh to mix with the likes of us' and she did not even come to Arthur's wedding in 1928. Much later, when Dorothy's son Peter married in January 1946, neither Charles nor Arthur received an invitation to the wedding. Incredibly, Peter's wife, Leonie Mitchell, would recall that in all their thirty-five years of married life she never once had occasion to meet any of the family.

The lack of close family ties caused Arthur little concern. He was much too preoccupied with thoughts of becoming a professional cricketer.

2

1927-29: A professional start

ARTHUR HAD TO COMPLETE TWO YEARS of residence in Somerset before he could play for them in the County Championship. It is difficult to conceive how the modern player would have tolerated such restraint of trade. However, the amateurs who dominated the game regulated the Laws of Cricket and treated the professional cricketers little better than hired mercenaries. The amateurs of course had different standards for their own kind and there are many stories of dubious Somerset qualification. T.C.Lowry played for Somerset while at Cambridge on the strength of being 'born at Wellington' but the club omitted to point out they were referring to Wellington, New Zealand not Wellington, Somerset. R.C.Robertson-Glasgow, was another amateur player without the slightest Somerset connection but with friends in high places. The rule on residential qualification required the player to live in a bona fide residence within the county throughout the year. It was strictly enforced, at least where the professionals were concerned, so it meant that Arthur had to leave his family and friends in the Bexley area and take up lodgings in Somerset.

The next two years would be very frustrating for Arthur and it was the one aspect of his life about which he would later show signs of regret and bitterness. He was at the peak of his powers and had already lost some of his best cricketing years; a further two years delay was rubbing salt into the wound. Taking a year off his age had been a bizarre thing to do but it suggests he was anxious that Somerset might reject him for being too old by the time he had served his qualification period.

Meanwhile he lodged with the Andrews family in Weston-Super-Mare and, as a member of the Taunton ground staff, became the local professional for Weston Cricket Club. The arrangement between Somerset and Weston was that Arthur's wages would be shared on a 50:50 basis. The Andrews family lived in Clevedon Road, Weston-Super-Mare and the cricket-mad household included two brothers who would both play first-class cricket. The younger brother, Jack, played as an amateur wicketkeeper for Hampshire. The elder brother, William Harry Russell Andrews, known to all as Bill, would become an integral part of Somerset cricket for the next fifty years.

Bill Andrews recalls, in his book *The hand that bowled Bradman*, the first time he met Arthur at the Weston cricket ground:

Our new professional soon completed our education in every way. I can remember Arthur arriving on the ground for the first time, wearing a very flash suit, an equally bright tie and garish shirt. If we thought this well-built newcomer was up from the country we certainly found out quickly we had another think coming to us.

This first meeting in 1927 was the start of a lifelong friendship between the two men. They came from contrasting backgrounds and had very different personalities but they shared a passion for cricket. Their relationship was as close as was possible to that of blood brothers with Bill, six years junior to Arthur, exhibiting the full range of fraternal emotions normally associated with the younger brother. He idolised Arthur but was also jealous of his superior ability and constantly having to live in Arthur's shadow. It created a keen sense of friendly rivalry on and off the cricket field with Bill usually the one striving to keep up with his more talented friend. Arthur, on the other hand, never seemed to have to work hard at his game and this would rankle all the more. Arthur was also more circumspect about their friendship and in a condescending way often took advantage of Bill's eagerness to please. It did not seem to matter much because Arthur could do no wrong in his friend's eyes. Bill's autobiography provides ample evidence of the high esteem in which Arthur was held.

Lawrence Hawkins, the Weston cricketer who played 46 times for Somerset, was also present when Arthur first walked into the clubhouse. He called him a 'spiv in a sharp suit', a very perceptive description, and it is not hard to picture the scene of their first meeting. Arthur, always a natty dresser, had jet black hair, greased back in the fashionable style of the period. He spoke through the corner of barely parted lips with a Suburban London accent, which to the West Country ear must have sounded like that of a cockney barrow-boy. Laurie's opinion of the young 'Londoner' soon mellowed once they were in the nets.

Arthur's sense of dress was not the only thing that made an instant impression on the Weston players. Like the Somerset professionals in later years, they would quickly appreciate that Arthur's talent at cards was the equal of his talent at cricket. Arthur's card skills, acquired during his mis-spent youth at *The Black Horse*, would become legendary. Arthur was an exceptional cardplayer because he could remember every card played and whole sequences of play. He became an excellent bridge player - he had a good teacher, R.J.O.Meyer - but for now his preference was for pontoon, brag, solo whist or cribbage. His favourite card game was poker but few would risk betting against him. After practice evenings and Saturday matches at Weston it would be into the clubhouse and out with the cards.

Bill Andrews recalled those early card schools in his autobiography:

Even though my wages in the solicitor's office were up to 30 shillings *[£1.50p]* a week, this didn't last long after pontoon with Wellard. I was soon getting up at 5.00 am as the season wore on, picking mushrooms at well-chosen spots and selling them at 4d a pound.
In fact, all the time I've known him - that includes all those wet summer afternoons stuck in the pavilion and his many visits to my home - I've seldom outwitted him at cards.

Arthur's professional duties at Weston involved coaching the younger players and helping the groundsman, Bert Stokes, to prepare the wickets. Playing for Weston at the weekend served as a useful apprenticeship while waiting in the Somerset wings. There were, however few memorable performances, although he soon had a reputation for losing more balls out of the ground than all the other players put together. Weston had a formidable side by club standards and would field six or seven regulars with first-class experience, including Evelyn Hill, George Hunt, Jim Bridges and Lawrence Hawkins. With Bridges and Hill, both quite quick, Arthur often had to wait his turn to bowl and he was usually only required to bat in the end of innings slog.

Arthur could usually be found at the County Ground when not at Weston. He helped out with the maintenance of the ground and took every opportunity to improve his bowling technique in the nets. Arthur needed no encouragement to bowl and he soon gained a following among the Somerset members who would sometimes watch him in the nets in preference to watching the game. His reputation as a promising fast bowler was also growing and there were many amateurs and club members anxious to face this bright young prospect. It was not just the Somerset amateurs who faced him in the nets. In May 1927, after the match with Surrey finished early, Percy Fender had to wait some time for his train and chose to have a net. Arthur bowled to the Surrey captain and twice uprooted his stumps. It caused such an impression on those watching the net that the incident made the local papers.

Arthur also played for the Somerset Club and Ground team and it was not long before the local papers were reporting his exploits. The papers soon had their first headline match report, which appeared in July 1927:

A.WELLARD CAPTURES 8 WICKETS FOR 15 RUNS

The match was against Frome and the Club and Ground scored over 200 before declaring. According to the local paper there was a 'bright innings of 38 from Wellard, the fast bowler, including a quartette of fours.' Arthur, with some deadly and accurate bowling, had at one stage taken eight wickets for 15 runs and finished with nine wickets for 41 runs. The Frome side were all out for 73 runs and only the Somerset amateur, C.C.C.Case, withstood Arthur's onslaught.

Later that month, Bexley Cricket Club arranged for Arthur to return to play in their Cricket Week. It gave him another opportunity to play against Kent Club and Ground and he did not waste the chance to prove what Kent were missing. He took six wickets for 21 runs, including the wicket of G.J.V.Weigall. Arthur also contributed 39 runs to Bexley's score of 159, which was sufficient, by two runs, to record an exciting and deserved victory. Gerry Weigall was of the 'Old School' of players. He had played his 130 games as a Kent amateur while Queen Victoria had been on the throne. It had been Weigall, as the club coach and 2nd X1 captain, who marked Arthur down as unreliable. Weigall approached Arthur during the break for lunch and tried to persuade him to change his mind and sign for Kent. Arthur pointed out in no uncertain terms that he had not been given the chance to explain the incident the previous year. He told Weigall that Somerset were being very good to him, so Kent could forget their interest. Weigall should have known better. Arthur had signed a contract and as far as he was concerned that was that. Arthur had his principles and would not have considered breaking a contract; it was a matter of honour.

Arthur told his Weston team-mates that Weigall ended the conversation by telling him that he would never be a cricketer as long as he had a hole in his ass! This does not sound like Gerry Weigall but it does suggest there was no love lost between them. Bexley recalled Arthur for their cricket week in 1928 to play Kent Club and Ground. It provided a further opportunity to vent his feelings of frustration on the Kent batsmen. On this occasion he took eight wickets for 32 runs and six of these wickets were clean bowled. Gerry Weigall, now in his last year as club coach, was included in this number. He no doubt received an encouraging word as he passed the jubilant bowler on his way back to the pavilion! Kent just managed to win the game with their last pair at the wicket.

At the beginning of August 1927, Arthur played for Somerset against the New Zealand tourists at Weston-Super-Mare. The pitch appeared favourable to run-getting but also proved helpful to the bowlers. New Zealand made scores of

150 and 128, the latter being their lowest innings score of the tour. Bill Greswell did most of the damage in the first innings but Arthur did manage to take his maiden first-class wicket. He produced a good length ball that kept low and bowled the middle-order batsman, M.L.Page, before he had scored. Arthur also took two catches to dismiss T.C.Lowry and C.C.R.Dacre. J.C.White took eight wickets for 28 runs in New Zealand's second innings and with the skipper in such fine form it was not surprising that Arthur saw little of the ball. He bowled only five overs for 10 runs, which did nothing to ease his growing sense of frustration. If the New Zealand batting was bad, Somerset's was abysmal. Somerset scored 117 in the first innings having been 63 for eight wickets when Arthur walked nervously to the crease. He started anxiously but soon settled and scored 29 valuable runs before being bowled by Merritt. According to *Wisden,* Arthur batted 'in good form', which is more than can be said for his team-mates. New Zealand won the match inside two days after Somerset were all out for 67 in their second innings. Arthur could not have been impressed with his team's performance.

Arthur's next major game was against the West Indians the following year. The 1928 side could not be compared with any of its more modern counterparts. The tourists lost badly in all three tests against England and *Wisden* wrote somewhat ironically that, 'whatever the future may have in store, the time was certainly not yet when they could challenge England with any reasonable hope of success.' The match against the West Indies was at Bath starting on the 1st August 1928. Arthur again did well enough to show the Somerset public that they had a player of great potential. He bowled only four overs in the first West Indian innings; Bill Greswell and George Hunt opened and shared most of the bowling with J.C.White. The West Indies were all out, after four hours of dull batting, for 130 runs with Greswell and White taking four wickets apiece.

Somerset scored 216 runs thanks mainly to J.C.MacBryan and by the end of the second day West Indies were only 32 runs ahead having lost four wickets. Arthur took the wicket of F.R.Martin. Rain prevented any play until mid-afternoon on the last day and spoiled any chance of an interesting finish. The tourist batted on for the remainder of the day and were all out for 230 runs at the close. The slow scoring caused frequent barracking from the crowd but they did see Arthur take three more wickets to finish with an analysis of four wickets for 59 runs off 34 overs.

When his commitments to Somerset and Weston Cricket Club were over for the 1928 season, Arthur returned to Bexley to marry Vera Alexandra Trengove. Vera was known to everyone as Jack, a childhood nickname given by her father, Reginald, in deference to her size. The marriage took place at St. John's Church Bexley on the 29th September 1928.

It was neither a whirlwind romance nor what might be described as a 'marriage made in heaven'. Jack, born on the 1st January 1902, was just three months older but was considerable more mature. They had been in the same year at Old Bexley School but were not romantically linked during their teens or early twenties. They did, however see quite a lot of each other because Arthur visited the Trengove home regularly, to call on Jack's two brothers. Jack had many admirers and was far too busy receiving her male callers to notice Arthur. The Trengove family lived in Victoria Road, a short distance from *The Black Horse*, but came from a very different social background. Reginald Trengove's publishing interests had provided this middle-class family with a comfortable upbringing. Jack's father, however, drank more than was good for him and the family fortunes were now in decline. Even so, Arthur would not have been regarded as a potential suitor for Jack. If there were any dormant feelings for each other they were well concealed. There was also more than just their feelings of ambivalence to overcome; they had contrasting interests and personalities.

Jack was an attractive young lady, petite, vivacious and flirtatious. She was an incredible romantic, loved dancing and never had any shortage of young men vying for her affections. Arthur's interests lay in sport, shooting and gambling so there was not much time for the opposite sex; not that he ever seemed bothered about the need for female company at this or any other stage of his life. It was not through any lack of interest on the ladies' part but he would appear shy in female company and lacked the necessary confidence to engage them in conversation. He certainly never had a steady or serious relationship until Jack took an interest in him. Jack was involved with Bexley Cricket Club, making the teas. She didn't like cricket so it can be safely assumed that she was there for the players rather than the game. Jack could not help being impressed by Arthur's exploits on the field. After Somerset offered him a contract and Arthur became a local celebrity, Jack saw the young man she had known since their school days in a very different light. She was attracted to the glamour of professional sport as much as anything else and Arthur did not stand a chance once Jack had set her mind on courting his attention. From then onwards, his bachelor days were numbered.

The wedding reception at the Fremantle Hall was as unromantic as the courtship. With the formal proceedings at an end, most of the guests took to the dance-floor. Arthur did not enjoy dancing, which he regarded as an affront to his masculinity. He had to be dragged onto the floor for the traditional opening dance. The pair made a striking contrast as their wedding photograph reveals. Jack was a tiny creature, not five feet tall, Arthur towered above her. Jack was an excellent dancer, Arthur had two 'left feet' that needed squeezing into size thirteen boots! Jack was not too perturbed by Arthur's reluctance to dance and spent the evening with other young men at the reception, many of whom had been her previous suitors. Arthur slipped away to the club next door to play snooker with the lads and, in the process, got paralytically drunk!

The newly-weds never had a honeymoon and after a few days staying at Victoria Road, the pair returned to Somerset to complete Arthur's period of residential qualification. Prior to the wedding, Arthur had been living with Bill Andrews and his family. When Arthur and Jack returned to the West Country, they lodged with Len and Minnie Wade who lived at 111 St. Augustine Street, Taunton. The house was conveniently situated close to the County Ground. It was also conveniently situated for the *Ring of*

Bells and the *Crown and Sceptre*, where Len Wade's brother used to work! The Wades made the couple most welcome, especially Jack who was feeling homesick and quite neglected. It was alright for Arthur; he had plenty to occupy his mind, not least with thoughts of the coming season. There was also much to be done at the County Ground and Arthur, being a member of the ground staff, was expected to play his part.

The head groundsman, Harry Fernie, and his staff were busily employed during the close season. The stands and the woodwork of the enclosure were repainted and everything was looking spic and span. The club had also just acquired the triangular piece of land near the bridge, which was bounded by the river, Priory Bridge Road and the original perimeter of the ground. The land was levelled, trees were planted and part of the ground was prepared for a new net practice area. A roadway was also constructed to provide a new entrance to the ground, which was seen as proving a great convenience to people coming from the direction of the railway. Arthur put his back into the heavy labouring, which helped build up his impressive physique as well as whiling away the days before the start of the season.

In March 1929, Arthur was sent on a course of training at Major Faulkner's Cricket School in Walham Green, London. It was the excuse that Jack Wellard needed to return to her family in Bexley for she had never settled in her new surroundings. The training was an excellent opportunity for Arthur as this famous school was run by Aubrey Faulkner, the South African Test all-rounder and one of the great coaches of all times. The Major had set up his school after serving with distinction in the First World War. Arthur never took to the Major - who was inclined to bouts of depression as a result of his war experiences and took his own life the following year - but he did gain considerable benefit from the tuition he received. Arthur went to the school with the Somerset wicket-keeper, Wally Luckes, and it was while at the school that Wally's debilitating heart condition was diagnosed. The heart weakness would keep him out of professional cricket for most of the next three seasons, which would be a great loss to Somerset and in particular to the Somerset bowlers. Arthur returned to Somerset impatient to start his professional career.

Somerset's first game of the 1929 County Championship season was against Worcestershire at Bath, starting on Saturday the 11th May. The weather was dull and threatening but Somerset's diehard supporters soon had something to cheer about. Worcestershire were put into bat with Arthur and George Hunt providing the opening bowling attack. All the pent-up energy from the last two years came flowing out of Arthur. After only three balls of his first over he bowled B.W. Quaife with a ball that moved into the right-hander. It was a beautiful delivery, which shattered Bernard Quaife's wicket and prompted him to later remark that he had not even seen the ball. Arthur should also have been credited with Nichol's wicket in the same over if an easy slip catch had been taken. It was the first of numerous disappointments with the Somerset fielding, which would cost him countless wickets during his career.

Nichol did not last long. He was caught by Arthur, off George Hunt's bowling in the next over and the visitors were two wickets down without a run on the board. They were 45 for four wickets at one stage but Gibbons and Wright came to the rescue and by lunchtime the score had climbed to 111 for four wickets. Arthur produced a splendid ball to clean bowl Gibbons immediately after lunch and he bowled Wright in similar fashion when the latter had made 99 runs. Worcestershire were 253 all out and Arthur was content with his figures of three wickets for 77 runs off 32 overs. Rain interrupted play on Monday but there was sufficient time for Somerset to be bowled out for 108 runs and for Worcestershire to start their second innings. The match was abandoned when it became clear that no play would be possible on the Tuesday. Arthur did manage to take one of the five wickets to fall in Worcestershire's incomplete second innings; the hapless Quaife was bowled by a similar ball, this time for one run.

Arthur continued to make a good impression during the next few matches. Somerset travelled to Cardiff for their next game and Arthur took another five wickets during the match. Curiously, his first eight victims in first-class cricket had all been clean bowled; his ninth was leg-before-wicket. He followed this with four wickets in Hampshire's first innings at Taunton, again all clean bowled. The ball that bowled C.P.Brutton was a magnificent delivery, which all but silenced the large bank holiday crowd. One of the bails sailed high into the air eventually landing just in front of the members gathered in the pavilion. Tom Young went to retrieve the bail, slowly measuring the distance as he returned to the wicket. It measured 50 yards! Arthur took a further three wickets in Hampshire's second innings, helping Somerset to win by a comfortable margin. This first victory of the season owed much to Frank Lee who had top-scored in both innings and scored his first of twenty-three centuries for the County. The appreciative holiday crowd gave freely to a ground collection, which netted £35.9s.4d. The organisers gave £23.12s.10d to Frank Lee and the remaining £11.16s.6d went to Arthur for his contribution to the victory. Arthur could be forgiven for thinking that first-class cricket was a 'piece of cake'. His share of the collection was the equivalent of four weeks wages!

There was no stopping him now; in the next match on the same ground he took ten wickets against Kent. The Kent side included three of the players from the Club and Ground side that had played at Bexley so Arthur was particularly anxious to impress. On the first day he bowled flat out for 41 overs and his figures of six wickets for 108 runs did not do him justice. Apart from the catches that were missed, he repeatedly beat the bat. G.B.Legge, the England middle-order batsman, had a particularly torrid time and was all at sea when eventually clean bowled by Arthur. In Kent's second innings, Arthur was said to have bowled very fast and the visitors collapsed in sensational fashion. They started their innings at 2.16pm and by 3.22pm - one hour and six minutes later - they were all back in the pavilion for 63 runs. Arthur took four wickets for 28 runs and was particularly pleased to have taken the wicket of Les Ames in both innings. In the second innings, Ames was none too pleased to see all three stumps cartwheeling out of the ground!

If Arthur's bowling had been nothing short of phenomenal, his batting had been abysmal. Going in at number ten or eleven, he had so far made sixteen runs from six appearances at the wicket and this total included an innings of twelve runs against Kent. He had faced the wily old Worcestershire professional Fred Root and the even more artful 'Tich' Freeman of Kent and neither had much trouble in taking his wicket. The next match at Trent Bridge – his fifth – against Nottinghamshire and Harold Larwood at the peak of his career would provide the ultimate test of his batting.

Arthur in a heedless show of bravado made light of his confrontation with Larwood. He would, almost fifty years later, recall the match in conversation with the playwright Harold Pinter:

He was a bit quick, Larwood. Quickest thing I ever saw. First time I faced him was at Trent Bridge, that was my first season with Somerset. Who's this Larwood? I said, supposed to be a bit pacey, is he? I didn't reckon the stories. He's a bit quick, they said. A bit quick? I said. We'll see about that. I'd faced a few quickies in Kent. Well, I went out there and I got four balls from Larwood and I didn't see any of them. The first I knew about them was Bert Lilley throwing them back. The fifth ball knocked my hob over and I didn't see that one either. I'll tell you he was a bit quick, Harold Larwood.

Arthur was much too modest to tell Harold Pinter that he had bowled Larwood for a duck in Nottinghamshire's only innings or that his 21 not out in the second innings almost avoided the innings defeat.

Arthur's bowling was improving with every match and after another fine spell in the next match against Derbyshire – he took five wickets for 96 runs off 43.1 overs – he completed his one and only 'hat trick' of his career. The match, at Leicester, beginning on the 5th June 1929, was affected by rain on an uncovered wicket. Despite only three hours of play during the first two days, Leicestershire completed the victory by five o'clock on the third day. Somerset were all out in their first innings for 105 and Leicestershire took a decisive first innings lead of 21, after being at one stage 83 for eight wickets. With eight wickets down, Somerset, in typical fashion, missed three vital catches before the first innings lead was established. J.C.White had good figures of four wickets for 44 runs but Arthur proved even more effective with his pace and fine length. He took six wickets for 55 runs including the 'hat trick' wickets of the middle-order batsmen, Armstrong, King and Coleman. Armstrong and King were the 'not out' batsmen at the start of the third day's play but were quickly separated as Arthur took the first four wickets to fall. He scattered Armstrong's wicket, got King taken in the slips with the next delivery and then bowled Coleman. Somerset were all out for 61 runs in their second innings. Astill, the Leicestershire and England right-arm bowler, took eight wickets for 23 runs and was almost unplayable. Astill's bowling certainly managed to confuse Arthur; taking his wicket in both innings without a run scored in either. The home side, set 41 to win, still contrived to lose six wickets in the process with Arthur taking a further two wickets for 31 runs. The 'hat-trick' ball was kindly presented to Arthur by the Leicestershire authorities after the match.

As if this sensational start was not enough, Arthur surpassed all previous performances in the next match, starting on the 8th June at Taunton, against Somerset's old adversaries, Gloucestershire. Although Gloucestershire won the match by 64 runs, all the honours went to Arthur. In a low-scoring match, he took eleven wickets for less than 16 runs apiece and scored 130 runs. With Hammond and Goddard, like J.C.White, engaged in the Test Trial at Lord's, Gloucestershire's main hopes for runs were pinned on their opening batsmen, Alf Dipper and Reg Sinfield. They got off to a fine start after some erratic bowling allowed them to score 95 runs. Arthur then came back for a second spell and immediately took both their wickets, followed shortly by the wickets of Harry Smith and Charlie Barnett. His figures for the first innings were six wickets for 82 runs.

The Somerset batsmen quickly found themselves in trouble but Arthur, in a typically belligerent mood, attacked the bowling. His batting surprised his team-mates and the crowd for he had not previously shown himself to be a hitter. He reached his fifty in as many minutes and finished with 75 runs, including two sixes and nine fours. His score of 75 accounted for over half of Somerset's paltry innings total of 144 runs. This was the Taunton crowd's first opportunity to witness Arthur's powerful driving. Arthur took five wickets for 93 runs in Gloucestershire's second innings including the repeat wickets of Dipper, Sinfield and Barnett, and Somerset were set 277 to win. They started well and Guy Earle, who on his day could hit the ball as hard and as far as Arthur, scored fifty in fifteen minutes. It was a bold effort but by the end of the second day Somerset still required 127 runs with four wickets left. Gloucestershire needed less than an hour of the third day to win the match and Arthur, completing his second fifty of the match, merely delayed the ending. He completed his fifty with a splendid drive to the rails past mid-on and in the next over lifted Sinfield high over the shilling stand *[next to the old pavilion]*. He was caught off the next ball trying to repeat the shot. Arthur's fine all-round performance deserved better from his team-mates who gave him no support.

A few games later, towards the end of June, Arthur had his first experience of playing at Chelmsford. Essex batted first and Arthur had some initial success, taking the wicket of the opening bat, Cutmore. Little else happened of note during the morning session but the locals had plenty to think about after lunch. Arthur was now bowling appreciably faster, which forced the wicket-keeper, Walter Wilde, to stand back. Seven runs came from his first over after lunch but then Wilde took a neat catch to get rid of Morris. O'Connor, who had been batting at the other end with some success, collected two fours off Arthur but a dramatic collapse was to follow. He had O'Connor caught behind, then took the wickets of Raison and Sheffield who both went without scoring. His figures for this bowling spell were:

$\underline{O}$	$\underline{M}$	$\underline{R}$	$\underline{W}$
7	1	9	4

He closed the innings in spectacular fashion by

uprooting two of Wade's stumps. The crowd of 5,000 were stunned; Arthur's figures for the innings were six wickets for 47 runs and Essex were all out for 109 runs. Arthur took four wickets in the second innings and scored 32 runs in the run chase, which should have secured a fine victory but for some poor batting from the rest of the team.

Despite the rigours of playing county cricket six days a week, Arthur still had time for his pals at Bexley. It had seemed that Arthur would miss their Cricket Week at the beginning of July but a two-day finish against Sussex at Brighton gave him a rare day off. He went home to Jack, intending to spend the day with her, but was easily persuaded to turn out for Bexley against the MCC. Arthur bowled throughout, taking seven wickets for 64 runs, but the MCC's score of 164 was too much for Bexley despite a spirited 35 runs from Arthur. There was time for only the briefest of reunions with Jack because he had to be in Taunton for a championship game the next day.

Less than two months had elapsed since Arthur's championship debut yet he gave all the appearance of a seasoned campaigner. His aggressive approach to cricket on the field and his carefree manner off it made him an instant success with the crowds, particularly the younger elements. The Somerset public quickly adopted him as one of their own. He seemed to show no signs of nerves or of being overawed by any occasion. Perhaps this was because he was having far too much fun to think seriously about his impact on Somerset cricket. It was a fantastic experience for him as he rubbed shoulders with the living legends of the game. Some, like Hobbs and Sandham of Surrey, Hirst and Rhodes of Yorkshire and Woolley of Kent had direct links with the 'golden age' of pre-war cricket. Jack Hobbs, whom Arthur rated as the best he ever bowled against, was his favourite and he did not have long to wait before witnessing firsthand the brilliance of the 'Master'.

Somerset played Surrey at the Oval in Mid-July. Jack Hobbs scored 204, giving only one chance, in Surrey's score of 555 for four wickets declared. Arthur got off quite lightly, taking one wicket for 59 runs before badly straining the ligaments in his left side. He had overstretched himself and was called for a no-ball before having to leave the field. The wicket was that of Jack Hobbs' opening partner, Andrew Sandham, leg-before-wicket for 74 runs. The ligament strain saved him from the punishment meted out to the other Somerset bowlers. Alec Bedser refers to Arthur's first encounter with Jack Hobbs in his book *Our cricket story*:

There is the story of Arthur Wellard's first ball against Jack Hobbs. Arthur, who served Somerset so well, sent down an outswinger-the first of the match, mark you-well wide of the off stump. Jack Hobbs, not content to allow the ball to pass through to the wicket-keeper, swept it by square leg to the boundary. Big Arthur just couldn't believe his eyes, and running to his captain asked in sheer despair, 'Just what do I have to bowl to keep him quiet?'

Arthur missed the next three championship games before returning to face the South African touring team at Taunton. The tourists won comfortably by an innings and 34 runs. Somerset's batting again let them down and Arthur was left to set an example to his more experienced team-mates. He scored 46 out of his side's second innings total of 146 runs. In one over from Mitchell, he hit two sixes, one of which went clean out of the ground. Soon after this match, Arthur had his first experience of Weston festival cricket. He had an excellent start, taking twelve wickets from the first two matches against Essex and Glamorgan but Somerset lost both games. During the Glamorgan game, he took his hundredth wicket of the season and received a rapturous reception from the large holiday crowd. The third and final festival match was against Surrey and resulted in another defeat for Somerset. It had been less than a month since their visit to the Oval and this time, Hobbs scored 134 in Surrey's first innings. He hit two sixes and sixteen fours in what was described as a faultless innings. Arthur failed to take a wicket and most of the 70 runs scored against him came from the bat of Hobbs. His baptism in professional cricket was all but complete.

Towards the end of the season, in late August, he took five wickets in an innings on two further occasions. By some curious coincidence, his last wicket of the season was the same as his first. Bernard Quaife was caught Hunt, bowled Wellard for nought. Quaife had lost his wicket to Arthur in all three innings against Somerset that year for a combined score of one run! Despite missing the three matches in July, Arthur took 131 first-class wickets for Somerset at just over 21 runs apiece. *Wisden* in the report on Somerset's season paid Arthur some encouraging compliments:

Some compensation for the misfortunes *[of the season]* was forthcoming in the success of the new professional bowler, Wellard, who became qualified by residence. A fast medium right-hander, with a natural off break and quick off the pitch, this young player was one of the finds of the season. A strained leg kept him out of three matches in July, and fortune by no means favoured him, numerous catches being missed in the slips off his bowling. No less than 69 of his victims were clean bowled-a remarkable proportion. Tall and long limbed, Wellard has the ideal physique for a bowler of his type. When he shared the attack with White the pair made a most effective combination.

The fact that such an extraordinary number of Arthur's victims were clean bowled suggests that the *Wisden* comment concerning missed catches contained more than a grain of truth. During this period of Somerset's history the team was usually to be found towards the foot of the County Championship table and the fielding was regarded as a particular weakness. Arthur's bowling in the early years relied on pace and swing, mixed with the occasional break-back and out-swinger, so Arthur depended on catches being taken by the close fielders.

There is also no doubt that his figures would have been better still had Somerset been able to call on a reliable substitute for their stricken wicket-keeper, Wally Luckes. Following the diagnosis of his heart condition, it was months before the London specialists would give him the all-clear. Meanwhile, Somerset employed various keepers, none of whom were much better than club standard. Walter Wilde of Weston played seven games, mostly at the start of the season, followed by the Reverend F.E.Spurway, Stanley Amor of Bath, M.V.Spurway and Alan Marshall, another keeper from a well-known local family. Wally Luckes returned for the last nine games, taking five stumpings and thirteen catches. This was almost as many as the five aforementioned keepers had taken on the nineteen occasions that they were asked to keep wicket.

The *Wisden* reference to the combination of Arthur and J.C.White was the one encouragement for Somerset in 1929 and it would be the start of a useful bowling partnership for a few years to come. Despite a long and strenuous tour of Australia the previous winter, J.C. White took over 100 championship wickets for the season. While the bowling was relatively strong, Somerset's batting let them down and they languished in 15th place in the Championship at the end of the season. They had managed to lose 17 games out of a total of 28!

Despite all the disappointments of the season, the Somerset public could claim that they had a rising star in their midst. Arthur was an attractive cricketer in every sense and in keeping with the style of Somerset cricket. He was talked about as the natural successor to S.M.J. 'Sammy' Woods, the great all-rounder who played for Somerset between 1891 and 1910. The Secretary, A.F.Davey, was rightly pleased with the County's acquisition and reported to the members in glowing terms:

In Wellard it looks as if we may have found a real bowler. He did splendidly in his first season to take 131 wickets and as he gets experience may do even better. He is also a fine field, will make runs, and is altogether a promising recruit.

The summer of 1929 marked the beginning of a nomadic existence for Arthur that would last the best part of twenty-five years. Almost every match for Somerset was an away fixture for him and his home matches were those at Maidstone, the Oval and Lord's. Throughout his Somerset career he never had a permanent address in the area so took lodgings when necessary, stayed with the Wades, Bill Andrews or other friends and supporters. If all else failed he would stay at *The County Hotel* in Taunton, a short walk from the ground. He did not drive or own a car in his life so travelled by public transport like most of the professionals of the day. After the War, when car ownership became slightly more common, he would rely on lifts from his fellow players, particularly Bill Andrews. Bill never seems to have considered it an inconvenience to transport Arthur around the country.

During the period up to the start of the Second World War he would return to his true home in the South East when the season was over. He was usually not seen in the West Country until the following April. In 1929, he returned to Bexley and his wife Jack. They were lodging with Jack's parents at Victoria Road together with Jack's younger sister Betty and brother Cecil. They were to lodge with Jack's parents for another five years.

Jack was heavily reliant on her mother, Celina and seemed to need the strong support of her close family. Later, when her mother died, Jack's dependency shifted to her younger sister, Betty, despite the fact that there was a seventeen-year age difference. Jack was never far from her family. If Betty moved house, Jack would soon follow without any regard for Arthur's views on the matter. Their moves to Sutton and Eastbourne, were both prompted by Jack's need to be close to Betty and her family.

During the winter months, Arthur never gave any thought to looking for work and in all his adult life, he never had a job that did not involve cricket. He was a naturally lazy person and much preferred the attractions of the local pub or the snooker hall. It is extremely unlikely that Arthur returned to the South East for the winter with much to show for his efforts during the summer. Arthur had a simple attitude to money; it was there to be spent. He was a generous man and, like most habitual gamblers, could never hold on to money for long. Jack also had no employment so the couple had to manage on little or no income during the early years of their marriage. They were able to live frugally thanks to the patronage of Jack's parents. Jack's sister Betty remembers these days of almost seventy years ago very clearly. Jack would put a ten shilling note in the silver cigarette case on the dining room table as a contribution to the couple's keep for the week. More often than not, Arthur would 'borrow' it, without Jack ever realising, and her parents, who were very fond of Arthur, never let on!

Arthur hated the winters and he would just mark time waiting for the following cricket season. The winter of 1929 was particularly trying after such a dramatic start to his professional career. He was so keen to get back to the game that shortly after the New Year he returned to Somerset. He could not wait to get back to the West Country and spent his time working at the County Ground before reporting for professional duty in April.

3

The early thirties

UNDERSTANDABLY, THE SOMERSET PUBLIC were anticipating further progress from Arthur but the 1930 season fell well short of everyone's expectations. The season got off to a bad start with exceptionally poor weather affecting their April training schedule. The County did not have any indoor facilities at their disposal so the professionals resorted to skipping and roadwork until the weather improved. By the third week in April they had not yet been able to play on turf but were using coconut matting to provide a surface for net practice. Tom Young, as senior professional, was in charge of the nets and was having great difficulty in restraining Arthur's enthusiasm for fast bowling. It was hardly proper preparation for a bowler but worse was to come in the traditional pre-season trial match at Taunton. Arthur was playing for Mr White's Team against Mr Ingle's Team and during his very first over, he strained a muscle in his leg.

The injury was caused by the lack of adequate pre-season preparation and kept him out of contention for three weeks. He missed the first four championship matches - three of which Somerset lost - and when he returned he could not find any sort of form with the ball. His first game back was at Lord's and he did at least signal his return by fairly belting the ball with some fine aggressive batting. He scored from 19 of the 24 deliveries he faced, including a gigantic six off Harry Lee, which landed on top of the clock tower [now behind the Compton Stand].

Arthur had a lot to learn about cricket at this level and it was almost inevitable that he would not recapture the form of the previous season. He accepted the failures with great stoicism, suggesting a character to match his physical strength. He was eager to improve and readily took advice from his fellow professionals who were extremely supportive. Arthur was especially friendly with the Lee brothers with whom he shared a common bond; being 'Londoners' in a 'foreign' environment. Jack Lee had joined Somerset in 1925 and his brother Frank followed the same route from Lord's in 1929. Arthur and Frank Lee made their championship debuts in the same match and, as the 'new boys', instinctively shared in each other's triumphs and lent support during the leaner times. Frank Lee and his wife Ruby remained family friends, long after the Somerset connection ended. Jack was killed in action during the Normandy D-day landing in June 1944.

Of all the professionals, Tom Young and Jack Lee gave Arthur the most help with his game. They were especially helpful with Arthur's batting, which lacked finesse and the most rudimentary defence. Tom Young, however, was quick to recognise that Arthur had enormous potential, provided the power of his hitting could be controlled. Young spent many hours in the nets with Arthur, imploring him to hit straight and teaching him how to play spin. Apart from his brief spell at Major Faulkner's School, this was the closest Arthur came to receiving proper coaching. Arthur's vulnerability to spin bowling was much in evidence when Somerset played Yorkshire in 1930. They had not played them in 1929 so it was Arthur's first experience of meeting another 'golden age' cricketer and one of the greatest ever slow left-arm bowlers, Wilfred Rhodes.

Wilfred Rhodes was in his last county season and was altogether too cunning for Arthur. At Bradford towards the end of June 1930, Rhodes drew Arthur into a soft caught-and-bowled in the first innings for one run. Bowes got his wicket in the second - before Rhodes could get to him - but not before Arthur had smashed Emmott Robinson out of the ground. Arthur still fancied his chances against Rhodes and looked forward to the return fixture at Bath, two weeks later. He made a point of finding out if Rhodes was playing and vowed he would 'hit the old bugger out of the ground.'

He was almost true to his word as in successive deliveries he lifted him well over the ropes and then cracked him through mid-wicket. The old campaigner soon had his revenge. Arthur was caught in the deep by another veteran, Percy Holmes, while attempting to put the ball in the river. He was out to the same combination in the second inning, playing the same shot!

Arthur's batting was not always this disastrous. In the next game against Leicestershire he hit probably the longest six ever seen at Taunton, although others described in this book come close. Arthur hit 45 out of 61 runs scored in less than thirty minutes with C.C.C.Case. It would have been quicker but two of his three sixes had to be retrieved from the roadway. The six off Haydon Smith went miles over the pavilion and landed by the main gate from where it bounced up and onto the roof of Starkey's brewery on the opposite side of St. James' Street. The distance from the river end of the wicket to the main gate is 170 yards, which would rival the recognised longest first-class hit. It is also close to the distance achieved at Bombay in 1938, which Arthur and others maintained was his best and longest six.

There was more bold hitting against Nottinghamshire at Taunton in late June when he hit 51 runs in forty-six minutes. Larwood was not playing but Arthur hit out against his partner, Bill Voce. One huge drive landed in the River Tone and prompted S.M.J.Woods, sitting in the pavilion, to shout, 'well hit, young Wellard.' Arthur also hit out at Bath against Northamptonshire where his 28 not out came from six deliveries, including a six which went high over the Recreation Ground pavilion and into the road at the rear. Arthur was gaining a reputation for big hitting. Others had noticed a peculiar fondness for clouting balls out of cricket grounds and into football grounds. At Bradford, the six off Robinson had soared over the stand and landed on the 'spot-kick' in the Park Avenue ground. At Cardiff, he hit a ball from Eddie Bates into the Cardiff Rugby Football ground.

His batting tended to be inconsistent but did improve towards the latter part of the season when, with the harder wickets, the ball came more on to the bat. In the last seven matches of the season he scored over 300 runs, which accounted for almost half of his tally for the whole season. He hit 55 runs in a forty-minute innings against Essex that including three sixes. He hit 61 runs in a fifty-minute innings against Warwickshire that included two straight drives for six. He also scored 75 against Hampshire at Portsmouth in late August. It was achieved in less than an hour and he was trying very hard to get his first century. He might well have succeeded but the new ball, taken when the Somerset score had reached 400 runs, was the cause of his undoing. His late scoring prompted Somerset's president V.T.Hill to remark that 'he had showed considerable advance as a bat with promises to still further improve.' In all his matches for Somerset this year, he scored 775 runs at an average of 22.79 runs per innings.

Arthur had also batted well against the Australian tourists at Taunton in July. He scored 38 out of Somerset's first innings of 121 runs and 17 out of their second innings of 81 runs. With little respect for reputation, he hit Clarrie Grimmett for two sixes. The first was a massive hit, which went far and away over the pavilion roof. The second, in the same direction, disappeared into the upper tier of the pavilion. Grimmett had the last laugh, however, by taking ten wickets in the match and Somerset lost by an innings and 158 runs.

Arthur did not help the Somerset cause by dropping Archie Jackson when he had scored 6 runs. He went on to score a fine century, as did Don Bradman. It was the first of a number of opportunities that Arthur had to bowl at Bradman. Arthur never captured Bradman's wicket but usually made him appear uncomfortable at the crease, especially during the early stages of his innings. The Australians' scorer, W.H.Ferguson, said that Bradman paid a great tribute to Arthur's bowling on the first day of the match. Bradman reckoned that it had been the most accurate he had met for such a long spell of bowling. Arthur's first eight overs against the rampant Australian batsmen had yielded just ten runs.

Arthur's bowling was not generally this tight during the 1930 season. An inspection of the Somerset scorebook reveals that he rarely took more than one wicket in an innings. In his fifteen full seasons with Somerset, he took five wickets in an innings on 108 occasions but this year he managed it just once, against Gloucestershire. He played in all but the first four matches and took only 37 wickets at over 46 runs apiece. These were easily his worst figures of his career and in such marked contrast to the excellent results from his first season. The opposition is always better prepared for a bowler in his second season and this may have had an effect on Arthur's figures. In addition, he was troubled throughout the season by the injury that had caused him to miss the early matches. There were occasions when he hardly bowled at all and during one spell in early August when he was completely out of sorts, he bowled just 23 overs in four consecutive championship matches. Altogether, he bowled four hundred fewer overs in his second season. Somerset's fielding had also shown no discernable improvement and many catches were missed, particularly behind the stumps. Wally Luckes suffered a recurrence of his heart problem and played in only the first six matches, four of which Arthur missed. Various club keepers were tried – six in all – including Seymour Clark of Weston whose infamous batting record has endured longer than his reputation as a keeper. Despite his injury and having little luck all season, Arthur never gave up trying nor made excuses for his bowling.

The following year Arthur showed a welcomed return to form and there were several memorable performances with bat and ball in the 1931 season. In early May at Birmingham, he was largely responsible for Somerset beating Warwickshire. He scored 83 in Somerset's first innings – his highest score yet – and played the fast bowling with great confidence. He had come in when his team were struggling at 196 for six wickets and, thanks largely to his efforts, Somerset extended their innings to 320 runs. He then kept a splendid line and length in Warwickshire's first innings. His 25.2 overs included a remarkable sequence of fourteen balls *[11W... .W..W4 .W]*, which took the last four wickets.

Arthur finished with six wickets for 42 runs and took three more wickets in the second innings. Somerset won by the narrow margin of 49 runs.

Unfortunately many of his better performances this season would find him on the losing side. Two games later, he took six wickets for 39 runs in Kent's first innings and, in a valiant attempt to save the match, scored 39 out of Somerset's second innings total of 121 runs. A few days later at the end of May, in yet more rearguard action at Trent Bridge, he hit 81 runs, scored in sixty-one minutes. Arthur was particularly proud of this innings because it was against Harold Larwood at the peak of his form. Earlier in the day, the Somerset first innings batting had been eclipsed by Larwood who was described as 'bowling like lightning'. J.C.White's peculiar dismissal, given out 'hit wicket', gives some indication of Larwood's speed. The bowler broke White's bat and a large splinter of wood from the bat removed the off bail. Larwood took seven wickets for 25 runs - Arthur was one of his victims - to force the follow-on, a situation that none of the shell-shocked Somerset batsmen looked forward to with much relish. In Somerset's second innings, J.C.White scored a typically stubborn century and shared a partnership of 116 runs with Arthur. Arthur's innings included four sixes and ten fours and one of his sixes off Robinson went over the Radcliffe Road stand and into the gardens of the *Trent Bridge Hotel*. The partnership staved off an innings defeat but was not enough to save the match.

Shortly after this match, Arthur made his first of the six appearances for the Players against the Gentlemen. The matches between the Gentlemen and Players had been an important feature of the English cricket scene. The fixture was introduced in 1806 but came into prominence during the days of W.G.Grace. The traditional prestigious meeting between the Gentlemen and the Players took place at Lord's in mid-July but between 1857 and 1934 an additional fixture was played at the Oval.

Arthur's invitation was for the Oval fixture, a three-day match starting on the 10th June 1931. His selection may have come earlier than was merited or expected but ten of the first-class counties were engaged in the Championship. The Players could still boast Hobbs, Sutcliffe, Leyland, Verity, Mitchell and Bowes in their side and the Gentlemen included R.E.S.Wyatt, D.R.Jardine, P.G.H.Fender and M.J.C.Allom. Somerset's C.C.C.Case also played as a late replacement for the Gentlemen and came in for some harsh treatment from Arthur. At one stage, a ball from Arthur hit him painfully in the small of the back and he was out shortly after, caught by Arthur off the bowling of Bowes. Arthur took five wickets for 45 runs in the Gentlemen's first innings, including the prized wicket of Douglas Jardine. Sir Pelham Warner, writing some ten years later in his book *Cricket between two wars*, praised Arthur's bowling and vividly recalled the ball that defeated Jardine. The strong defensive batsman was well set when he received a ball from Arthur that pitched on the middle and leg stumps and hit the top of the off stump.

Somerset continued to lose most of their games and it was not until the end of June that they achieved their second win of the season against Northamptonshire. Arthur contributed with both bat and ball in a rare all-round team victory but it was Jack Lee, with a century and eight wickets in the match, that turned the game in Somerset's favour. It was a remarkable victory given that the players were exhausted after a gruelling week of travel. This week's itinerary provides a fascinating example of what the county circuit was like in an age without the advantages of fast cars and good road networks. The previous Tuesday they had left Kidderminster bound for Nelson in Lancashire. They did not reach Preston, the nearest vantage point to Nelson, until 3.00am and were roused again at 7.30am for a connection to Nelson. Fortunately they won the toss but not surprisingly were all out for 141 runs. The match against Lancashire, a ding dong affair, went the full term and it was 7.20pm on the Friday evening before the team could start the nine-hour journey to Northampton, arriving at 4.00am. After taking the full three days to beat Northamptonshire, they travelled to Dewsbury for the match against Yorkshire, again arriving in the early hours of the first day's play.

Understandably, Yorkshire beat Somerset by an innings. Arthur bowled 49 overs in Yorkshire's innings, taking five wickets for 114 runs. In the course of these four away fixtures, Arthur had bowled almost two hundred overs. It would never have occurred to him that he was being overworked but as a consequence he was rarely free of injury. There were few chances to rest tired muscles and no physiotherapist on hand. He would carry on playing because he could not afford to be out of the side so the strain of the day would be strapped to provide rudimentary protection. Finger injuries came in for similar treatment. Arthur was the expert on 'cracking' dislocated digits and fractured ones received the same cursory attention. Tony Sibley, a Somerset Committee member from Street, remembers one particular incident at Weston, which illustrates the point. Arthur had a broken finger and was clearly in a great deal of discomfort at net practice. Tony enquired how long the injury would keep him out of the game. 'Till eleven-thirty when we start,' was Arthur's pithy reply! Tony remembers him bowling the full two hours in both morning and afternoon session; his one concession for the day was to field in the outfield.

The players returned from Dewsbury to play the Bath festival and met with some success when comfortably beating Middlesex. Arthur took six wickets in the match after bowling another 53 overs. He was tired and also fed up, having missed Bath races, but there would be no immediate respite. They had to be at Cardiff the next day for the match against Glamorgan where Arthur was in action straight away. He worked like a trojan and generated an astonishing pace. Arthur's opening spell of bowling lasted seventy-five minutes and he bowled for an hour after tea. He bowled 35 overs in total taking five wickets for 79 runs. His efforts were to no avail as the game ended in stalemate.

Arthur would see his best efforts wasted again in the next game against Lancashire. Somerset were made to bat on wet turf and were all out for 116 runs; Arthur top-scored with 30 after coming in when Somerset were 25 for five wickets. Somerset showed no improvement in their second innings when they scored a total of 106 runs. Arthur scored

35 of these runs and also took five wickets for 39 runs in Lancashire's first innings. He took six of the eleven wickets that fell and five of these were clean bowled, including the England batsmen, Ernest Tyldesley and Eddie Paynter *[twice]*. It was not enough to prevent a nine-wickets defeat and Arthur would have been justified in berating the efforts of his team-mates who had shown no application. Not unnaturally, Arthur's stamina was being stretched to the limit and this may have caused the decline in his bowling performances for the duration of the season. The drop in performance was unfortunately timed because the England Selection Committee were taking a keen interest in him. P.A.Perrin who was one of the selectors, certainly watched him closely at Leyton in late July. He took two wickets for 70 runs off 31 overs and, although he bowled well, appeared to have lost the extra yard of pace that had been so evident earlier in the season.

By the end of the season, Arthur had taken 85 wickets for Somerset at 26 runs apiece but only 22 wickets came from the last third of the season. Arthur bowled over 1,000 overs; only J.C.White bowled more and took more wickets during the season. Jack Lee was the only other bowler to take more than 50 wickets for the County. Bill Andrews and George Hunt, who played in nineteen matches apiece, had poor seasons, contributing just 36 wickets between them. It is therefore not surprising that Arthur had to shoulder most of the responsibility for the opening pace attack. It was a burden that should have been more properly shared but Arthur was his own worst enemy, being at times too willing a workhorse.

Arthur scored 756 runs for Somerset during the season, slightly fewer than in 1930. Although his batting showed signs of growing maturity, he was still too anxious to hit the ball out of the ground irrespective of its line and length. As far as Arthur was concerned the ball was there to be hit and the temptation sooner or later became too strong to resist. Arthur had provided the appreciative county cricket followers with various demonstrations of his striking ability but there was no better example of his hitting power than at a Sunday match at the end of the season. He played for R.A.Ingle's X1 against a strong Bath side that included four county players, Bertie Buse, Louis Powell, Stanley Amor and Walter Whiting. The latter who played eight matches for Somerset in the early Twenties, took six wickets for 13 runs to reduce the County side to 52 for six wickets. Arthur's batting was never more needed as he walked out to the middle and within an hour the Somerset total had increased by 177 runs. Arthur scored 147 of these runs in an innings that included thirteen sixes and nine fours. Several sixes cleared the pavilion and the limes at the road end of North Parade that were said to be at least 60 feet high even in those distant days. There was a large crowd to witness the occasion and no doubt many of them were hoping that he could repeat the performance in first-class cricket; everyone in Somerset felt Arthur's maiden century to be long overdue.

Somerset, fared no better in 1931 than they had done in the previous two years and there was little improvement to their position in the championship table. They finished thirteenth in 1931 compared to thirteenth equal in 1930. The situation was no better off the field of play. The weather had seriously affected the gates this year and Somerset suffered a heavy loss of £1,050. It took the club's overall deficit and overdraft to over £2,400, which was so damaging that the players and paid officials volunteered to take a 5% pay cut.

At the end of the 1931 season Arthur returned to his family for the winter and to unfamiliar territory. The Trengove family, including Jack, had moved from Bexley during the summer. A further decline in fortunes led to the move to 442 Footscray Road, New Eltham; a large edwardian semi situated off the High Street. It was to be the end of Arthur's long association with Bexley since there were no remaining family ties in that vicinity. He did, however, return to Bexley Cricket Club occasionally when in the area to visit friends. Arthur quickly adapted to his new surroundings and the ex-servicemen's club, less than five minutes away, at the top of Eltham High Street very soon became his second home. The club offered snooker and bowls among other attractions. Jack's brother Cecil who was a very keen snooker player quickly made himself a reputation at the club.

Arthur was a gifted snooker and billiards player himself and could have played snooker at the highest level if he had taken the game seriously. However, it was just a source of recreation for Arthur and the aptitude he had for the game was never exploited. Cecil Trengove would complain bitterly to his sister about Arthur. Cecil would practice religiously all day whereupon Arthur would put down his pint, drag himself away from the bar or a card school and proceed, in usual nonchalant style, to beat him without seemingly appearing to try!

During Arthur's time at the club, he became so good at snooker that he beat Fred Davis who, with his brother Joe, dominated world snooker for four decades. This was at a time when Fred, world champion during the late forties and early fifties, was approaching the height of his powers. True to form, Arthur never mentioned this achievement to anyone outside his immediate family. The ex-servicemen's club in Eltham High Street would become Arthur's 'winter retreat' for the next ten years. He even tried his hand at bowls and was soon bringing home honours and trophies much to the chagrin of the established bowlers.

Arthur returned to Somerset in the spring of 1932 and after the improvements of the previous season, he was again expected to do well. However, 1932 was to be an indifferent season for him with the ball although there were some encouraging signs of development in his batting that suggested further potential as an all-rounder. The season again got off to a bad start when the poor weather prevented any sort of bowling practice. The weather also badly affected Somerset's opening match at the Oval although there was a bright moment in Arthur's spirited innings of 28 runs. Eighteen of these runs came from a Bob Gregory over, which included one shot that hit the stonework of the centre portion of the pavilion. The ball bounced off the pavilion wall back into play where it was 'caught' by Barling, fielding on the boundary. His claims of a catch greatly amused the crowd as it did Arthur when he eventually saw the funny side of Barling's deception.

Somerset did manage to win their next game but it was the spinners that took the honours with Arthur having a modest match by his standards. The team travelled to Bristol for their next match, which became another casualty of the weather. Arthur bowled just 9 overs in the match but did hit three rasping leg-side sixes off Goddard in a brief innings of 26 runs. The rain continued throughout the Bath festival and produced treacherous conditions for bowlers and batsmen alike. The Worcestershire game was washed out and even the Yorkshire side struggled to 115 all out. It was still enough to give them a nine-wickets victory! Hazell for Somerset and Verity for Yorkshire did most of the damage, which meant Arthur had only a few token overs. Batting was difficult throughout and only Herbert Sutcliffe had the ability to cope with the conditions. In an uncharacteristic innings, Arthur took thirty-nine minutes to score 5 runs! The next match, the return fixture with Worcester, saw no improvement with only one completed innings in the entire match. It was hardly the start that Arthur had been looking for and the comments in *The Somerset County Gazette* did not ease his concern:

In the match against Worcestershire at Worcester he did not send down a ball and 53 overs were bowled. He is dropping catches too! Let's hope he has not struck a bad patch.

It was now into June, a quarter of the season completed, with Arthur having taken just seven wickets from the seven matches played. He would, however, look forward to the next match at Trent Bridge where a pace bowler's wicket would be guaranteed. Nottinghamshire batted first and Arthur struggled for his two wickets off 36 overs bowled. The home side scored 351 runs and let Larwood and Voce loose on the Somerset batsmen. Somerset were all out for 117 and, in following on, made an even greater mess of their second innings. At one stage, Somerset were 21 for eight wickets; the situation was custom-made for Arthur. Larwood and Voce were bowling at terrific speed but Arthur treated all the bowling the same. He hit an undefeated 41 runs in 35 minutes, which included two sixes and four fours. Arthur ran out of partners with the score on 72 and although Nottinghamshire had won the match by a huge margin, Arthur's spirit had not been broken.

The team's morale could hardly have plumbed greater depths but surprisingly, they immediately bounced back by beating the same side in the very next county match. It was their first win against Nottinghamshire since 1893 and Somerset's slender victory owed much to Arthur's positive approach. He hit Voce over the shilling stand during his first innings of 21 runs, which helped Lawrence Hawkins to guide Somerset to a respectable total. They finished on 242 all out after being 117 for seven wickets when Arthur and Lawrence Hawkins went out to bat after lunch. J.C.White with five wickets and Arthur with three wickets restricted the visitors to 219 all out but hopes of a big lead were soon dashed. Larwood sliced through the top-order batting and Somerset collapsed to 129 for seven wickets. For the second match in succession, it was left to Arthur to take up the gauntlet against Larwood and Voce. Later in the year, on the Bodyline Tour of Australia, this pair would decimate the Australian batting during the Sydney Test match. For the moment their sights were set a little lower. Arthur took no liberties with Larwood but hit Voce twice into the pavilion for six. He was caught on the boundary by William Keeton, bowled Voce but not before he had scored 40 priceless runs and provided Somerset with a decisive lead of 219 runs. Nottinghamshire were bowled out for 206 runs, which gave Somerset a famous victory.

The highlight of Arthur's season was his highest score to date, 93 not out against Northamptonshire at Kettering in July 1932. He would have undoubtedly achieved his first century had it not been for the weather and a peculiar incident towards the close of play. Rain had affected play on the first two days and fine drizzle prevented cricket on the last day until nearly 4.30pm. The only interest in the game was that Somerset might overhaul Northamptonshire's first innings score of 464 to secure first innings points. Arthur had already hit four sixes and eight fours when the last over was due to be bowled. He needed seven runs for his first ever century and Somerset required just two runs for first innings points with one wicket to spare. Arthur, curiously made no attempt to score off the last over thinking that the play would be extended to 6.30pm if necessary.

Bill Andrews who was sharing the last wicket partnership explained to David Foot what happened:

When the last over was called, we needed just one to tie and two to win (sic). But, Arthur, the slogger, had for some reason gone into his shell. He'd gone into a bit of a trance, not realising that the close of play on the third day was six p.m., and he wasn't taking any notice of my frantic gestures. Matthews bowled that final over and Arthur, to my horror, let the first three balls pass outside the off stump. The next three were played defensively. I ask you.

Bill was dropped for the next match because Reggie Ingle, in his first year as skipper, blamed him for not goading his partner into action. Bill lost his home match fee of £6 but he held Arthur in such uncritical esteem that Arthur's mental aberration was soon forgiven. Arthur had previously been quite severe on Matthews and regretted the lost opportunity in the last over. He was desperate to get his maiden first-class century and had decided to take no unnecessary chances. It was still the highest score of his career so far but an excellent opportunity had been thrown away. Arthur had much to learn about the game and the mistake would not be repeated. In retrospect it seems strange that the captain had not sent word to Arthur when it was clear what was happening.

Bill Andrews was not the only Somerset professional dropped by Reggie Ingle that year. In late August, on the northern tour that called at Sheffield and Blackpool, Arthur and another professional were guilty of an undisclosed misdemeanour. On the train journey back, Ingle sent for them and in the privacy of his compartment, gave them a severe dressing down. 'I'll let you know when I want you to play for me again' he said as they made their exit. Arthur was dropped for the next match at Taunton and the Somerset public never found out the reason for his absence. It was the only occasion in his professional career that he was dropped for any reason. Arthur bore Ingle no grudge. He had the greatest respect for the Somerset skipper who was better than most at bridging the amateur and professional divide.

It had been a brave thing for Ingle to do because Arthur had been in his best form of the season after a month of indifferent cricket. He had produced a match-winning performance against Lancashire at Weston-Super-Mare, just before the start of the northern tour. On a sticky wicket in a low-scoring match, Lancashire were set a modest total of 144 runs to win. They were 15 for one wicket overnight but on resumption lost Hopwood to a fine catch by Luckes off Arthur's bowling. Iddon was bowled by White who then dropped Tyldesley, off a delivery from Arthur, when the Red Rose County were 26 for three wickets. Arthur was bowling at a tremendous pace and fully deserved the two more wickets taken with successive deliveries. He struck Eddie Paynter on the foot and as umpire Hardstaff called 'out', Paynter collapsed in a heap, his leg numb from the force of the delivery. After Paynter had been helped off the field, Butterworth came and went, his uprooted leg stump somersaulting way past Wally Luckes who was standing back. Butterworth was to tell Arthur later that he never saw the delivery. This was the last ball of the over and spectators waited expectantly for Arthur's 'hat-trick' ball. Beattie survived, allowing the ball to pass his off stump, but the damage was done and there was no further resistance. Lancashire were all out for 92 runs. White took four wickets for 43 runs and Arthur four wickets for 16 runs off 17.2 overs, nine of which were maidens.

Arthur missed the match against Derbyshire at Taunton as a result of his indiscretion on the northern tour. He returned for the penultimate match against Warwickshire at Taunton, which Somerset won easily, and scored 50 in Somerset's only innings. He followed this with a fine score of 83 against Sussex at Hove to finish the season. It looked all over that he would get his maiden century but a brilliant boundary catch by Cook ended a delightful innings that had lasted a minute over the hour. He had scored 83 out of a partnership of 116 with his captain and his score contained two sixes, a five and ten fours. The crowd gave him a standing ovation as he walked defiantly back to the pavilion. It was a good ending to a disappointing season and probably helped save his flagging career.

Arthur finished the season with only 43 wickets at over 38 runs apiece. He did manage to score 759 runs in the championship at an average of just over 21 runs per innings but this was poor consolation for his bowling failure. There had been the usual collection of match-winning performances but there was no consistency in either his bowling or batting. Arthur came very close to being sacked at the end of the 1932 season after the Somerset administration decided that they could not afford to retain both Arthur and Bill Andrews. Neither player could have expected more than a year's contract but this would have provided some job security at a time when the Country was in the grip of the Depression. Unemployment was so rife that the Somerset authorities had been forced to offer a 50% reduction in admission fees for the unemployed. On production of an unemployment card, they could now watch a day's cricket for six old pence [2.5p]!

It is highly likely that Arthur's batting improvement tipped the balance in his favour and fortunately for Arthur they chose to dispense with the services of Bill Andrews, the first of his many exiles from Somerset. Bill soon found alternative employment as the professional with Forfarshire Cricket Club. John Daniell had given him a glowing reference to help him find new employment. The two-page handwritten testimonial, which Bill kept in one of his many scrapbooks, is full of praise for his ability as a cricketer. John Daniell also mentions in the letter that 'it was a mere toss-up whether we *[the Somerset Committee]* should let Wellard or Andrews go.' It clearly suggests that Arthur may have been closer to the sack than he ever realised at the time!

The season of 1932 had been a better year for the club and there were some encouraging signs of progress. They advanced to seventh in the table. J.C.White had another good year taking 102 wickets at less than 16 runs apiece and Reggie Ingle had been very influential with the bat and in his new role as captain. They would have been even closer if the Somerset players had held their catches. *The Somerset County Gazette* resorted to publishing the names of the guilty parties, presumably in the hope that they would be shamed into becoming a better fielding side. By the middle of August, their reporter had identified over seventy dropped catches. John Daniell was a fervent supporter of the paper's campaign. His often repeated motto was, 'catch your catches, win your matches.'

Somerset made a wise choice in not sacking Arthur because the 1933 season saw a change in Arthur's fortune and a return to something like the form of his first season. He exceeded 1,000 runs and 100 wickets in the championship and was the second player in Somerset's history to achieve the cricketer's 'double'. J.C.White was the first, in 1929 and 1930, after the number of matches increased from twenty-four to twenty-eight, making it easier to achieve. Arthur achieved his 'double' despite the number of matches being reduced to twenty-six.

Arthur was fitter than he had been for several seasons and appeared to be giving more thought to his bowling. In the previous two seasons he had bowled well above fast medium pace but this had been obtained by sacrificing his line and length. His bowling action was more rhythmical and he began to rediscover the movement off the pitch that had accounted for so many of his wickets in his first season. Arthur had a good early start but his first real test came with the eagerly awaited visit of the West Indians at the beginning of June. The West Indies were at full strength and Arthur must have had nightmares on seeing the perfect batting wicket that Harry Fernie had prepared. The West Indies took good advantage, scoring 482 runs, which included a fine double century from the 'Black Bradman', George Headley. His innings of 224 runs was faultless and contained thirty-one fours. Despite such an onslaught, Arthur bowled his 28 overs with fine control and was unlucky not to have captured more than his one wicket for 83 runs. Arthur produced an onslaught of his own in Somerset's second innings. His 28 runs, followed by a plucky unbeaten ninth-wicket stand between Jim Priddy and Wally Luckes, saved the match after an early batting collapse. Arthur's brief innings included sixes into the River Tone and the churchyard before being caught in the deep attempting a third.

The highlight of his championship season was against Hampshire at Portsmouth in June 1933. The match was dominated by Arthur and *Wisden* wrote:

The excellent all-round work of Wellard, who scored 137 runs and took ten wickets for less than 11 runs apiece, was mainly responsible for Somerset winning by 107 runs.

Somerset began the match badly, collapsing to 38 for six wickets before Arthur restored some respectability to the innings. He reached his fifty in forty minutes and was eventually out for 77, scored in a partnership of 94 runs with Jack Lee. Arthur's innings included four sixes and he was out to a fine catch on the boundary line by the Arsenal and England footballer, Ted Drake. By mid-afternoon and before a delayed tea interval, Hampshire's first innings reply was in tatters. Arthur bowled so well in his 10 overs that he took the first four wickets that fell for 18 runs. Not content to take a well-deserved rest, Arthur bowled unchanged for the rest of the first day. He finished with six wickets for 41 runs leaving Hampshire 103 runs behind with one wicket standing. The following morning he took the final wicket and in due course came out again to compile a second innings score of 60 that was no less spectacular than his first innings. In the space of fifty minutes he and H.D.Burrough put on 89 runs for the seventh wicket. Arthur's vigorous driving included two sixes, one of which was hit clean out of the ground on to an adjoining railway embankment. Arthur had still not finished with this match; he took three wickets for 66 runs in a fine spell of fast bowling, which lasted 29.2 overs.

This was to be the beginning of a most prolific period of bold and fierce hitting. Between the middle of July and the end of August he would register scores of fifty or more in seven different matches. Against Hampshire at Bath, he hit 66 out of 96 runs in an eighth-wicket partnership before being caught from a skier in the deep. He received just thirty-five deliveries, scoring off twenty-two of them, and in one over from O.W.Herman he scored twenty off four consecutive deliveries. His fifty came in twenty-five minutes and his innings contained five sixes and five fours.

Arthur followed this match with a typically aggressive innings of 66 runs at the Oval, scored in less than an hour. He then returned to Taunton where, against the Essex bowlers, he hit 52 out of 78 runs scored in forty minutes. His two sixes off Smith both went over the pavilion. There was another big hit recorded against Gloucestershire at Ashley Down, Bristol, also known as Fry's Ground. The hit went well into the old Rugby enclosure and prompted some of the old time members to reckon that it was the biggest six ever seen on the ground. As Gilbert Jessop had often played on Fry's Ground, this was a great compliment. Similar scores were made at Northampton where he hit 61 out of 88 runs, including two sixes. His first six injured a woman spectator who committed the cardinal sin of not keeping a sharp eye out when Arthur was batting.

Arthur took a particularly liking to the Glamorgan bowlers during this second half of the season. At Weston in early August, he scored 65 in a forty-five minute innings that included five sixes and five fours. He hit Emrys Davies for three sixes in one over, two of which went out of the ground. He also struck a massive blow off J.C.Clay, which landed high up on the roof of St. Paul's Church. It is the longest ever six hit at Clarence Park measuring 155 yards from the centre of the wicket to the foot of the outside wall of the church. It is only when standing in the centre of Clarence Park that it is possible to appreciate Arthur's awesome power with the bat. This hit prompted Clay to throw himself to the ground in mock surrender. The holiday crowd were then treated to the comical sight of Clay bowling under-armed lobs in order to avoid a repeat of the stroke and to stem the flow of runs. There was the even more comical sight of Arthur losing his wicket to one of these lobs. He drove the ball straight back to Clay with such ferocity that the umpire took evasive action, missing Clay's stinging return catch.

The Glamorgan bowlers fared no better against Arthur in the return match at Cardiff later in the month. This time, Glamorgan declared at 373 for seven wickets leaving Somerset to bat on a rain-affected pitch. They were quickly in trouble and at one stage J.C.Clay sent back five men for five runs off twenty-two overs! Just when it appeared that Somerset would have to follow on, Arthur saved the situation. He immediately set about the bowling and took three sixes and one four off the next four overs. He punished Clay who was then taken off and when the bowler was tried at the football end, Arthur hit him for another 18 runs off his first two overs. He hit four sixes all told, two of which went out of the ground and through the construction works being carried out on a new stand at Cardiff Arms Park. He scored 59 out of the 78 runs put on for the seventh wicket to save the match.

Arthur maintained this rich vein of scoring right up to the last championship match of the season, against Nottinghamshire at Taunton. On the second day of the match, he hit 70 runs, included five sixes and four fours. It was a great day for Arthur who had already taken his one hundredth wicket in the previous match. This innings now took him past his one thousandth run. In appreciation of his efforts, a collection was taken at the ground, which received a ready response from the large crowd. The collection realised £16.13s.5d!

There were similar exploits with the ball from Arthur during this period. Against Kent at Tunbridge Wells he finished with seven wickets for 59 runs in Kent's first innings to set up a Somerset victory. Kent had virtually lost the match in the first hour of play after collapsing to 31 for six wickets; Arthur took four of these wickets at six runs apiece.

There was another match-winning performance against Worcestershire at Stourbridge. After a blank first day, Somerset scored 214 on a difficult wicket and Worcestershire finished the day on 81 for five wickets. Arthur had no luck whatsoever having bowled 12 overs for 16 runs without any success. When play resumed the following morning, Worcestershire slumped to 90 all out and were

forced to follow on. It was Arthur's opening spell that
created the havoc. His figures were:

O	M	R	W
6	3	5	4

Worcestershire never recovered. Tom Young, playing his
last season for Somerset, took seven wickets in their
second innings and Somerset won by ten wickets.

It had been a splendid year for Arthur. He had
operated without his bowling partner, Bill Andrews, and
without a replacement in the pace attack. Arthur appeared
to relish the extra responsibility and work. He had taken
104 championship wickets at an average of 25.58 runs
apiece. It was his batting, however, that had been the more
remarkable. In the season he scored 1055 runs at an average
of 26.38 runs per innings. His tally of sixes in the season
was 51, the first of four occasions that he would exceed
fifty sixes in a season. The other remarkable thing about
his batting this year was the proportion of runs scored
from boundary hits. Apart from the sixes, he hit 89 fours,
so two thirds of his runs came from boundaries. *Wisden*
wrote of Arthur:

His batting bold and enterprising as ever frequently served to extricate
his side from awkward situations and whatever the aspect of the game, he
usually punished the bowling mercilessly and without fear. No other first
class cricketer hit so many sixes during the course of the season.

Somerset wasted no time in securing Arthur's services
for the coming season. It was well known that he had
received some tempting offers to play league cricket. One
substantial offer from Bacup, the Lancashire league club,
was sent by telegram to the Chilvers Coton Ground at
Nuneaton while Arthur was playing for Somerset against
Warwickshire. Bacup's offer was worth a great deal more
than Somerset could afford to pay him. Arthur kept Somerset
in suspense for some time before signing a new contract but
there was never any serious intention on his part to go
into league cricket. The offers did, however, enable him to
negotiate some marginal improvement in terms.

There was someone else who had appreciated Arthur's bold and enterprising cricket. Arthur's innings of 66 at the Oval in late July had impressed Jack Hobbs so much that he asked Arthur to play for his charity team at Wimbledon later in the season. Arthur, greatly honoured by the invitation, readily agreed to play. The Jack Hobbs' X1 was quite formidable and included such famous names as Sandham, Gover, Squires, Barling and Santall. Jack Hobbs would not be disappointed by Arthur's performance. An article in a 1992 *Somerset Wyverns Newsletter* by John Stark, recalled the occasion very clearly:

My gaze concentrated on Wellard, bowling not, I suspect, at full pace but good enough to take several wickets. He batted halfway down the order, by which time Hobbs was cruising comfortably. The fireworks started on Wellard's arrival. He batted for little longer than fifteen minutes or so and scored forty runs. Few were singles and the boundaries included straightly driven fours and five sixes. Three of these cleared the tall netting surrounding the perimeter of the ground; of these, two hit parked cars and the third smashed a bedroom window. The fourth six also went out of the ground and the fifth landed near the apex of the roof of a four storied house. That hit, in my book was worth the entrance money alone.

Jack Hobbs was content to play second fiddle during this brief and masterful display of hitting. He sent Arthur a commemorative pen with a typically fine letter. Arthur kept the letter which is reproduced opposite:

TELEPHONE: STREATHAM 1819. WIMBLEDON 3406.

DARRAWELLA,
23 DUNSTALL ROAD,
WIMBLEDON,
LONDON, S.W. 20.

WOODTHORPE,
39, ATKINS ROAD,
CLAPHAM PARK,
S.W. 12.

Oct. 6/33

My dear Arthur,

No, I have'nt forgotten about it! . Here is the pen which I hope will reach you safely and please you .

Thank you for playing for my team at Wimbledon.

With kind regards to Mrs. Wellard & yourself and hoping you will winter well

Yours sincerely
Jack Hobbs,

Arthur Wellard Esq.
442, Footscray Road
S.E. 9

Arthur did winter well as Jack Hobbs had wished but on his return to Taunton in the spring of 1934 there were nagging fitness problems that would affect his bowling throughout the season. There were few high spots in his bowling performances during the season but his batting continued to improve. He would also reach an important milestone when at last scoring his maiden century.

The century was scored in mid-June, fittingly against Surrey at the Oval and in the presence of Jack Hobbs. He was dropped in the slips by Garland-Wells when on 22 but his innings was otherwise very disciplined and restrained. His innings of 112 runs took two hours and twenty-five minutes - slow-going by Arthur's standards – and included three sixes and fourteen fours. He brought up his hundred with a beautiful on-drive and followed this stroke with his third six. He came as near as anyone to striking the gasometer after glancing the roof of the east stand. In desperation, Garland-Wells handed the ball to Laurie Fishlock, a very occasional bowler, and Arthur sliced his drive to mid-on, into the hands of the relieved Surrey skipper. In the context of the match, Arthur's century was extremely valuable because Somerset were staring defeat in the face when Arthur strode to the crease. At lunch on the third day, they were 123 for seven wickets and still needed 126 runs to avoid an innings defeat. Thanks to Arthur and some determined support from Hawkins and Luckes, the match was saved, proving beyond doubt that he was more than just a slogger. For all that Arthur gave the appearance of not caring, he was always immensely proud of this century and the fact that it had been scored at the Oval.

The match would be as memorable for Jack Hobbs as it was for Arthur. Although not apparent at the time, it was to be his last first-class match at his beloved Oval. Jack Hobbs, at fifty-one years of age, was playing irregularly but was still driven by the desire to score three more centuries to complete his two hundredth century. He batted, unaccountably, at number four in Surrey's only innings and was caught by Arthur, bowled P.J.Davey for fifteen.

There were several occasions in 1934 when Arthur almost repeated his three-figure score and, in contrast to the Oval century, all of these scores were achieved in rapid time. A new competition had been introduced featuring a prize of £100 for the scorer of the fastest hundred during the season; it was later referred to as the Lawrence Trophy. This was a substantial sum of money, equivalent to £2,500 at today's prices, and Arthur naturally fancied his chances of winning the prize. In July, he hit 81 runs against Worcestershire at Frome in the space of forty minutes. The first 49 runs came in thirteen minutes before he lost the bowling!

He came closer still in the next match against Glamorgan at Swansea when the time to beat for the fastest century was sixty-five minutes. When Arthur came in to bat, Somerset required 123 runs to avoid an innings defeat, with four wickets standing. Arthur needed a crisis before he could summons the necessary determination but the prize of £100 was also a powerful incentive. His first 39 runs came in eight minutes but then C.C.C.Case collared the bowling and the minutes ticked by. In the end, Arthur scored 96 out of 156 runs in just under ninety minutes. His innings included five sixes and nine fours. He hit the refreshment marquee twice and one of his other sixes was the biggest seen at Swansea in living memory. It cleared the seating accommodation and landed alongside the members enclosure. It is a long way from the pavilion to ground level at St. Helens as anyone who has negotiated the eighty or so steps can confirm. Arthur's innings merely delayed the inevitable and Glamorgan still had plenty of time to secure a nine-wickets victory.

The visit to Taunton of the Australian tourists was the eagerly awaited event of the season. The match was at the end of June and the small Taunton ground was packed to overflowing. On the first day, Somerset were completely flummoxed by the bowling of Bill O'Reilly who took nine wickets for 38 runs. Had it not been for a gritty performance from Frank Lee who carried his bat for 59 runs, Somerset would have got nowhere near their feeble total of 116 runs. Australia overhauled this score by the close of play finishing on 148 for two wickets, with Woodfull and Darling in good form. Arthur bowled exceptionally well on the second day and was given a tremendous ovation when he came off the field. His morning's effort had brought him six Australian wickets for 67 runs and the tourist had been restricted to a modest total of 309 runs. All Arthur's good work was soon wasted and this time it was Fleetwood-Smith who created problems for Somerset. They started disastrously, were 52 for four wickets, then Reggie Ingle and H.D.Burrough followed after a few more runs had been added. By the time Arthur came in with six wickets down, the game was all but over so he decided to give the large crowd their money's worth. He twice drove Fleetwood-Smith out of the ground and it took a magnificent catch from Chipperfield to end the fireworks. The match finished shortly afterwards, Australia winning by an innings and 77 runs.

Arthur managed an appearance for his old club Bexley during 1934. The Saturday of their Cricket Week coincided with a free week in the Somerset calendar so Arthur travelled over from Colchester where Somerset had just lost to Essex. Arthur's appearance for Bexley against a Bank of England X1 had been billed as the main attraction of the week and some 3,000 spectators turned up for the match. They were not disappointed and Arthur gave the large crowd a treat by scoring a magnificent 149 out of his side's 260 runs. He was stumped, going down the wicket, trying to reach his 150 in style. The match is still talked about today and for excitement and atmosphere this was probably the most memorable occasion in the club's history. Arthur opened the bowling and took the wickets of both openers for one run before being discreetly removed from the attack. The bank finished on 181 runs and the crowd had good value for their money with Arthur enthusiastically taking around the collection tin for the club and the groundsman.

Arthur remained in the South East to make his second appearance for the Players against the Gentlemen. In this match, which was again at the Oval starting on the 11th July, Arthur produced his best performance for the Players. The small Oval crowd was treated to an orgy of run-making by the strong Players team, which amassed a first innings total of 651 for seven wickets declared. Arthur scored 91 quick runs coming in at number seven and at one stage adding 85 runs in thirty-five minutes with R.G.Duckfield of Glamorgan. He batted for an hour and fifteen minutes and hit a huge, high trajectory six into the pavilion. There were further lusty blows and, in total, he hit fourteen fours. The Gentlemen were bowled out for 192 and 154 losing by an innings and 305 runs. Arthur took four wickets for 60 runs off 17.3 overs in the first innings and three wickets for 53 runs off 13.5 overs in the second. Sir Pelham Warner writing in his book *Gentlemen v Players 1806-1949* commented on 'Wellard's clever use of a slow ball'. Arthur relished these challenges and loved to 'put one over' the amateurs whom he could never quite fathom. At the end of the match he was heard to naively comment to E.R.T.Holmes, 'I can't understand it. We get paid for this but you chaps are doing it for fun!'

Arthur made his third appearance for the Players at Folkestone in September. Folkestone was a lower-key fixture and one of five grounds, other than Lord's and the Oval, to stage a handful of Gentlemen v Players matches. The match would be remembered for being Jack Hobbs' last appearance for the Players but Arthur would have few memories of this fixture; he did little with either bat or ball.

At the end of the season, Arthur could reflect on his batting performances with some pride. There had been three scores of ninety or more, all made on away grounds, and his 91 runs for the Players had secured him a total of 1,000 first-class runs for the season. His bowling had not been so impressive and, apart from his performance against the Australians, it had been a very poor season with the ball. He ended the season with 62 wickets at a cost of just under 42 runs apiece. Somerset's fielding again let them down and Arthur seemed to suffer more than most. *Wisden* wrote:

Time after time, missed catches at important periods of the game meant all the difference between gaining an advantage or conceding it and it says much for the bowlers that they never lost heart.

It was true that Arthur never lost heart and never complained, although he played at times in great pain.

Arthur was not one to make much of his knee problems and he regularly played when not fully fit. It did not do to be out of the game when your livelihood depended upon being able to play. Arthur returned to the South East and another change of surroundings. Arthur and Jack bought their first house together, although it says much about their relationship that the move was arranged and completed during the summer. Jack paid £850 for a newly built house in Cadwallon Road, which was less than half a mile from her parents' house in Footscray Road, New Eltham. Arthur, always one for the quiet life, went along with Jack's decision to move. It gave the couple the chance to be alone for the first time since their marriage but little else changed in their lives. Arthur still had the snooker club nearby, now even closer, and Jack spent most of her spare time back at the family home with her mother.

The move was short-lived. Jack was already regretting the decision to move when her father, Reginald, suffered a stroke at Christmas. Arthur and his young sister-in-law Betty kept a vigil at his bedside but he died a few days later. Reginald Trengove left very little money and so Jack seized the opportunity to sell the house in Cadwallon Road and buy the family home in Footscray Road. Before a year was up, Arthur and Jack had returned to the bosom of the Trengove family and life resumed as normal.

4

1935: Fortunes change

HAD ARTHUR TAKEN STOCK of the past five summers he could not have been satisfied with his progress. He could be justifiably pleased with his achievements in his first season of 1929 and in his 'double' season of 1933. Between these seasons and after, his bowling had been indifferent and, at times, poor. Excuses could be found for his bowling but if Arthur was ever to become something more than just a journeyman cricketer, his fortunes would need to change quickly. His batting technique had improved out of all recognition and he could now be genuinely regarded as an all-rounder. What he now needed was to achieve greater consistency in his bowling in order to gain wider recognition.

One of Arthur's problems was that he never did trouble his head about his career and the direction it was moving. Somerset rarely gave their professionals long contracts and Arthur was content just so long as he could secure a further renewal. However, it is just possible that by the time Arthur returned to Somerset in the spring of 1935, he had realised the need for a 'make or break' season. There certainly was a more steely resolve to his game that was apparent from the opening day of the county season on the 4th May 1935. Somerset were at the Oval to play Surrey and Arthur, who was beginning to get a liking for the ground's open spaces, almost scored the second century of his career. He hit a magnificent 99 runs after going in at number seven. He drove Alf Gover high over the long-on boundary and then, from the Vauxhall end, he hit Whitfield for a gigantic six, which dropped into the top balcony on the pavilion roof. Later, off Berry, he provided the Oval crowd with the rare sight of a straight driven six over the railings at the Vauxhall End; a minimum carry of 125 yards. Altogether, he hit four sixes and six fours in his innings. Somerset had much the better of the game throughout and declared their second innings closed after Arthur hit a brisk 37 not out, which included a six and five fours. Surrey were left to score 246 to win but when stumps were drawn, they were in desperate trouble at 36 for five wickets. Arthur had taken three wickets for 19 runs and Bill Andrews, returning for his second spell with the club, took the other two wickets for 10 runs. Arthur had appreciated the extra support from the opposite end of the wicket and the two friends left the field, arms linked, to fine applause from the Surrey crowd.

In the next game, against Northamptonshire, Arthur had a five-wicket haul in the second innings, which but for some poor batting from his team - being all out for 75 - would have secured a Somerset victory. Other fine bowling performances followed and by the end of May, Arthur had taken almost half as many wickets as he had taken the previous season. There had also been some bold displays of hitting. This included a six at Lord's, off R.W.V.Robins, which went over the clock tower *[now behind the Compton Stand]* and a six at Trent Bridge which dropped into the West Bridgford Road. The old Nottinghamshire player, Jack Carlin, reckoned it was the biggest six he had ever seen. The match at Trent Bridge was a controversial affair after rain had made the pitch dangerous. Arthur and Bill Andrews were getting the ball to rear up and the crowd were screaming 'get 'em off'. Arthur hit Joe Hardstaff twice in an over and sportingly bowled the last ball off two paces. The pair were subsequently removed from the attack. The pitch does not appear to have bothered Arthur; his 68 runs came in twenty-nine minutes before the anticipation of winning the £100 prize spoiled his concentration.

This was also the month in which Somerset beat Essex at Frome, thanks to Harold Gimblett's debut performance. He went in when Somerset were 107 for six wickets and reached his century in sixty-three minutes. It turned out to be the fastest of the season and won him the Lawrence Trophy. Arthur had earlier taken pity on the youngster and lent him a bat. Harold's own bat, which Arthur referred to as a 'lump of wood', appeared to be held together by strategically placed tape and string. Arthur gave Harold Gimblett the bat afterwards; he reckoned he had earned it! Arthur also contributed to Somerset's victory having taken five wickets for 66 runs in the Essex first innings. It was their first win of the season and the team had to wait until the beginning of July before their next victory. They lost six matches during this period and significantly Arthur missed four of these games after he twisted a small muscle above the right elbow whilst fielding at Hove. The injury did not respond to treatment and after further examination, he was sent to Guy's Hospital, where the doctors operated to remove a small piece of bone.

When Arthur returned, he was quickly into the thick of the action at Taunton against Kent. Somerset had batted abysmally in their first innings of 85 and looked to be heading for an embarrassing innings defeat. In the second innings, Arthur played defensively up to the luncheon interval but afterwards batted with all the usual freedom and fluency. He compiled 75 runs in fifty-eight minutes, hitting five sixes and five fours. Three of the sixes came off J.G.Davies, including two into the river. In this twenty-minute spell after lunch he hit 44 runs. Arthur then turned his attention to 'Tich' Freeman, drove him for four and then hit him over the stand next to the pavilion. By the time Arthur was caught attempting another big hit, the innings defeat had been averted. Kent eventually won the match by eight wickets.

Somerset's second victory of the season was against Gloucestershire at Bath and Arthur's telling contribution of five wickets for 39 runs in Gloucestershire's first innings helped set up a narrow one-wicket victory. Somerset were now almost halfway through the county season with only two wins to their name. There was hardly much improvement during the remainder of the season, with Somerset achieving only three more victories. Their third win was against Glamorgan at Pontypridd but for once, Arthur's contribution was eclipsed by a match-winning performance from J.H. 'Snowball' Cameron who took eight wickets in the match. Arthur did, however, play a major part in the other two victories against Essex - for the second time in this season - and against Kent.

The match against Essex, at Clacton-on-Sea towards the end of July, was a thrilling affair. Arthur drove with tremendous power in Somerset's first innings hitting 57 runs. In one over from Boswell he hit three superb sixes and a four. He hit another two sixes in an over from Eastman. Arthur took a couple of wickets in Essex's first innings and by the beginning of the third day there was nothing between the sides. Somerset were just 48 runs ahead when Reggie Ingle took a calculated risk and altered the batting order to get runs quickly. The wicket for Somerset's second innings had deteriorated badly but Arthur was in determined mood and still had half an eye on snatching the £100 prize from Gimblett's grasp. He scored 83 out of 125 runs, made in just over the hour and hit four sixes, one five and seven fours. It enabled Somerset to declare and Essex, by now totally demoralised, were all out for 110 in an hour and fifty minutes.

Two of Arthur's sixes were hit clean out of the ground on to the railway track. One of these huge blows gave rise to the popular story - now a part of Wellard folklore - that Arthur hit the longest ever six. There is no reference to the hit in *Wisden* because it is supposed to have become the longest six by landing in a moving goods train bound for London; or so the story goes! As with many popular cricket tales, the story has benefited from a certain amount of embellishment. However, the ball, which was bowled by Evans, did land in the cab of a stationary engine about to leave Clacton where it was retrieved by a somewhat startled fireman!

News of the Essex match must have caused some trepidation amongst the Kent supporters knowing that Somerset were to visit Maidstone the very next day. They were well aware that Arthur always put in that little extra effort against them and this occasion was no exception. Somerset were put in on a difficult wicket and collapsed to

57 for five wickets by the time Arthur came into bat. Arthur's entrance met with the usual response from the opposition with fielders scattering to all parts of the ground but for four overs, Arthur belied his reputation. He took the odd single and played some exaggerated defensive strokes. He was paying due regard to Somerset's perilous predicament and at the same time sending messages to the dressing room that at least one member of the team could bat responsibly when necessary! Everyone on the ground knew that it was just a matter of time before he would open his shoulders so the defensive ring of boundary fielders stayed put. They did not have long to wait. He took 14 runs off Todd, which included a mighty six and in Todd's next over, he drove him into the trees. When Claude Lewis was brought on to bowl, he was immediately driven out of the ground for six. He reached his fifty with a polished leg-glance and hit Todd for another six before being caught on the long-on boundary. He had scored 74 in an hour, including four sixes and eight fours.

There was no respite for the Kent fielders in Somerset's second innings. As on the previous day, he went in when Somerset were struggling and completely altered the aspect of the game within a short space of time. Lewis took most of the punishment and was hit for three sixes but Todd was also pulled over the long-on boundary. He scored 70 runs before again being caught in the deep. Arthur had been the highest scorer in each Somerset innings. Kent still only had to score 170 runs to win but Arthur and Bill were in no mood to let the game slip from Somerset's grasp. Arthur with four wickets for 39 runs off 19.4 overs and Bill Andrews with six wickets for 65 runs off 18 overs reduced the shell-shocked Kent team to 117 all out.

In the course of five successive innings, Arthur had scored 334 spectacular runs. These included twenty-three sixes and twenty-five fours, almost three quarters of the runs scored. It brought his season's tally of sixes to forty-four. This prolific run of bold hitting attracted great interest and all the national newspapers covered his exploits. *The Sunday People* even published a poem to celebrate his achievement.

Ray Brock of Bristol committed the verse to memory and can still recite the poem despite the passing of some sixty years:

> *When Wellard wields the willow*
> *He hits the Welkin ring*
> *His slashes o'er the meadow*
> *Make him the hitting king*
>
> *From Wells fair field to Maidstone*
> *He's clashed the ball with shocks*
> *His sixes number twenty three*
> *In five successive knocks*
>
> *How can a ball of leather*
> *Roll calmly off the turf*
> *When Somerset's son of Ajax*
> *Sends it flying off the dirt*

The ground was almost full for the following match against Middlesex at Taunton. The supporters had turned up in large numbers hoping that Arthur would continue his rich vein of form with the bat. Somerset batted first and he might have given them what they wanted had it not been for a controversial umpiring decision. Somerset were in their customary precarious position at five wickets for less than fifty runs; the situation was made for Arthur and the Somerset supporters waited in eager anticipation. Arthur hit a two, two singles and a six off the first five balls he faced but was then caught by Joe Hulme on the boundary line. The Arsenal and England soccer player, had leapt into the air to take the catch but fell over the line. Everyone but Joe, the fielders and the umpire felt it was an obvious six but Arthur was given out. The disappointed crowd howled for him to be called back but the decision was left to stand. Somerset were all out for 117 runs and even a fine spell of bowling from Arthur - taking six wickets for 91 runs - could not prevent Middlesex building an unassailable first innings lead. The visitors achieved a comfortable nine-wickets victory.

Arthur had an excellent Weston festival taking nineteen wickets at around 22 runs apiece but all three festival matches were drawn. This year's festival would also be memorable for an Arthurian six that is still remembered by those people fortunate to see it. In the game against Nottinghamshire, he hooked Harold Larwood clean out of the ground and into the adjoining park. It was his forty-ninth six of the season and he took his tally to fifty-one in a brief second innings of 24 that was enough to complete his 1,000 runs for the season.

Not surprisingly, Arthur's exploits were attracting a great deal of press speculation about him playing for England. Many good judges were confidently predicting that Arthur would be selected for the final Test against South Africa at the Oval in mid-August. They were suggesting that he should play as an all-rounder at number 6 or 7 in the order. South Africa had only to draw the match to win the rubber - a feat not previously achieved in England - so the forecast was for an attacking English line-up. The selectors, however, ignored Arthur's obvious credentials and took an even greater gamble in choosing H.D.Read and J.C.Clay for their first Test appearances. Read and Clay were both amateurs and Wykehamists, which probably gave them a head's start. The captain, R.E.S.Wyatt, put South Africa in on a perfect wicket and neither bowler produced a match-winning performance. The game was drawn, South Africa won the series and neither Read nor Clay played for England again.

Arthur had already played the South Africans earlier in the season at Bath when he took four wickets in each innings. On the strength of his bowling throughout the season and in this match in particular, it is surprising that he was not being tipped for an earlier Test. He was fitter than for a long time and bowling as fast as ever. The South Africans were probably relieved that Arthur had been ignored throughout the summer. W.H.Ferguson, the 'universal' scorer, who toured with the South Africans, reckoned that Arthur was the fastest they had faced up to their match at Bath, which incidently followed the tourists' comprehensive victory in the second Test at

Lord's. The South Africans were certainly disturbed by
Arthur pace at Bath as H.B.Cameron, the hero of the second
Test, would have testified. Cameron, who was a powerful
hitter, drove Arthur's first delivery through mid-off for
four and repeated the stroke off the next three balls.
Arthur, looking extremely perplexed, bowled a much quicker
ball that Cameron deflected on to his head. He had to be
taken to hospital, needed four stitches to mend the gash in
his head and took no further part in the game. Jock Cameron
died tragically of enteric fever only days after returning
from the tour of England.

It is tempting to speculate what might have happened
if Arthur had been playing in the final Test. Meanwhile,
Arthur contented himself with playing against Surrey at
Yeovil. He made runs and took eight of the twelve wickets
to fall, including six wickets for 69 runs in Surrey's
first innings. Somerset still managed to lose the match by
eight wickets in under two days. The poorly prepared wicket
and the new leg-before-wicket rule were blamed for the weak
batting display. Arthur top-scored in Somerset's first
innings with 41 out of a total of 149 runs.

Only three county games remained to be played after
Surrey's victory at Yeovil. The first of these was against
Lancashire at Old Trafford and it was a game that Arthur
would remember with great pride. He scored his second
century, matching his previous best total scored at the
Oval the previous year. It came a good deal quicker than
his first and was a more typical Wellard innings. His
performance delighted the crowd of about 7,000 people, many
of whom had turned up especially to see him bat. He went in
when Somerset were in trouble at 109 for five wickets.
Arthur hit five sixes and ten fours in his innings of 112
runs, which was made from a total of 145 runs scored in
about ninety minutes. He reached his fifty in thirty-five
minutes and at this stage, appeared to be in with a chance
of beating Harold Gimblett's time of sixty-three minutes to
take the Lawrence Trophy. However, he received less of the
bowling and his century eventually took eighty-five minutes
to complete. All five of his sixes were huge blows that
would live in the memory of those present. A ball from Jack

Iddon was hit over the former ladies stand *[now the MacLaren stand]* before smashing the screen of an adjacent car and another almost cleared the Hornby stand. Len Hopwood's delivery was driven out of the ground into the Warwick Road and the ball from Frank Sibbles went over the square-leg boundary hitting one of the towers on top of the pavilion. Another ball from Sibbles landed near the railway station. He was out leg-before-wicket to Sibbles and when he left the field every member 'stood to' and gave him a wonderful reception. C.L.R.James, the highly respected cricket writer, described this innings as extraordinary. Another reporter described it as 'the finest display of vigorous hitting seen at Old Trafford for many years in a performance that would be long remembered.'

Arthur rounded off the county season with a fine all-round display at Taunton in a rain-affected match against Sussex. When Somerset eventually started their innings, they soon found themselves in their customary position. Arthur joined J.C.White with his team five wickets down for 28 runs. With White defending stubbornly, Arthur reached his fifty in thirty minutes with some bold driving. In all, he made 68 out of 77 runs scored in an hour for the sixth wicket. Fifty of these runs came from eleven scoring strokes; three sixes and eight fours. Sussex just managed first innings points in the time available despite Arthur's five wickets for 44 runs.

Arthur took 105 wickets for Somerset at 20.53 runs apiece, ranking a close second in the Somerset averages to Bill Andrews who also took 100 wickets. The return of Bill Andrews - with Forfarshire since his release in 1932 - had provided Somerset with a penetrating opening attack. The pair were christened 'the terrible twins' and proved an ideal combination with one usually making the ball leave the bat and the other making it come into the bat. Somerset's other bowling, however, had been ineffective. Somerset's batting was no better and they finished the championship in fourteenth position, losing eleven of the twenty-six matches played. Arthur also finished second in the batting averages having scored 1232 runs at an average of 32.42; it was his second 'cricketer's double'.

Before leaving the review of his county season, it is interesting to note that Arthur received around £350 from Somerset for his magnificent efforts in 1935. His contract paid him a retainer of £3 per week and a further £2 per week for acting as 'Ground Bowler' during April. He received £6 for each match played in Somerset and £8 for those outside the County. The difference was to pay for accommodation and evening meals so it is not surprising that the professionals went to extraordinary lengths to save on their expenses. This included pitching tents on the ground, as close to the beer tent as would be allowed, and resorting to three or four sharing a room or even a bed. Bill Andrews would recall the comic occasion they shared a double-bed. Bill woke to find Arthur's false teeth sticking into him! When they played in a weekend match, other than those in Somerset or Gloucestershire, the professionals received an extra £1 for their expenses. This barely covered their living costs, not to mention their Saturday night entertainment, so any available bed at Arthur's house in New Eltham was commandeered when the professionals were in Town.

Within the next few years, as Arthur's worth to Somerset increased, his match fees went up to £8 for home games and £12 for away games. This still only provided a modest income of less than £450 but it was the going-rate for a cricketer at the top of his game. Arthur continued to receive many tempting offers from the league like the one from Bacup in 1933. The offers were always turned down because Arthur was not motivated by the money. His simple wish was to play county cricket and Arthur genuinely believed that asking too much from Somerset might risk putting him out of the first-class game. He was probably correct and the fact that few professionals had contracts lasting more than a year merely served to heighten their extreme sense of insecurity. Arthur's Northern league offers did extract one concession from the Somerset administration for they agreed to count only Taunton matches as home games. This had been a bone of contention with Arthur for some time since all Somerset home games were effectively away games for him.

The 1935 county championship season ended after the final day of the Sussex game on Tuesday, 3rd September 1935 but Arthur's cricket season was far from over. With the match heading for a draw, Arthur was able to slip away and catch the train to Folkestone. He was due to make his fourth appearance for the Players against the Gentlemen starting on the Wednesday. His hurried journey proved unnecessary as rain meant there was no play on the first day and with further interruptions for bad weather the game was played out to a draw on Friday. Arthur - promoted up the order to set up a declaration - scored 37 out of 50 runs scored in the space of fifteen minutes before he was brilliantly caught on the long-on boundary. His brief knock included three sixes and two fours. He was able to spend the weekend in New Eltham but then had to travel to Scarborough to play for H.D.G.Leveson Gower's X1. He was asked to play in a match, starting on the 11 September, against the previous winter's MCC team that had toured the West Indies. The matches at Scarborough were prestigious events in the cricket calendar. It was Arthur's first taste of Scarborough Festival cricket and Arthur planned to make a holiday of the occasion with his wife Jack.

All the cricketers privileged to receive an invitation looked forward to the Scarborough Festival. It was a chance to unwind and forget the rigours of a hard county season. Although the cricket was not without it's serious intent, the matches were also played for fun. Arthur's game complemented this approach and it is not surprising that he took to the Scarborough Festival in the same way that he had taken to Weston and Bath. There was still the same class differences as would be found in county cricket including the usual segregation of the amateurs and professionals. The Festival was organised by the Scarborough Cricket Club with lunch and tea being provided for the amateurs and their guests in the President's tent. The professionals had their lunch on their own but they were expected to attend the lavish dinners held at the Grand Hotel where their ladies would dine separately under the aegis of Mrs Leveson Gower. The dinners were followed by balls and dances, organised at various venues, which were black tie affairs. Arthur was a reluctant attender. He hated the dancing and the formal attire and Alf Gover remembers that Arthur would refer to these occasions as a 'right bleedin' business'. Most professionals tolerated the class distinction and there were plenty of less formal functions where they could relax and enjoy themselves.

The professionals could also be relied upon to find entertainment on the field of play. It was quite common for the first delivery of the innings to be a tennis ball or a tomato and there was always a sense of theatricality. Patsy Hendren, a Festival favourite, would don the most inappropriate cricket wear and one day borrowed Arthur's sweater - too big even for its owner - but on Patsy it came down to his calves, much to the amusement on the crowd.

Arthur had a moderate game by his standards, taking three wickets and scoring 35 not out and 16 in his two innings. His batting had been unusually subdued but he had done enough to secure further invitations to play at the Festival in the years up to the War. The offers would be readily accepted although Jack never accompanied him again. She had enjoyed Scarborough as there had been precious few chances to have a holiday together but the emphasis on cricket was too much for her. Arthur and Jack returned to London immediately after the match because Arthur still had another important game to play, at the Oval.

He was selected to play in the annual fixture between the Rest of England and The Champion County, which was Yorkshire. R.E.S.Wyatt captained a strong Rest of England side but Yorkshire, who had lost only one match in the season, won the match by 149 runs. It was the first defeat for the Rest since 1905. Arthur opened the bowling with H.D.Read and bowled at a lively pace taking three wickets for 41 runs in Yorkshire's first innings of 238 runs. This compared with Read's figures of three wickets for 107 runs, which may have given R.E.S.Wyatt further cause for reflection on the selectors' choice of bowlers in the final test against South Africa. The Rest's batting let them down in both innings and Arthur did not stay too long at the crease. He took two wickets for 20 runs in Yorkshire's second innings. His selection was further indication that the cricket authorities were taking a keen interest in him although not sufficient to win him a place on the MCC tour of New Zealand that winter. *The Somerset County Gazette* were moved to conclude that, 'had Arthur been a home county player, he most certainly would have been on the tour.'

Arthur ended the season with 114 first-class wickets at 20.68 runs apiece. He scored 1347 runs at an average of 31.32 runs per innings. His batting had been of a consistently high standard throughout the season although, much to the chagrin of the Somerset supporters, seven of his ten scores of fifty or more were made outside of Somerset. These seven scores included his three highest innings for the season. Arthur always reserved his best innings for away fixtures, which contradicts the widely-held view that his prolific scoring was assisted by the small, cosy grounds of Somerset.

Arthur's batting was also remarkable for the high number of sixes that the scores contained. In total, he was credited with seventy-two first-class sixes, which accounted for 35% of his total for the season! This record number of sixes was reduced to sixty-six exactly half a century later when another Somerset all-rounder, Ian Botham, scored eighty in a season. Arthur did not live to see his record overtaken and would not have appreciated its downward revision; the result of research undertaken by the cricket writer and renown expert on six-hitting, Gerald Brodribb.

Arthur would, however, have graciously acknowledged Botham's record, achieved in a lesser number of first-class matches. As a result of Botham's efforts in 1985, a new record for 'MOST PERSONAL SIXES IN A SEASON' was included in *Wisden*. The four other entries in this category, which equal or exceed fifty sixes, all belong to Arthur! Full details of his batting record and six-hitting in 1935 are included in the Statistical Appendices. It provides further evidence to refute the argument that Arthur was assisted by the small Somerset grounds as two-thirds of his sixes in 1935 were scored on grounds outside Somerset. In Ian Botham's case, two-thirds of his sixes in 1985 were scored on Somerset grounds.

Arthur was disappointed not to be going to New Zealand but was confident that national recognition was round the corner. It was a mystery to all concerned why the selectors continued to ignore his claims. His cavalier approach to cricket was never going to endear him to the England selectors but there was some support for him even in this camp. Pelham Warner, the most influential selector, paid Arthur a glowing tribute when he wrote his account of the Somerset season:

Somerset's Wellard hit no fewer than seventy-two 6's - surely a record in first-class cricket since hits over the boundary have thus been reckoned - and was one of the outstanding personalities of the year. A modern Jessop, though entirely different in style, he was hailed with delight wherever he played. A powerfully built man he timed the ball exactly, bowled fast-medium excellently, being especially difficult with the new ball, and fielded keenly. He was a tower of strength to Somerset.

To top all his achievements in this year, Arthur was one of the *Wisden* 'Cricketers of the Year' in 1936. He was described as 'one of the most attractive personalities in the last season'. The final four paragraphs of *Wisden's* account were especially complimentary:

As a batsman he has developed from a raw, if fearless hitter into a master of sound defence and stroke play without losing any of his power and aggression. Wellard is an example of how natural ability can be developed without the aid of excessive coaching. He says he has never had a days coaching in his life though a few hints, particularly from Young and J.W.Lee proved valuable.
Wellard is an attraction to the public as well as a match winner. No matter how badly his side is faring he is always likely to alter the course of a game.
Of his fielding nothing but praise can be written. Whether in the slips or at short leg or silly mid-off he is wonderfully good.
Unlike the other four Cricketers who appear this year he has not appeared for his country or taken part in a tour but his claims for a place in the team for the final test last season were seriously considered.

Arthur was very pleased with these comments and the timing of their publication, in the spring of 1936, provided the fillip needed for the start of the season.

5

1936-37: England beckons

ARTHUR RETURNED TO SOMERSET in the Spring of 1936 anxious to build on the successes of the previous season. His confidence was boosted by being a 'Cricketer of The Year' and he reckoned on an outside chance of Test selection against the Indian tourists. He also had a genuine chance of securing a place on the winter tour of Australia so there was much to play for when the season began. Arthur soon proved that his previous season's form was no fluke. He had an excellent start in Somerset's first match, which was against All India at Taunton. Somerset won by nine wickets thanks largely to Arthur's second innings bowling performance. His wickets included India's main batting threats, C.K.Nayudu and V.M.Merchant, but not before the latter had hit 151 runs. It is interesting to compare Arthur's bowling figures, which show that he had 52 runs scored off him in each innings. He took no wickets at all in the first innings but claimed six victims in the second, four of whom were bowled. The contrast in wickets taken was nothing to do with Arthur who had bowled consistently well throughout the match. The difference was due to the Somerset fielding, which missed seven good chances off Arthur's bowling in the first innings. Arthur accepted the fielding lapses with the usual good grace even though they may well have cost him a place in the England team for the first Test in June.

Later that same month, the selectors were at Kettering to watch Somerset's game against Northamptonshire. They were there primarily to watch Harold Gimblett but a telling contribution from Arthur could have caught their eye. On a difficult batting wicket, Gimblett duly obliged the selectors with a century before lunch and virtually sealed his place in the England side for the first Test. Arthur went in at number five to hasten the scoring along but managed only 15 runs; he was caught going for another big hit having already hit a six and two fours. Arthur bowled tidily in Northamptonshire's first innings but had no success. The pitch gave him little assistance but it was ideal for Horace Hazell who had match figures of fourteen wickets for 139 runs. Arthur would have to wait a little longer for his England call!

Arthur remained in good form on the county circuit during the next few games. At Taunton in early June, in the traditional bank holiday fixture against Gloucestershire, he hit very hard and with Bertie Buse almost a spectator, scored 52 out of 64 runs. His innings included three sixes and four fours. One of his drives went over the pavilion and into the car park and only a brilliant leg-side boundary catch by Monks halted his progress. He also took five wickets in Gloucestershire's only innings, including the prized wicket of Hammond. Arthur took Sinfield's wicket, caught behind by Luckes, to bring the great batsman to the crease. The crowd of more than 6,000 people had been eagerly awaiting his appearance but Arthur shattered Hammond's stumps with his second delivery.

This match was followed by a typically outstanding performance against his native county, Kent. On this occasion at Frome, he was able to make the ball swing both ways, taking seven wickets for 61 runs in Kent's first innings and five wickets for 77 runs in their second innings. Arthur twice took two wickets from consecutive balls and his twelve wickets were remarkable for the fact that nine of these were bowled. Somerset still managed to lose the match, despite Arthur's splendid contribution!

He continued his impressive start with the ball in the next match at Hove, where he took six wickets in the first Sussex innings. On the last day of this match, he learnt that he had not been selected for the North versus South trial the following week. This ruled out any chance he might have had of playing for England in the first Test. By now, Arthur must have wondered what he could possible do to attract the selectors' attention. The Somerset players travelled from Hove to Tunbridge for the return match against Kent. Arthur bowled well without luck and was the only Somerset batsman that showed any sense of purpose. 'Tich' Freeman caught Arthur in the first innings when he was well set but Arthur 'caught' Freeman when batting in his second innings. Freeman, in his final season of a distinguished career, conceded four sixes and three fours in the course of sixteen deliveries. Altogether 53 runs were taken off the little man in six overs before he was removed from the attack. Arthur scored 41 out of a dismal Somerset total of 123 runs and Kent won by six wickets.

Arthur had another fine game at Bath, in late June against Northamptonshire, when he took twelve wickets for 123 runs in the match. *Wisden* records that none of the Northamptonshire batsmen found an effective way of dealing with Arthur's fast bowling. Besides this impressive contribution he also hit 70 runs in Somerset's first innings. The innings included six sixes and three fours and was achieved in just over an hour. Three times, in four deliveries from Perkins, he sent the ball high over the sight screen. He also drove two successive balls from Buswell for six and hit Matthews so far over the boundary that it struck the Pulteney Street wall. This time, his efforts were at least rewarded with a Somerset victory.

His good form with the ball continued. In the match at Yeovil against Worcestershire in mid-July, he was virtually unplayable. Helped by the showers that interrupted the game, Arthur generated considerable pace and brought the ball off the pitch at a great rate. At one stage, Worcestershire were 10 for five wickets in their first innings after Arthur had taken four wickets for 2 runs off 19 balls. Gibbons and Quaife staged a minor recovery but Bernard Quaife could not shake off his Wellard jinx for long and was soon bowled by Arthur. Worcestershire were all out for 60 runs and Arthur finished with five wickets for 16 runs. Arthur's bowling in the first innings was described as unusually quick and it suggests he had something to prove.

In the second Worcestershire innings on a drying wicket, Arthur tried something completely different. Much to the surprise of the crowd and the opposition, he bowled off-breaks round the wicket and achieved some startling success. He finished with five wickets for 29 runs - including the wicket of Quaife - having at one stage taken five wickets for 11 runs off 8 overs. He had been experimenting with his off-breaks in the nets for some time, particularly when muscle and knee strains prevented him from bowling at full pace. Arthur had not until now found the right conditions to use this type of bowling and was as surprised as anyone to see the wickets tumble. It is difficult to bowl both types at the same time as the spinner's action requires the bending of the elbow in the bowling arm whereas the pace or swing bowler requires, more or less, a stiff arm action. Quite a number of bowlers have progressed from pace to spin but few have perfected the two actions at the same time. For the rest of Arthur's career, he was treated as a dual-purpose bowler and it would be even more difficult to get the ball off him. Bill Andrews, in his book *The hand that bowled Bradman,* remarked:

This second string for Wellard didn't please me too much. It appeared he was *always* bowling - either fast or slow. Often he'd go up to the skipper and say he thought the ball would turn. He was given a go and naturally I was taken off at the other end with the shine hardly off the ball!

Somerset beat Worcestershire by 170 runs, thanks mainly to Arthur's contribution. The Press Association reporters were openly talking about Arthur going to Australia and were referring to him as the best 'stock' cricketer in England. His Worcestershire wickets brought his total for the first-class season to ninety but it was still not enough to attract the attention of the selectors. His name was absent from those chosen for the second Test against India. His name was also missing from the names selected for the Gentlemen versus Players match, which was played on the day following Somerset's game against Worcestershire. Arthur was very upset at not being selected for the Players because this match had a much greater significance. It was well known that the selectors were using the match as a trial on which to base their final decisions for the MCC winter tour of Australia. He was not alone in his disappointment, his absence was regretted by the national press. *The Times* wrote:

If a reward for sheer merit during the last two months were to be paid, we might have expected to see Wellard in the Player' side. As it is, it seems extremely doubtful whether the selectors will go far beyond those taking part in the match.

The selectors prolonged Arthur's agony by gradually announcing the names of those selected for Australia. The first seven were announced on the 21st July, the next four on the 31st July and the remainder on the 10th August. The suspense created by the trickle of news from the selectors did not help Arthur's performances for Somerset. He passed the hundredth-wicket mark at the beginning of August by bowling Haynes of Gloucestershire but otherwise did nothing exceptional. It was not until the second Weston festival match, after all the selectors' announcements had been made, that Arthur began to recover his form.

He took sixteen wickets in the last two festival matches and had further success with his newly acquired bowling option. It was the final festival game against Sussex that produced the most spectacular results. Arthur had opened the bowling in the opposition's first innings by bowling fast-medium but after three catches had been dropped at a cost of eleven runs, he went round the wicket with his off-breaks. The move was so successful that he took six wickets at a cost of 7 runs! Horace Hazell took the other four wickets and Sussex were bowled out for 47 runs in just under 26 overs. Somerset won the match by 62 runs. Arthur was threatening to go over to off-spin full-time. 'Not such hard work, cock,' Arthur would exclaim.

Despite all the disappointments, it had still been an extremely good season for Arthur and there was still further excitement to come. Against Worcestershire at Kidderminster, he hit 64 in thirty-nine minutes to help his side secure victory. His hurricane hitting included seven sixes; two off Howorth went way out of the ground beyond the railway track. The very next match, the penultimate of the season, produced a spectacular climax for Arthur. The match was against Derbyshire at Wells on the 28th August 1936. Derbyshire, the eventual county champions, had only to avoid defeat in one of their two remaining matches to secure the championship. They were wary of Somerset because they had already lost to them earlier in the season at Ilkeston and Arthur had played an important part in the victory. Derbyshire's confidence was high and they could not have imagined that Arthur would again be the cause of their undoing. This was the game in which he first achieved the record of five sixes in an over. The unlucky bowler was T.R. 'Tosser' Armstrong, an occasional player and left-arm bowler, whose 58 matches as a professional for Derbyshire spanned a remarkable twenty-two years. Tommy Armstrong was employed in the office of Clay Cross Company owned by the family of Guy Jackson, the old Derbyshire captain. Tommy was allowed time off whenever the county needed a good left-arm spinner but on this occasion he probably regretted leaving his desk.

It was a remarkable game for Arthur. He was one of only four players to reach double figures in Somerset's first innings and he took nine wickets for 99 runs in the match. He came to the wicket in Somerset's second innings with his side staring defeat in the face, on 140 for five wickets and needing a further 131 runs to win. He went on to score 86 out of a stand of 102 runs and enabled Somerset to achieve a narrow one-wicket victory.

His innings contained seven sixes and eight fours. Arthur gave a early chance to Denis Smith, which was dropped in the deep and went for four runs. Armstrong was the bowler and in the same over, Arthur hit him for two successive sixes that disappeared into the surrounding countryside. Armstrong, instead of winning the game for his County, had seventeen taken off the over and was removed from the attack. Neither Copson nor Pope looked like getting Arthur out so Armstrong was brought back with the idea of getting Arthur to offer another chance. Arthur never needed much in the way of enticement but played the first ball quietly to leg. His partner, Reggie Ingle, refused Arthur's call for a single, which is just as well for Arthur despatched the next two deliveries into the car park. The fourth was hit out of the ground, lost forever, and the last two easily cleared the boundary.

George Langdale, who played for Somerset after the Second World War, was twelfth man for Derbyshire and reckons that this match brings back his clearest memories of Arthur. He was actually scoring the match at the time and recalls that one of Arthur's sixes was caught by R.C. Robertson-Glasgow who had been standing by the sight screen with Ben Travers, the playwright and Somerset vice-president. Travers mentioned this occasion in his book *94 declared* and thanked fortune for planting him on the right spot to witness such an outstanding performance. It must have been an awesome sight! A total of 47 runs were scored off Armstrong's two overs and this included seven sixes hit off ten successive deliveries! Armstrong's analysis was:

$$0,0,4,6,6,1,0,6,6,6,6,6$$

Arthur was eventually caught on the boundary by Townsend, bowled Copson for 86 runs. He had been in for sixty-two minutes and was on target for keeping the Lawrence Trophy in the West Country. Canon Kenneth Thomas, who was present that day, recalls:

I can see him now - sweat pouring from his face as he made his way round the ground to the beer tent - where most of Somerset were ready to buy him a drink!

Arthur was proud of the fact that the innings featured in the *Guinness Book of Records*. Arthur would equal the record in 1938 but it remained the record number of sixes in one over for thirty-two years, until Gary Sobers hit six consecutive sixes off Malcolm Nash at Swansea in 1968.

Arthur's innings was full of towering straight drives and powerful pulls to the mid-wicket boundary. His innings was uniquely recorded by a Somerset member, Mr A.G.Jones of Wells. Archie Jones, a prime mover in securing the fixture at Wells, recorded Arthur's innings for posterity on a stroke chart and presented it to Arthur after the match.

Arthur kept it for the rest of his life, unlike most of his other cricketing memorabilia. The chart is shown below:

Archie Jones would also be present at Wells two years later when Arthur repeated his record-breaking hitting. By this time, Archie had a more partisan interest in the game as his eighteen-year-old son, A.T.M. 'Trevor' Jones, was now playing for Somerset.

By the time Somerset's county championship season had ended, Arthur had taken 143 wickets at just over 18 runs apiece. His batting had not reached the heights of the previous season but he had scored runs at crucial times and was only 60 runs short of the 1,000 mark for all first-class cricket. His all-round performance was a major factor in Somerset's improved championship position, winning nine matches and finishing in seventh place, which equalled their best since 1919.

Arthur's success in the championship made up for the disappointment of not obtaining a place in the MCC team to Australia for the winter of 1936-37. The selectors chose Allen, Farnes, Voce and Copson for their pace bowling attack and it is difficult to challenge any of these selections. They had all performed well during the season, particularly Copson whose 160 wickets at 13.34 runs apiece helped Derbyshire win the championship. The quality and pedigree of this bowling quartet provides a good measure of the competition that Arthur faced throughout his career. Pelham Warner considered on reflection that the committee made some hurried choices and that the variety in England's bowling was insufficient. He did not, however, provide any clue to suggest that Arthur was ever seriously considered. It seems more likely that Arthur was still regarded by Warner and his establishment cohorts as a blacksmith cricketer who did not fit their image of a Test cricketer. Feelings in the West Country ran high, fuelling the popular notion that Somerset were far too unfashionable a county to warrant national interest. *The Somerset County Gazette* was most indignant about Arthur being continually overlooked:

It is inexplicable that our valiant all-rounder is consistently ignored for big cricket. In conversation with MCC members at HQ the writer learnt that he was apparently not considered there as more than a good "stock" county bowler.

Harold Gimblett with equally strong claims for a place in Australia was also unlucky, although he had been given his chances in the trial matches and in two of the three summer Tests. Harold's season, which had started brightly, failed to live up to the early promise but Arthur had been a model of consistency. He was by this time becoming extremely frustrated in his attempts to earn recognition from the England selectors.

Arthur played for 'An England X1' immediately after the end of the last championship match but the team was far from representative and included seven Kent players. The match was against India at Folkestone and Arthur left Taunton for the last time in 1936, stopping overnight at New Eltham before arriving on the morning of the match. The match ended in a draw and Arthur had an ordinary game but there was still the Scarborough Festival with which to finish on a high note. The first match of the festival was the following day against the MCC Australian side so there was no time to lose in making the long train journey northwards from Folkestone.

Arthur had a point to prove against the MCC side chosen to tour Australia but he toiled in vain during the MCC's first innings. The MCC scored 397 runs, thanks to the best innings of the match from E.R.T.Holmes who withdrew from the tour at the last minute. In reply, H.D.G.Leveson Gower's X1 were immediately in trouble and the team owed everything to a furiously hit sixth-wicket partnership of 111 runs between Arthur and Freddie Brown. The team still only managed to compile a total of 206 runs. The sixth-wicket partnership score was achieved in forty-eight minutes and Arthur was particularly severe on Ken Farnes. When Sims was brought back to dislodge Arthur, he was hit over the long-on boundary, out of the ground and then swept to long-leg for another six. Arthur was eventually caught by Duckworth, bowled Verity for 65 runs after hitting three sixes and seven fours. Arthur took the wickets of Hardstaff and Holmes, both bowled, for 45 runs in the MCC's second innings and Leveson Gower's X1 held out for a draw. Arthur could be forgiven for showing a tinge of resentment as the MCC side left Scarborough to prepare for their imminent tour. He was consoled by his team-mates, many of whom felt that he should have been picked for the tour. Arthur stayed on for the match against the Indians, which started the following day. The match became something of an anticlimax and finished a disappointing draw. It was the third occasion of the season that Arthur had played the Indians and his mind had not been fully on the game. It did not stop him hitting three sixes however, including two huge drives off Amir Elahi.

Arthur, having harboured hopes of spending the winter in Australia, settled for the more limited horizons of New Eltham. Like the previous winters he found comfort in the local snooker club and waited in keen anticipation of the coming summer. Farther afield, Australia retained the ashes winning the series 3-2 after having been 2-0 down. Arthur was entitled to feel that national honours could not be too far away as long as he maintained his form and consistency. He would not have that long to wait.

Arthur's early-season form in 1937 was steady if unspectacular but he was very much involved in an exciting game at Leicester in late May. Apart from taking six wickets in the match, he featured in the match-saving partnership with G.M.Bennett. Somerset had collapsed to 27 for five wickets, chasing 153 runs to win the match, when Bennett and Arthur began their partnership. Arthur hit 41 runs and would have almost certainly won the match for Somerset had he not been run out by Bennett who was captaining the side in Ingle's absence. Their concentration may have been broken when Berry, attempting a boundary catch to dismiss Arthur, caused much comical amusement by falling over a dog! Arthur was run out off the next ball. There was a look of relief on the faces of the Leicestershire players as Arthur made his way back to the pavilion and Somerset settled for the draw, thirty runs short of their target. Arthur hit two sixes in this innings; one bounced off a car into the road, the other pitched into the player's dressing room.

Soon after this match, Arthur took 10 wickets at Northampton for just 81 runs, including five clean bowled. Bill Andrews took seven wickets for 46 runs in the same match and Somerset won by an innings. Arthur followed this match with five wickets in an innings against Nottinghamshire and a further five-wickets haul against Leicestershire in the return fixture at Frome. He also hit 50 not out at Frome in an innings that lasted less than half an hour and included five sixes. There were several delays while the ball was retrieved from the adjoining fields.

Somerset's next match was at the Oval in June where Surrey were bowled out for 35 runs in their second innings. Overnight rain, followed by powerful sunshine, had transformed the pitch and the ball began to lift at disconcerting angles. Bill Andrews achieved career best figures of eight wickets for 12 runs off 6.4 overs. Arthur maintained a tight grip at the other end, which was not quite so fiery, taking the remaining two wickets for 23 runs off 7 overs. Bill Andrews, not known for his modesty, claimed that Arthur had been the better bowler on the day but Arthur, normally such a good judge of ends, had made the wrong choice. As the senior pro, Arthur always had the choice of ends when he and Bill opened the bowling. Trevor Jones recalls that Arthur would hold up his hanky to gauge the strength and direction of the wind. The hanky could be waving frantically in the breeze but Arthur would say to Bill, 'Not much in the wind today old cock I'll take this end,' pointing to the one that would give him the breeze behind his back!

This game produced Surrey's lowest score for 44 years. Somerset, however, needed 178 runs to win and the ball was still coming off the pitch at incredible angles. They were quickly in trouble and the batting crumbled to 43 for seven wickets. The situation was made for Arthur, walking nonchalantly to the wicket. He was probably thinking to himself, 'the bleedin' batsmen have let the side down again. I'll show 'em how to bat!' He began hesitantly and gave chances in the slips and the deep but gradually settled to the task. His driving looked in ominous good shape and while Luckes and Hazell kept one end secure, Arthur hit out to all corners of his favourite ground. He drove Freddie Brown for two fine sixes; one went out of the ground and across the road. The ninth-wicket partnership with Hazell added 67 runs and a Somerset victory began to look a distinct possibility. When Hazell departed, the Somerset amateur P.S.M.Molyneux joined Arthur with 29 runs needed from the last-wicket pairing. Arthur steadily reduced the runs required and he was only nine runs short of his century, with Somerset needing 12 runs for victory, when he ran out of partners. With Arthur facing the last ball of an over from Watts, the pair devised a rash plan to keep Molyneux away from Alf Gover at the other end. They decided, after a mid-wicket conference, to run whatever happened. When Watts sent down the last ball wide, Arthur let it go and set off for the run. The wicketkeeper, Ted Brooks, fielding twenty yards back, anticipated the run and Molyneux, who was batting at number eleven because of injury, was well out of his ground.

Wisden described the attempt to steal a run as a 'foolish run-out' and it almost certainly cost Arthur a notable century and a famous victory. Alf Gover remembers Arthur walking off the field cussing and swearing. He turned to Alf Gover on the way and muttered darkly, 'bleedin' amateurs, don't know why they play them!' His remark was probably justified; the Somerset team included six amateurs who had contributed 27 runs between them in the second innings. Arthur soon calmed down and the matter was forgotten over a pint or two.

The Bath festival followed and it was to produce some noteworthy performances from Somerset's opening pace attack. In the first match against Worcestershire, Arthur and Bill Andrews took the first eighteen Worcestershire wickets to fall and secured a thrilling three-wickets victory for Somerset. Arthur, who was reported as having made the ball swing both ways, again demonstrated this exceptional ability to turn the course of a game. Having taken six Worcestershire wickets, he scored 31 not out to ensure first innings points when it looked a decided improbability. Sid Martin, who had taken the first seven Somerset wickets, was hit for 14 runs in an over to overhaul the Worcestershire total. Arthur's five wickets in the second innings produced match figures of eleven wickets at 11 runs apiece. In the second match at Bath, Kent were bowled out for 116 and 73, with Arthur and Bill Andrews taking sixteen wickets between them. Somerset won by an impressive margin of 419 runs.

During this period, Arthur seems to have produced something special in virtually every match played. He was never out of the headlines as the press searched for new superlatives to describe his performance. Somerset went from Bath to Ilford for their match against Essex. They were immediately in trouble, being all out for 94 runs, and it says much about the Somerset batting to record that Arthur scored 48 of these runs, hitting a six and six fours! He also took eight wickets in the match which was won comfortably by Essex. There was another sparkling performance from Arthur against Hampshire at Wells and this time it would earn Somerset a much needed victory. After Somerset had made 315 runs, Arthur found the pitch very much to his liking and was able to turn the ball sharply. Arthur ran through the top-order batsmen and took four of the first five wickets for 2 runs apiece. He finished with five wickets for 50 runs and was then promoted up the order to achieve an early declaration. He scored 58 very quick runs and took four wickets in Hampshire's second innings to secure victory by 69 runs.

The visiting tourists in 1937 were New Zealand and England were expected to win the three-match Test series comfortably. Despite the early season form, Arthur was never in contention for the first Test as he was again ignored for the North versus South trial in Mid-May. The selectors preferred Gover and Farnes as the South's strike bowlers and both bowled well enough to secure their places in the Test side. The first Test ended in a disappointing draw and the England bowling had been far from impressive. Sir Pelham Warner, one of the selectors, was particularly critical of the bowling of Gover and Voce, which had been too short for most of the time.

The annual Gentlemen v Players fixture at Lord's started on the 14th July midway between the first and second Tests. Arthur was selected for the match, which was to be his only appearance for the Players at the Lord's venue. The Gentlemen v Players fixture started at Lord's in 1806 and this venue always retained a distinction of its own. It had been one of the fixtures of the year before Test matches began and an invitation to play was deemed a great honour. More importantly for Arthur, this fixture was often used as an unofficial Test trial and he knew full well that he now had a good chance of playing in the second Test match. The traditional Gentlemen v Players fixture would be confined to history after 1962 but in the Thirties there was still considerable interest in the match. As an indication of the interest generated by the 1937 fixture, 10,000 paying spectators attended on each of the two days required to complete the match.

It is not surprising that such a large crowd attended this fixture considering the formidable array of talent on display. The Players team comprised Hutton, Barnett, Hardstaff, Hammond, Paynter, Compton, Ames, Langridge, Wellard, J.Smith and Goddard. As expected, they were much too strong for the Gentlemen and the Players won the match within two days. Arthur did nothing of note with the bat but turned in a creditable performance with the ball. His figures were four wickets for 62 runs off 21 overs and two wickets for 44 runs off 17.5 overs. Most observers considered that Arthur had done enough to earn his Test debut. When the names were announced it was no surprise that nine members of the victorious Players team were included and, not before time, the name of A.W.WELLARD was among the nine on the selectors' list. The selectors had made four changes for the second Test at Old Trafford, three of which were bowling changes. Out went Gover, Voce and Verity, in came Arthur, Tom Goddard and Jim Smith. The second Test began on the 24th July 1937.

The weather conformed to Manchester reputation; it was cold and sunless and the rain interruptions were frequent. The weather was so bad that fewer than 15,000 people, including members, attended the three days of play. England won the toss, chose to bat and made 353 for nine wickets by the end of the first day's play. Arthur contributed just five runs and appeared strangely quiet at the crease. He had decided to bat responsibly in keeping with what was expected of a Test player so he suppressed his natural hitting instincts. When play resumed on Monday, England immediately declared and New Zealand were made to struggle on a pitch that had become faster over the weekend. By 1.00pm, thanks mainly to Arthur's attacking bowling, half the side was out for 119 runs. Walter Hadlee, coming in when four wickets were down, rescued his side with a brave innings of 93 runs. Hadlee struggled against Arthur early on but gradually played himself in. Just when he was beginning to get on top of the bowling he slipped and kicked his wicket down while attempting to turn a ball from Arthur 'round the corner'. New Zealand were all out for 281 runs. Arthur, whom *Wisden* described as the most impressive England bowler, had bowled 30 overs and taken four quality wickets for 81 runs. He had worked hard without much luck, kept a splendid length in making the batsmen attempt strokes and bowled with plenty of life.

England went in for the last hour of the second day in poor light and going for the runs. When the light got too bad to continue, they were 37 for three wickets. England took their score to 187 the following day - Arthur was caught in the deep-field going for a big hit - and New Zealand were set the task of making 265 runs for victory. They went in just before lunch with Arthur and Jim Smith opening the bowling. Neither bowler had any luck but when the new Zealanders had reached 50 runs without loss, Arthur broke the wicket and ran out Moloney. The wickets were not coming quickly enough so Goddard and Hammond were brought on. The change of bowlers had a dramatic effect and the New Zealand batting collapsed to leave England the victors by 130 runs. It was Tom Goddard who caused the collapse after finding a spot that had worn badly. Arthur bowled fourteen overs for 30 runs in the second innings but did not take a wicket. England had not won in convincing style but Sir Pelham Warner in his book, *Cricket between two wars,* did mention that Wellard bowled 'uncommonly well'.

Arthur maintained his good form in the next few matches, especially with the bat. Against Gloucestershire at Bristol, he took eight wickets and hit 52 runs, which included four sixes, two off Goddard in one over. This match was followed by the Weston festival, which included a fine knock of 70 against Surrey when Alf Gover came in for some harsh treatment. His four sixes included one onto the pavilion roof and one - a tremendous straight drive over the sightscreen - went out of the ground.

Arthur was quietly confident about retaining his place for the third and final Test at the Oval in August. He had been pleased with his bowling in the second Test and was in good shape with both bat and ball. However, when the team was announced, his named was missing. Jim Smith, who had done nothing as a bowler in the second Test having bowled too short, was also dropped. The pair were replaced by Ken Farnes and A.D.G.Matthews. The inclusion of Farnes was no surprise; the amateur, a favourite with the selectors, had not hitherto been available owing to his scholastic duties. Matthews, however, was a strange choice which took everyone by surprise. Matthews had played for Northamptonshire since 1927 with moderate success before dropping out of first-class cricket at the end of the 1936 season. He was appointed coach at Stowe School but then returned to Glamorgan, the county of his birth, just three weeks before his selection! Arthur was entitled to feel aggrieved after waiting so long for his chance to play for England and the unaccountable haste with which Matthews achieved his selection just added insult to injury. Sir Pelham Warner described Matthews as a 'trialist', which suggests that, as England were one up in the series, the selectors were turning their attention to the visit of Australia in 1938. Arthur obviously did not figure in these plans or he would have been given a further chance to prove himself. Arthur felt let down by the selectors and extremely unlucky to be dropped from the team but accepted the news with a resigned shrug of the shoulders. The third Test ended in a draw, Matthews failed to impress and was never selected again.

There was some consolation for not being selected because, while the third Test was in progress, Arthur was told that he was in Lord Tennyson's party to tour India during the winter. Somerset were playing Kent at Dover when the third Test was being played in mid-August. Arthur needed no incentives when playing Kent but the combination of receiving news of his Indian tour and his disappointment at being dropped from the Test side was bound to induce an exceptional performance. From the beginning of the game, he got the ball to lift and fly off the pitch at alarming pace. Arthur took seven wickets for 62 runs in Kent's first innings and reduced them to 134 all out. Nine of their batsmen fell to off-side catches, including seven in the slips. Somerset made 346 runs, with Arthur contributing 38 runs out of 39 added with J.H.Cameron, including the obligatory six off Woolley. Somerset still let Kent off the hook, thanks to some poor fielding, a score of 193 from Woolley and a century from Todd. Arthur took the wickets of the century-makers - he captured four wickets in total - but these were taken at a high price. He was hit for 156 runs but the tables would be turned at Wells the following year when Arthur had his revenge on Woolley! Somerset let Kent escape from certain defeat and then contrived to lose the match by 85 runs after a poor batting display.

Arthur had an immediate chance to prove 'the buggers at HQ' wrong when Somerset played Middlesex at Lord's the day after the Oval Test. Middlesex scored 393 despite Arthur bowling very well and finishing with four wickets for 80 runs. Somerset started their innings strongly but surrendered to Robins and Sims losing nineteen wickets for 167 runs and the match by an innings. Arthur was the only one to show any resistance. In an over from Robins, he hit a soaring straight six, crashed the next ball over the railings at deep mid-on and then hit another high into the Grand Stand. He enjoyed his brief innings of 34 runs all the more with Pelham Warner looking on. It was also no coincidence that Robins - regarded by Arthur one of the 'establishment' - was the unlucky bowler.

In all first-class cricket, Arthur took 156 wickets and reached 1,000 first-class runs - for the third time in four seasons - at the Scarborough festival playing for Leveson Gower's X1. Arthur played in two festival matches. The first was against an MCC Australian Team drawn from the players that toured Australia the previous winter.

Leveson Gower's X1 scored heavily in their first innings - Sutcliffe with 74, Hutton with 83 - and Arthur chipped in with 42 runs. He started his innings slowly but then off-drove Verity for a six that sent the ball running up the terracing. He then hit Sims for six before being caught on the long-on boundary in the same over. Arthur's team started their second innings with an advantage of 131 runs but lost wickets cheaply until Arthur and Freddie Brown came together. They put on 99 runs to set up the declaration. It was the second year running that Freddie Brown and Arthur had rescued the Leveson Gower batting. Arthur's innings of 66 runs included three sixes and six fours. In one over from Verity he scored 17 runs including two amazing off-drives for six. He also hit Verity for a straight-driven six, which was a particular pleasure since Verity was Arthur's *bête noire*. Hedley Verity was quick to take his revenge; he had Brown stumped, Smith was bowled by his next ball and Arthur was later caught off his bowling by Hardstaff fielding at long-on. During this innings Arthur completed his 1,000 first-class runs and so became the eighth player to achieve the first-class double that season. The MCC lost seven wickets in their second innings just managing to avoid defeat.

The following day, Arthur played against the New Zealand Tourists. Arthur had missed out when bowling against the MCC Australian X1 so was anxious to do well in his final match of the season. He took four wickets for 55 runs in the New Zealand first innings and two wickets for 26 runs in the second. The Leveson Gower's X1 won by 145 runs, which rounded off a very successful season for Arthur. In the review of Somerset's season *Wisden* remarked:

Wellard's energy and zeal again bore fruitful results. Sending down more than a thousand overs he deservedly claimed most wickets. Excellent as were his figures, like those of Andrews and Hazell, they were adversely affected by poor fielding which cost Somerset more than one match.

Arthur's bowling partner, Bill Andrews, had an exceptional season in 1937. Bill also had his best year with the bat scoring over 1,000 runs and becoming the third player, after Arthur and J.C.White, to complete the 'cricketer's double'. Despite the exceptional performances from Arthur and his bowling partner, it was not enough to prevent Somerset from slipping to 13th place in the championship. The side was too unsettled and team spirit was often lacking. The County won seven matches and lost fourteen out of a total of 28 matches.

Arthur returned to the South East in a great frame of mind and was eagerly anticipating the tour of India with Lord Tennyson's team. In the weeks leading up to the start of the tour, Arthur became very excited by the prospect of his first trip abroad and the chance to continue playing cricket during the winter. A good tour would also improve his chances of further Test selection. Jack was pleased for Arthur but not enthusiastic about the tour. She had become accustomed to Arthur being away for most of the summer returning occasionally to New Eltham when playing in a nearby fixture. Even on these occasion there was rarely time for any intimacy for, apart from sharing the house with members of her family, Arthur would often turn up with a fellow professional, anxious to save on expenses. Five months away from home was a different thing altogether and the period leading up to Arthur's departure for India was not without tension.

The glamour of being a cricketer's wife had long since worn off for Jack. She had never taken a great interest in cricket and had hardly ever taken the trouble to watch Arthur play. She never created the opportunity to establish herself within the circle of Somerset cricketers' wives and very few people in Somerset got to know her well. Jack had made a few trips back to the West Country since spending the winter of 1928 in Taunton. However, these were mainly to attend the Weston festival, staying with Bill Andrews and his first wife, Joan. The previous year's Scarborough visit had been a pleasant interlude but she declined Arthur's offer to repeat the trip, preferring instead to be with her mother and sister. Jack resigned herself to spending the winter with them and to the prospect of a family Christmas without her husband. Arthur could not wait for the tour to begin.

6

India

ARTHUR'S SELECTION FOR THE LORD TENNYSON TOUR of India in 1937/8 was a fitting reward for the efforts of the past three seasons. The family photograph of him, looking resplendent in his Tennyson blazer, shows that Arthur was rightfully proud of his selection. Lord Tennyson's visit to India took on a greater significance than it might have done had there been an official MCC tour during this winter. D.R.Jardine had captained the first MCC tour of India four years previously and as far as the Indians were concerned, this was an 'England' team in all but name. The tour would be accorded due ceremony and the matches against the All India X1s would be referred to as 'Unofficial Tests'.

The Honourable Lionel Hallam Tennyson had succeeded to the title, the 3rd Baron Tennyson, in 1928. He played for his country nine times and captained England in the last three Tests of 1921. He had been famous for his heroics with a broken hand against Gregory and McDonald, had played for Hampshire as far back as 1913 and captained them from 1919 to 1933. His final first-class match in England had been for the MCC a few months earlier. This was to be his third tour as a cricket ambassador having previously taken tours to the West Indies and South Africa.

Tennyson's cricketing pedigree was therefore of the highest order but he was now forty-eight years of age and weighed seventeen stone. The social aspects of touring were therefore as important as the cricket and he was looking forward to touring a country still described as the 'jewel in the crown'. There was another motive for taking on the tour. He was permanently in debt and had just lost £40,000, a very considerable sum in 1937, so one of the reasons he had agreed to bring the side to India was to avoid his father who was furious with him. Tennyson made a splendid diplomatic and throughout the tour was addressed as 'My Lord, the Captain'. He had the easy confidence of an Old Etonian and his aristocratic connections made him an excellent choice as captain. His connections included being on first-name terms with the Viceroy of India, who Tennyson claimed, had been his fag at Eton.

Lord Tennyson had assembled a team of fifteen players. Chapman, Hammond and Goddard had declined to tour and Leyland was not released by Yorkshire. Nevertheless, it was a strong team that included eleven present or future England players. It comprised of Bill Edrich (Middlesex), Paul Gibb (Yorkshire), Alf Gover (Surrey), Joe Hardstaff jnr (Notts), Tom Jameson (Hants), Jim Langridge (Sussex), Neil McCorkell (Hants), Jim Parks (Sussex), Ian Peebles (Middlesex), George Pope (Derby), Peter Smith (Essex), Stan Worthington (Derby), Norman Yardley (Yorkshire), Arthur and Lord Tennyson.

Touring India would always be difficult. There were the possibilities of political and civil unrest that had already caused the cancellation of two previous MCC tours during the early part of the decade. The heat and the dysentery would also present problems, which would sometimes mean that the team was selected from those capable of rising from their beds. There were, however, obvious compensations and Arthur was introduced to a world of luxury, lavish entertainment and privilege beyond any of his wildest dreams.

On the 13th October 1937, the Team assembled at Victoria Station for their journey to Marseilles where they boarded the *Viceroy of India*, a luxury liner bound for Bombay. Ahead of them lay five months away from England and an arduous tour of the Indian Continent that would include twenty-four matches.

To comprehend what touring India was like in those far off days it is necessary to understand how India had developed as an emerging cricket nation. In the early part of the century, cricket flourished under the patronage of the Indian princes. They had quickly learnt that a prince with cricketing connections carried political clout in the Chamber of Princes. The greatest and most influential of all these princes in a cricketing sense was Bhupendra Singh, the Maharajah of Patiala. There was a cricket ground within his palace, the Bardari Palace Oval. It was in an area as large as Lord's and with facilities that were the equal of anything in England. He had his own private team that included most of the best Indian players as well as professionals from England and Australia who would spend their winters playing and coaching. Hirst, Kilner, Leyland, Larwood, Sutcliffe, Hobbs and Rhodes all played here at some stage and the latter spent six winters here in the Twenties and Thirties. Patiala had organised and sponsored a tour of England as far back as 1911, winning two of their 13 matches, including one against Somerset. Later Patiala had helped to pay for the MCC tour of India in 1926-27.

The Maharajah of Patiala was Chancellor of the Chamber of Princes between 1926 and 1930 when he was succeeded by another cricketing prince, Ranjitsinhji. After Ranji's death in 1933, Patiala became Chancellor again. However, by this time, the Cricket Club of India had been formed, as the Indian equivalent of the MCC, to take control of cricket. Patiala still had influence in staging matches and providing venues that were also designed to press his son Yuvraj's claims as a future Indian captain.

Patiala was also a useful cricketer. He had actually played for the MCC tourists in 1933, as he was entitled to do, being a member of the MCC. Jardine picked him mainly to express his thanks for the lavish hospitality given to the tourists but Patiala acquitted himself well, scoring 54 without any apparent favouritism from the fielders and umpires. However, it was Patiala's money that would leave a lasting legacy to Indian cricket. He was always willing to provide financial backing to the Indian Board of Control, which in its infancy was invariable short of funds. His first gesture was to donate the trophy for the Indian Championships, which at his suggestion was called the Ranji Trophy.

The Board could not survive without Patiala's money. He had organised and funded an Australian touring side in 1935-36 but was politically outmanoeuvred when it came to organising the 1936 tour of England. This was a blessing in disguise however, for this tour proved to be a financial and cricketing disaster. Patiala was back at the helm, as President of the Board, by the time that Lord Tennyson's team arrived but his reign would be short-lived for he was to die a few weeks after Tennyson's tour had ended.

The Maharajah of Patiala was 46 years old and considerably overweight; his poor health was not a little unconnected with his lifestyle. He had 300 wives and was a habitual womaniser who was said to be not above abduction, rape or murder to satiate his appetite for the opposite sex. But Patiala had one last great act of cricketing patronage to perform and Arthur would be there to witness the gift first hand. Patiala had financed the development of the Brabourne Stadium in Bombay. The Stadium was named after the Governor of India in exchange for practically giving the land to the Board. Lord Brabourne had laid the foundation stone in May 1936 and the Stadium was almost ready. The opening, by Patiala, was planned for December.

The team's passage to Bombay would be spent like most other tours, playing deck games, cards and generally relaxing after a hard domestic season. Alf Gover, in his autobiography *The long run,* tells the story about Lord Tennyson who discovered a cricket net on board and insisted that the team had net practice. The team were not keen on the idea as it was then the hottest part of the journey. So having arranged with the crew who erected the net to leave a suitable gap the only ball was soon despatched into the sea once his Lordship had retired to shower!

The tourists disembarked at Bombay on the 25th October 1937 and had their first taste of an Indian welcome. Wherever they went, the welcome was full of excitement, noise and great ceremony; Bombay was no exception. The touring party were hustled away and taken in cars to their hotel at breakneck speeds with horns blaring. There seemed to be a total disregard for the milling mobs in the street. No expense seems to have been spared for India's important visitors. Each of the party had his own bearer for the whole of the trip and the bearers wore the team colours in their turbans and waistbands. After their rapid journey to the hotel they were given lunch and at 6.00pm they had to board the train for their opening game of the tour at Baroda starting the following day. The organisation throughout the tour was well meaning but hopeless and they spent a frightful all-night journey, four to a compartment with luggage pilled high all around them. After arriving at 6.00am, they were taken to a hotel for a hurried breakfast and shower before being expected to start the match at 11.00am. The temperature was 110 degrees in the shade, they were tired and had been given no opportunity to practice. The team stayed with the Maharajah of Baroda, the famous racehorse owner whose hospitality was legendary. The Maharajah's palace was in stark contrast to the abject poverty they had witnessed in the backstreets of Bombay. These first impressions of India would remain with the team forever. In later reminiscences, Arthur would refer to the Maharajah as 'the nice kiddy with a place upcountry the size of Buckin'am Palace,' which was not much of an exaggeration. Arthur's tales of the prince's enormous wealth would beggar belief but he had seen the priceless jewel encrusted necklaces and full-size cannons made of gold with his own eyes.

The two-day match at Baroda ended in a draw. Afterwards, the team immediately boarded another ship to take them to Karachi for their next match. This was the opening first-class match of the tour, against Sind, which also ended in a draw. Two minor games followed including a match at Peshawar against North Frontier Provence. This side was made up from army and RAF troops stationed in the area. At a party before the start of the match Arthur and Alf Gover enjoyed the Indian beer so much that it was 3.00am before they left. This does not appear to have affected their performance in the field and the Northern Command team were quickly dismissed to set up the first win of the tour. The other minor game at Lahore versus the Universities resulted in a draw and this match preceded the first 'Test' in the same City.

The All India X1 was to be captained by the brilliant Vijay Madhavji Merchant who had been the only success of the 1936 tour of England. Merchant was appointed for all four planned 'Tests'. Tennyson's side won comfortably by nine wickets after Merchant found little support from his team-mates. The Indian team also suffered from the absence of the great cricketer C.K.Nayudu, away on a world tour. Arthur made a fine start with three wickets for 39 runs in the first innings and two wickets for 64 runs in the second. During the second day of the 'Test' match, while Tennyson's side were fielding, an earthquake shook the ground so badly that it held up play for some time. It is said that the English fielders were extremely frightened, believing that the world was about to end!

Tennyson's team lost their next match by two wickets at Ajmer against Rajputana after a switch from playing on turf to matting; Arthur did not play. A drawn game at Ahmedabad followed and then the team went to Jamnagar to play the Jam Sahib of Nowangur's X1. The Jam Sahib was better known as Digvijayasinhji, brother of Ranji and uncle of Duleepsinhji who like Ranji played for Sussex and England. Digvi, himself a talented cricketer, fielded a strong team that contained four princes as well as Mankad and Amar Singh, India's fastest bowler.

Responding to the Jam Sahib's first innings of 206 runs, Tennyson's side were all out for 126 runs and only Arthur looked comfortable against Amar Singh. His score of 30 included three sixes! The touring side, set 304 runs to win, were quickly in trouble but Arthur almost turned the game. He scored 90 out of 269 runs, including another six sixes, and entertained the large crowd. Arthur and Alf Gover delayed the end by putting on 91 runs for the last wicket with Gover contributing just 18 runs. The partnership almost won the match but Tennyson's team ended 34 runs short of their target.

After the first day in the field the Jam Sahib entertained the party to a superb and overwhelming banquet that lasted until 1.00am. They were woken at 4.00am (for breakfast) and driven forty miles at hectic pace to the hunting grounds where a shooting party had been arranged for the whole team. It was a point of honour to the Indians that their guests should not leave without having shot something. Arthur's boyhood experiences on the farm at Bexley made him one of the best shots in the team. Some of his team-mates were not so good and at times the beaters were in more danger than the wild animals. Arthur had been partnered with Alf Gover because Alf did not know one end of his rifle from the other. It was soon taken away from him when, following a hare, he shot into the line of beaters, fortunately without causing any harm. They were back at 10.30am and playing cricket by 11.00am so it is perhaps not surprising that they produced a lack-lustre batting performance.

The tour had so far not met with much success on the field. After a total of eight games, the touring side had lost two, won two and drawn the rest. The next game was a two-day match at Poona against Maharashtra. D.G.Burridge, writing in the *Somerset Wyverns Newsletter* in 1987 had good cause to remember the match:

I was stationed in Poona with the Somerset Light Infantry. The Commanding Officer (Lt. Col. Roche) gave permission for those wanting to see the game to go. Arthur Wellard was one of the players we wanted to see play. He came to the stand and spoke to most of us, saying how pleased he was to see so many from the County and to be with the Regiment. When he went to get ready to bat he said he would hit the first ball into the stand for a six; this he did with the second another six into the stand. A fielder was positioned to stop a third six, which he did by catching Arthur's third attempt for six right on the boundary. Needless to say the fielder received some friendly booing. When Arthur had taken his pads off he came back to the stands to talk.

The game at Poona was drawn and the party returned to Bombay to play the Cricket Club of India at the Brabourne Stadium. The opening ceremony, which took place before the start of the match was the fulfilment of the Maharajah of Patiala's dream. Patiala had employed the veteran Australian all-rounder Frank Tarrant to prepare a good turf wicket and he had struggled for two summers to complete the task. Now on the 7th December 1937 everything was ready and Patiala performed the opening honours with the Bombay Governor, Sir Roger Lumley and his wife. Lord Tennyson, anxious not to be outdone, turned up in a top hat and Ascot-style dress suit before changing for the match. The match was drawn and two days later the second 'Test' began at the same venue.

The Brabourne Stadium covered 40,000 square yards and accommodated 35,000 spectators under cover. It had a magnificent three-storey stucco pavilion and had every conceivable amenity including rooms overlooking the square where the players could stay. On the first day of the 'Test', the stadium was packed tightly with excited spectators who watched their team struggle to 153 all out. Arthur took three wickets for 30 runs. 25,000 people saw Tennyson's side build a useful lead on the second day whereupon India again struggled to come to terms with the English bowling.

Arthur took an early wicket and then had a hand in dismissing India's last five batsmen. He had Qamruddin caught behind then fielding at square leg he made a magnificent left-hand pick-up to run Singh out. He followed this by catching Yuvraj at short-leg and bowled their last two batsmen. Tennyson's team eventually won the second 'Test' by six wickets. The Indian team selection was criticised and not least because Nayudu, who had been available and in the original fourteen, had been replaced by Mahamad Saeed. Saeed was a Patiala player who was not in the original squad and, as Patiala and Nayudu were old enemies, it was suspected that the Maharajah was responsible.

Bombay, where Nayudu was a legendary figure, did not take kindly to Patiala's interference, real or imagined. Such was the likelihood of civil unrest that it was announced during the third 'Test' at Calcutta that there would be a fifth 'Test' in Bombay, to be captained by Nayudu. The announcement of the fifth 'Test' upset Digvijayasinhji, the President of the Board, who had not been consulted. He issued a statement that it would not be played but the Board insisted and Digvi resigned.

There were three matches around Christmas at Lucknow, Indore and Jamshedpur before the third 'Test' at Calcutta; two were drawn and the one at Jamshedpur was won by ten

wickets. Nayudu was not selected for the third 'Test' but
the All India X1 won by 93 runs despite Arthur taking four
wickets for 69 runs in the Indian second innings.

There was a further game in Calcutta against the
Maharajah of Cooch Behar's X1, which the touring side won.
Arthur did not play in this game as he was taking a well-
earned rest. His absence from the field of play gave him
the chance to take advantage of the Maharajah's wining and
dining. Arthur and Joe Hardstaff became very friendly with
the Maharajah of Cooch Behar. He was more than useful as a
cricketer and as a well-known socialite with extremely
lavish tastes, he was a frequent visitor to London. There
would be quite a few visits to his palace and on one
occasion Arthur and Joe took part in a challenge that
resulted in the pair drinking the Maharajah under the
table. The Maharajah had obviously not heard of Joe
Hardstaff's reputation as a drinker but even Joe met his
match later in the tour against another Indian prince in
Madras. On this occasion he passed out at 5.00am - at which
point Arthur and George Pope helped him to bed - but still
managed a flawless double-century against Madras later that
day. Arthur was presented with one of the Maharajah of
Cooch Behar's team blazers as a token of their friendship.
It is a beautiful pastel blue colour with the Maharajah's
coat of arms emblazoned on the breast pocket. The buttons
are made of pure silver. When Arthur returned home he gave
the blazer to his sister-in-law Betty as it was too small
and ostentatious for Arthur's taste.

Tennyson's side left Calcutta to travel to Patiala and
play the Maharajah's team. The game was drawn but the
touring side had the upper hand on the first two days
thanks mainly to a brilliant all-round display from Arthur.
Wisden described his bowling as 'lively' taking six wickets
for 46 runs. He had the first three batsmen caught behind
and then bowled the Maharajah who was easily beaten for
pace. It was only a ninth-wicket partnership stand of 68
runs involving Amir Elahi that saved the Maharajah's side
from a complete rout. Arthur bowled 21 overs in intense
heat, the other four bowlers managing just 26 overs between
them. He followed this with a characteristic display of

pulling and driving, hitting five sixes and seven fours before being bowled by Amarnath for 78 runs.

After the day's exertions, the team would relax at the Maharajah's palace where almost anything was at their disposal. Bill Edrich, in his memories of the tour, recalled with fondness one facility that was available to the team. He remembered that while in Patiala the team played roller-skate hockey in the Maharajah's rink during the evenings, waited on by attendants ready to provide cooling drinks. The Maharajah had the rink built in a moment of admiration for the sport!

After Patiala and more lavish hospitality from another Maharajah the team travelled to New Delhi, Nagpur and Madras. The game at Nagpur was won by Tennyson's team and the other two were drawn. The team had, by now, travelled virtually the entire length of India. At Secunderabad in late January, the team lost their fourth match of the tour against the Nawab of Moin-ud-Dowlah's X1. Arthur scored 37 in the second innings and took five wickets in the match but the Nawab's side won comfortably. Tennyson's side won their next match at Bangalore versus Mysore, which left only the last two 'Test' matches to play.

The fourth 'Test' was played in Madras and despite the announcement of the fifth 'Test' there were characteristic demonstrations over the absence of Nayudu. The Indians took to the streets with placards announcing, 'No Nayudu, No Test.' Nayudu was invited to play but by now was so fed up with the political intrigue that he did not even reply to the invitation. India still managed to win the 'Test' without him. India batted first on a perfect pitch and then, following rain on the second day, Amar Singh exploited the conditions taking eleven wickets. *Wisden* records that apart from Wellard, who hit hard, no-one could deal effectively with Amar Singh's bowling. Arthur scored 40 of the side's second innings total of 163 runs.

With two victories apiece, the fifth 'Test' became the decider. It was played on the 12th to 14th February 1938 at the Brabourne Stadium in Bombay. With Nayudu still refusing to play and disputes over seat allocations, only 5,000 spectators attended. India let the game slip away and

Tennyson's side won by 156 runs. Arthur fittingly provided significant contributions with bat and ball. He had match bowling figures of nine wickets for 117 runs and *Wisden* records that Wellard batted skilfully in the second innings. He was eventually bowled by Mankad for 33 runs but not before India had been set an impossible target.

It was during this innings that Arthur hit his longest ever six against a fast-medium delivery from Amar Singh. He had just hit a ball from Mankad into the Club House and from the opposite end he hit the six off Singh, which according to Bill Edrich was the greatest hit he ever saw. Edrich described the event in his book *Cricket heritage*:

Wellard straight drove Amar Singh sky high over the sight screens, over the top of the stand behind it, and out of sight. I was sitting with Lord Tennyson at the other end of the ground, and I said, 'Good heavens, that one's gone right over the top!' Lord Tennyson said 'Don't be a damn fool; no one could do it.' This was interesting because Tennyson himself was a tremendous hitter. I confirmed my statement, and Tennyson said 'I'll lay you a pound you're wrong.' I took his bet and his money. It was 97 yards when we measured the distance from the wicket to the edge of the turf where the sight-screen stood; then there was a cinder track, then a series of open terraces, then the stand, over 60 feet high. The ball had skied over the whole lot into the blue Indian distance. One of our team-mates swore that on his last sight of the ball it was still going *UP*, but I think this was an exaggeration.

All the players rated the six as the biggest hit ever witnessed. Norman Yardley, in his book *Cricket campaigns,* believed it had approached, if not exceeded, the 'classic 500 feet that would have put it in the biggest hit of all time class.' Alf Gover recently confirmed the six as 'a low, skimming hit which made the umpire duck, and then went on and on and on, until it rose to clear the stand and vanish.' There is no doubt that, if properly measured, the hit would have challenged the *Wisden* 'RECORD HIT', achieved in practice at Christ Church ground, Oxford. The hit by the Rev.W.Fellows made in 1856 was measured as 175 yards from hit to pitch. As it stands, Arthur's six at Bombay is arguably the longest ever first-class six. It certainly out-distances the reputed longest hit of 160 yards made by V.S.F.Crawford for Surrey at Bristol in 1900. Arthur considered that this was his biggest hit and would say, 'I was a bit proud of that one.' His account, however, strangely contradicts those of his team-mates. He is the only one to claim it did not carry the stand as confirmed in the conversation he had with Harold Pinter some forty years later:

He wasn't a bad bowler, Amar Singh. He moved it about a bit. He dug it in. You had to watch yourself. Anyway, he suddenly let one go, it was well up and swinging. I could see it all the way and I hit it. Well, they've got these stands in Bombay, one on top of the other, and I saw this ball, she was still climbing when she hit the top of the stand. I was aiming for that river they've got over there. The Ganges. If it hadn't been for that bloody top stand I'd have had it in the Ganges. That wasn't a bad blow, that one.

Arthur and Amar Singh were well acquainted, having known each other since 1932 when Amar Singh first toured England. He later became a Lancashire League professional and even played with Arthur on the same side, in a charity match at Lord's in 1935. They had the same joyful approach to cricket and there was always a certain amount of friendly rivalry between them. Amar Singh was himself a big hitter who had punished the English bowling at Bombay and Jamnagar where he hit a brisk 81 runs. Singh had hit all the English bowlers for six during these encounters and one ball from Gover was sent high over the extra-cover boundary off the back foot! Alf Gover remembers Arthur playfully shouting across to Singh, 'if you do that to my mate again I'll do the same to you!' He did and Arthur was later true to his word. As the ball disappeared in the direction of the Ganges, Amar Singh jumped excitedly in the air, applauding the shot. He called out to Arthur - leaning nonchalantly on his bat and peering exaggeratingly into the distance - 'that's the greatest hit ever, Arthur!'

It was a fitting climax to the tour, which had been disappointing as far as the cricket was concerned. The team's performance was much affected by weather, wicket conditions, sickness and injury. Nearly all the players suffered ailments or injury; Gover, in particular had problems with his right knee and he played in only nine of the first-class games. While three of the five 'Unofficial Tests' had been won, they had lost five of their twenty-four fixtures.

Arthur's contribution with bat and ball had been exceptional. He had taken forty-seven wickets by the end of the tour and had almost as many catches dropped off his bowling. Arthur's forty-seven wickets were taken at 21.74 runs apiece and in his sixteen innings of the tour, he scored 433 runs at an average of just under 29. *Wisden* records that 'Deprived of many wickets by faulty slip fielding Wellard was always steady' and 'Wellard as a hitter of gigantic sixes was especially popular with the crowds.' Arthur had hit twenty-six sixes in the first-class games so there were plenty of these moments to savour.

David Foot, in his book *Sunshine, sixes and cider*, mentions that on his return to Somerset the following season, Arthur would refer to the dropped catches by saying 'So what's new, cock?' His rhetorical question would be accompanied by a resigned shrug of the shoulders. Arthur's tally of wickets would have also been much greater had the umpires been a little less partisan. They were often in the employ of the princes and would leap in the air, shouting shrill cries when giving the Englishmen out. Bill Edrich concluded that they had to get the Indians well and truly out before they *were* out.

This tour had marked the end of an era for Indian cricket and, with Patiala dead, the Maharajahs would never again carry such influence on the cricket field. The tour had also produced some encouraging performances from Indian players. Mankad, just twenty years old, had been largely responsible for the Indian's two victories in the 'Tests'. He headed both the batting and bowling averages and would be a force in Indian cricket for the next two decades. Amar Singh had taken thirty-six wickets at an average of 16.66 runs apiece but tragically he would die of pneumonia within two years and before his thirtieth birthday.

India was also to provide Arthur with one of his best and favourite stories. Eric Hill remembers hearing the story many times and always with the odd new inflection in his voice designed to have his audience in stitches. Alf

Gover tells the same story, in his autobiography *The long run*, about one of their excursions into the jungle at Porbander, just before the second 'Test' at Bombay. A panther shoot had been laid on for Lord Tennyson who was said to be a good shot. They had been staying at the Maharajah's palace and travelled to a small building in the jungle where they were lavishly wined and dined. After the meal at around dusk they set off in cars to the shoot. Alf Gover described what happened:

On arriving at the 'killing ground' we went into the muchan, the building accommodating the shooters. We were led up to the first floor, here were holes (slits) in the wall which were big enough to hold the 'shooter' and for him to push his gun through and see to take aim. Some thirty feet away on a stone plinth, about ten feet high by six feet wide, was a small goat tethered to a pole which had a light fixed to the top. We were told that the panther would soon be here, attracted by the bleating of the goat, so the maharajah handed Tennyson a rifle.

Now the skipper had wined and dined very well and as he worked himself into a comfortable position pushing his gun through the hole in front of him we reckoned the panther had a sporting chance of escape. The panther duly arrived and with a great leap and a swipe of the paw knocked down the goat and stood still making a perfect side on target. 'Now,' said the maharajah to the skipper who immediately pulled the trigger. The panther was away like a flash of lightning. The goat in it's death throes jumped and then lay back still. 'My God, skipper,' I said, 'you've shot the ruddy goat!' We had been accompanied by an agency press man and when we told him he reported it and the story reached around the globe. Tennyson was not too pleased to receive cables from his shooting pals congratulating him on 'getting the goat.' But he forgave us later, especially after we looked after him when he contracted a bad dose of dysentery.

This was the story that Arthur never tired of telling to anyone who would listen. He arrived back in England weighed down with curios and mementoes returning briefly to the family home in New Eltham. Shortly afterwards, he returned to the West Country for the start of the county season at the beginning of April 1938. He looked exceptionally fit with his swarthy face tanned even more than usual for this time of the year. He was in fine form and would remain that way; 1938 was to be his best and most rewarding cricketing year.

1. Bexley Cricket Club, 1925. Arthur is standing third from the left, Percy Waistell is seated centre

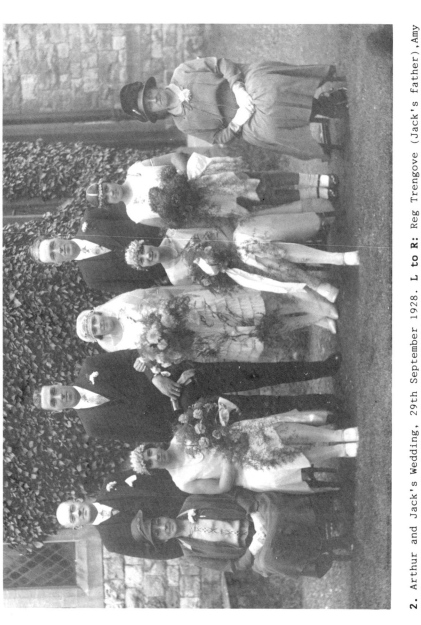

2. Arthur and Jack's Wedding, 29th September 1928. **L to R:** Reg Trengove (Jack's father),Amy Wellard (Arthur's mother),Clara Trengove (Jack's sister-in-law),Arthur,Jack,Sylvia Cook (Jack's cousin),Betty Trengove (Jack's sister),Charles Wellard (Arthur's brother),Celina Trengove (Jack's mother)

3. Somerset, 1929. **Standing L to R:** Luckes,Young,F.Lee,Wellard,Hunt, J.Lee. **Seated L to R:** Hawkins,Earle,White,Ingle,Case

4. Portrait photograph of Arthur in Somerset blazer, taken in his first full season, 1929

5. Arthur hitting the six that landed on the `spot-kick' at the Park Avenue Ground, Bradford, June, 1930 (right). Arthur Wood is the Yorkshire wicketkeeper

6. Signing autographs, c 1930 (below).

7. Early bowling action, c 1930 (left). Note characteristic leap in the delivery stride

8. Somerset v Australia, 1934 (below). B.A.Barnett batting, Luckes behind the stumps, Wellard at first slip. Note Arthur's huge hands

9. The `terrible twins' with Harold Gimblett, c 1936 (above). **L to R:** Andrews, Gimblett and Wellard

10. The formidable `Players' that beat the `Gentlemen' at Lord's, 1937 (below) **Standing L to R:** Hutton,Goddard,Smith,Wellard,Compton,Langridge. **Seated L to R:** Paynter,Ames,Hammond,Hardstaff,Barnett. All but Compton and Langridge were selected to play for England against New Zealand, Old Trafford, 1937

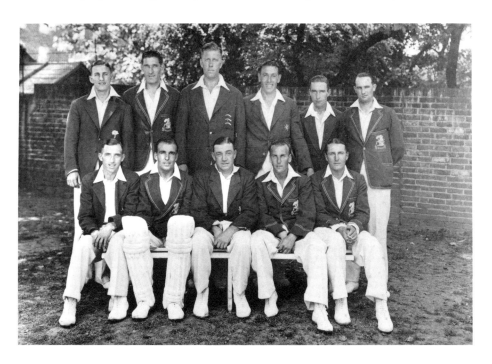

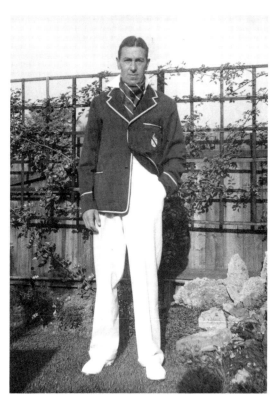

11. Arthur proudly displaying his Lord Tennyson blazer in his back garden at New Eltham, October 1937 (left)

12. Tennyson's Tourists, India, 1937/38 (below). **Standing L to R:** Langridge, Smith,Wellard,Pope,Hardstaff,Gibb **Seated L to R:** Gover,Worthington,Jameson, Tennyson,Peebles,Parks,Yardley **Seated on floor L to R:** McCorkell,Edrich

13. Sightseeing in India, (above). **L to R:** Neil McCorkell, Arthur, Peter Smith

14. England v Australia, Lord's 1938 (below). **Back row L to R:** Compton,Waite, Edrich,Chipperfield,Wright,Ward,Paynter,Barnes,Ferguson **Second row L to R:** Fingleton,Hutton,Brown,Barnett(Eng),White,Wellard,O'Reilly,Fleetwood-Smith, Hardstaff, McCormick **Seated L to R:** Ames,Barnett(Aus),Farnes,Jeanes,Hammond, Bradman,Rait Kerr,McCabe,Verity,Badcock **Seated on floor L to R:** Hassett,Walker

15. Lord's Test, 1938 (left).
Bowling practice in the nets

16. Lord's Test, 1938 (below). Presentation to King Gorge Vl. The King is
shaking hands with Hedley Verity, Arthur is next in line, followed by Charlie
Barnett, Joe Hardstaff and `Fanny' Walden, the umpire

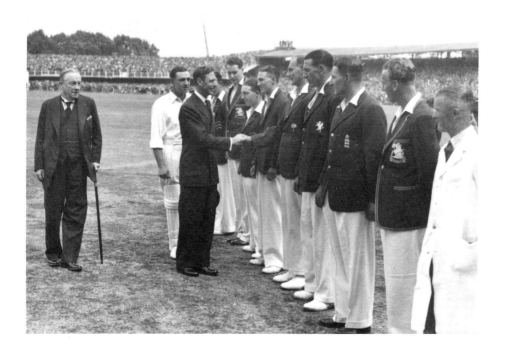

17. Lord's Test, 1938 (right). England 2nd Innings. Arthur bowled McCabe after scoring 38 precious runs

18. Somerset at Worcester, 1938 (below). **Standing L to R:** F.Lee,Hazell,Buse, Andrews,Pearce,Wellard,Gimblett,Luckes **Seated L to R:** Barnwell,Longrigg,Lyon, Jones

19. Central Mediterranean Forces X1, Lord's 1945 (above). **Standing L to R:** Merritt,Vaulkard,Pritchard,Smailes,Wellard,Emmett,Dollery,Hill,White,McIntyre **Seated L to R:** Moore,Hazlerigg,Martin,Henty

20. Arthur in England blazer at Weston, c 1947 (left). With Betty Andrews

21. Arthur in his last full season with Somerset, 1949 (right).

22. Postcard for Arthur's testimonial season, 1951 (below).

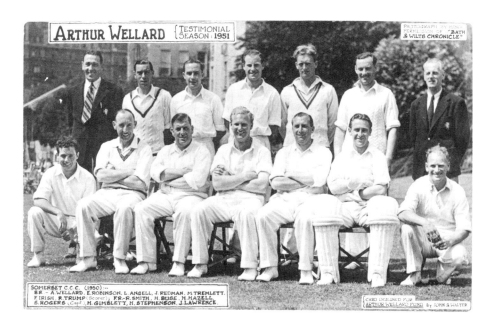

23. Coaching schoolboys at the Gover Indoor School, c 1960 (above).

24. Arthur's return to Weston-Super-Mare, 1968 (below). With Bill Andrews

25. Gaieties Cricket Club, early 1970s (above). Arthur is seated far right,
Harold Pinter is second from the left

26. `Old Somerset', Centenary Celebrations at Weston, 1975 (below). **Standing
L to R:** Lobb,Kitchen,Parks,Jones,Wight,Angell,Lawrence **Seated L to R:**
Burrough,Barnwell,Wellard,F.Lee,Andrews,Stephenson,Gimblett,Tremlett

50 NOT OUT FOR ARTHUR AND VERA

ONE OF cricket's great all-rounders, Arthur Wellard, and his wife, Vera, celebrated their golden wedding anniversary.

A fast bowler and hard-hitting batsman, Mr Wellard played for Somerset and England during the late 1920s, throughout the 1930s and for a short time after the war.

He played for England twice, against Australia in 1938 and New Zealand in 1937.

He is mentioned in the Guinness Book of Records for hitting five consecutive sixes, a record which was beaten by Sir Gary Sobers three years ago, and for hitting 72 sixes in one year.

Mr Wellard, now 76, retired from county cricket in 1950, but continued to play and coach for local teams until he was 74.

Mr and Mrs Wellard met when they were at school to-gether at Old Bexley, Kent. They became more friendly when Mr Wellard played for the local cricket team and Mrs Wellard made the teas. They were married at St. John's Church, Bexley. They have no children.

The couple moved to their home in Gainsborough Road, Langney, a year ago.

They celebrated their anniversary with a party for family and friends.

27. Arthur and Jack's Golden Wedding Anniversary announcement, 1978.

7

1938: A glorious year

THE LONG AND ARDUOUS WINTER TOUR of India had no adverse
effects and Arthur was quickly into his stride from the
start of the 1938 season. In the match against
Worcestershire at Taunton, he took three wickets for 47
runs in the first innings and five wickets for 65 runs in
the second. Bill Andrews also took eight wickets in this
match, which Somerset won by 53 runs. Arthur followed this
with five wickets in an innings against Derbyshire and in
the next match against Sussex, played on a lively pitch at
Taunton, he took six wickets for 40 runs to secure first
innings points. He had rarely played better and started in
sensational fashion by taking three wickets for 14 runs off
his first 3 overs. Somerset then went to Frome to play
Northamptonshire and Arthur took twelve wickets in the
match for 128 runs to secure a three-wickets victory. By
the end of May, he had taken thirty-eight championship
wickets compared with the eighteen taken by his bowling
partner, Bill Andrews.

Up to this point, there had been no success with the
bat but he made up for it in the Whitsuntide match against
Gloucestershire. He had already taken seven wickets in the
match when on the last day, a fine innings of 140 not out
from Wally Hammond enabled Gloucestershire to set Somerset
a target of 284 to win. Somerset were 172 for seven
wickets, needing 112 runs to win with an hour of play
remaining, when Arthur strode purposefully to the wicket.
A Somerset victory appeared most unlikely but the
Gloucestershire team knew full well that there was no room
for complacency while Arthur was at the wicket. After a

quiet opening, Arthur hit six sixes in an innings of 68 runs, which was scored out of 81 runs added in forty minutes for the eighth wicket. Three of his sixes, including two in succession, were off Emmett. The first six was the longest and most vigorous pull ever seen at Taunton. It soared out of the ground, over the Organ Works and eventually came to rest in the backyard of a house in St. Augustine Street. The hit is conservatively estimated at 170 yards but may have been much longer depending on the placement of the wicket and the exact pitch of the ball. Sinfield was hit into the car park and Hammond, coming on for Emmett was straight driven out of the ground. His final six off Scott, a huge drive, pitched on top of the stand and flew through the open window of the scorers' box. His bold hitting had taken Somerset to the brink of victory and the Taunton crowd gave Arthur a rousing reception. Wally Luckes hit two boundaries in the last over of the day for Somerset to win by one wicket. The crowd were said to have thrown up their hats and danced with delight!

The early season form undoubtedly helped to press Arthur's claims for Test selection against the Australians. The visitors were a fine young side, perhaps not quite as strong in their bowling without Clarrie Grimmett. The English chances were not greatly enhanced by the recent record of meetings between the two countries. Except for the body-line tour in 1932-33, Australia had been superior to England throughout the decade so far. They had won the previous two series in England, in 1930 and in 1934, also the series in Australia in 1936-37. Bradman, in particular, had treated the English bowling with disdain. In 1930 he scored 974 runs in Test matches at an average of over 139, which including the then record Test score of 334 at Headingley. In 1934 he had scored 758 runs at an average of just under 95 despite being far from well all season. His total included a score of 304 in the fourth Test at Leeds. In 1936-37 he scored 810 runs at an average of 90.

There seemed little prospect of stopping the run machine and England's bowling attack was the most worrying selection problem. The Board of Control chose P.A.Perrin, Pelham Warner, M.J.Turnbull of Glamorgan and A.B.Sellars of

Yorkshire as the selection committee. Turnbull and Sellars were interesting choices and departures from normal policy. They were still playing cricket and were presumed to be more in touch with current form. Hammond was chosen as the captain for the series and the batting of Hutton, Barnett, Edrich, Paynter and Compton almost picked itself. The bowling was a little more tricky with Voce, Allen and Bowes unavailable through injury. The selectors chose Farnes, Verity, Sinfield and Wright as their bowlers. Ames, the wicketkeeper made up the eleven.

Doug Wright, the leg-break and googly bowler, had been chosen to make his debut Test appearance on the strength of his performance in the England versus The Rest trial, held ten days before the start of the first Test. Arthur was disappointed not to have been chosen for the trial as he was in good early-season form and would have expected to be on the fringe of Test selection. He was well aware that Allen, Voce and Bowes were all unfit, which left the selectors with a tricky decision about who should partner Ken Farnes. They chose Reg Sinfield who had not played in the trial match but was in the best form of his long county career. He was picked to make his first appearance for England on the strength of his ability to supply accuracy of line and length.

The first Test at Trent Bridge was notable for the Test match debuts of Len Hutton and Denis Compton. Both made hundreds and the restored-to-favour Eddie Paynter made 216 not out, in a total of 658 for eight wickets declared. Stan McCabe played one of the most memorable innings ever seen at Trent Bridge when scoring 232 but Australia still had to follow on. Don Bradman scored 144 not out in Australia's second innings and made sure that the Test was drawn. Although the English bowling had been tidy, it had lacked penetration and had not resolved the selectors' bowling problems. The slower bowlers, Wright and Verity, had been used a great deal but mainly in a defensive capacity. Farnes had got wickets but Sinfield had been relatively expensive. He had kept a good length but off 63 overs in the match he had figures of two wickets for 123 runs. Selection committees seem prepared to allow batsmen sufficient time to prove they can play at Test level. They seem less tolerant towards bowlers who are discarded after an indifferent performance even when conditions, as at Trent Bridge, have been less than favourable. Sinfield would suffer this fate and he was never given another opportunity to play for his country.

The first Test ended on the 14th June 1938, the same day that Arthur and Bill Andrews were polishing off the Nottinghamshire batting at Taunton with four wickets apiece. Somerset went off to Chelmsford where they achieved another fine victory thanks mainly to their opening pace attack, which accounted for eighteen Essex wickets. Arthur took eleven wickets in the match. There was a break in championship cricket so he remained in the South East for the weekend. It was spent in heightened anticipation after a great deal of press speculation about likely changes in the bowling line-up for the second Test. Arthur's name was on the tip of everyone's tongue; the selectors would find it difficult to ignore his indisputable claims based on current form. He had now taken sixty-seven wickets for Somerset at 18.6 runs apiece with the season still less than half complete.

The invitation letter from the Board of Control Selection Committee, which Arthur kept all his life, was dated Sunday, 19th June. The letter from Pelham Warner, the Chairman of Selectors, begins 'Dear Wellard' and is amusing for its officious tone and the conditions attached to acceptance of the invitation. As instructed, he sent a telegram 'at once' to Lord's confirming his availability. His remuneration for playing in the match was £50 plus third class railway fare. The Board would also arrange for settlement of the bill from the Great Central Hotel, 'excluding drinks'! Pelham Warner provided the underlining. Had he been forewarned of Arthur's taste for pink gin?

Arthur as replacement for Sinfield was the only change made to the England team for the second Test. Australia also made one change, Chipperfield coming in for Ward. The other members of the side were Fingleton, Brown, Bradman, McCabe, Hassett, Badcock, Barnett, O'Reilly, McCormick and Fleetwood-Smith. The match started on the 24th June amid great excitement and pandemonium. There was not even a standing position to be found and the gates were closed well before the start of the match. The crowd had grown to such a size that spectators had begun to intrude on the playing surface. After some desperate consultation between officials it was decided to leave them where they were and move the boundary ropes. England won the toss, chose to bat and were quickly in trouble at 31 for three wickets, after a lively opening spell from McCormick. Wally Hammond came to the wicket at ten minutes past twelve and quickly stopped the rot. By the close of play at just after 6.00pm, he was 210 not out!

An even bigger crowd turned up for the second day to watch the England captain take his score to 240. The attendance was officially returned as 33,800 although the true figure was much higher. Once Hammond was out, England looked for quick runs from the tail-enders. Arthur only managed a four off O'Reilly to the square-leg boundary. He hit the next ball so high it took an appreciable time to come down but the patiently waiting McCormick held a good catch. England ended their innings on 494 runs.

Australia made a confident reply which included the second double century of the match from W.A. Brown, carrying his bat for 206 runs. When the Australians had scored 276 for three wickets, Arthur took the wicket of Lindsay Hassett. It was a key wicket for England. Hassett and Brown had put on 124 runs for the fourth wicket and *Wisden* described Hassett as 'batting with style and confidence'. Arthur had returned for a new spell and was now bowling from the Pavilion end. He had Hassett leg-before-wicket for 56 runs and in the same over bowled Badcock for a duck. The Australian innings continued into the third day and they were nine wickets down when three hours of rain transformed an easy wicket into one that was soft on top but hard underneath. When play resumed, Australia quickly lost their last wicket and were all out for 422 runs. Arthur took no more wickets after his mid-innings success and finished with figures of two wickets for 96 runs off 23 overs. His analysis would have been considerably better if the catch given by Brown, before reaching his double-century, had been held by the mid-wicket fielder!

England, starting with a valuable advantage of 72 runs, were quickly in trouble. The top batsmen struggled against McCormick who was now getting the ball to fly off the pitch. England finished the third day on 28 for two wickets and at one stage on the fourth and final day they were 64 for four wickets then 76 for five. Paynter, the not out batsman, was joined by Compton at this critical stage and much depended on the latter, just turned twenty and playing in only his second Test. Between them, they carried the score to 128 when Paynter ran himself out. Ames followed just after lunch with England still not safe at 142 for seven wickets.

It was Arthur's turn to come in and one can only imagine the tension of that moment as he made the long journey from the professional's dressing room, down the pavilion steps to join Compton. Another huge crowd was there to greet his entrance and if he felt nervous it did not show. Denis Compton describes Arthur's entry in *Playing for England*:

Then in walked Arthur Wellard, the cheery big-hitter from Somerset. Although he played his natural game, and tried to knock the cover off the ball, Arthur, for all that, did not ignore defensive play when the occasion demanded it, and together we gradually took the score along towards the safety mark. Eventually Wellard, after making 38, was bowled but only after we had added 74.

Arthur was not in any way overawed by the occasion nor did he seem to be inhibited by the situation in which the English players found themselves. He hit fiercely and his innings of 38 runs including a mighty six that landed on the balcony of the Grand Stand. It was an outswinger from McCabe, which was unceremoniously carted over the long-on boundary with one of Arthur's characteristic pulls. At one stage Australia had two men deep on the leg side but still failed to save the fours through mid-wicket. His innings ended when he was bowled by McCabe attempting to hit the ball so hard it would never be seen again. Not all the MCC members would have appreciated his brave batting. Pelham

Warner and others from the 'golden age' era would have been shaking their heads in disbelief but the crowd appreciated the innings and gave Arthur a rapturous reception on his return to the pavilion. His innings had relieved the tension that gripped players and spectators alike but more importantly had all but saved the match. Don Bradman, in *Farewell to cricket*, reckoned Arthur's batting 'offended every principle in cricket' but conceded that the runs had counted at a time when he thought Australia might win. The eighth-wicket stand had taken England's score from 142 to 216 and the match beyond reach. E.W.Swanton also felt that they had saved a match that would otherwise have been lost. Compton took the credit, deservedly so, but there is scarce mention of Arthur's contribution. The fact remains that had Arthur failed, only Farnes and Wright had still to come. While not exactly 'rabbits', their Test batting averages of 4.8 and 11.1 respectively would not have inspired great confidence in the England camp.

Hammond eventually declared at 242 for eight wickets setting Australia an impossible target of 315 runs to win in the two hours and three-quarters of play remaining. The game drifted into a draw with Australia finishing on 204 for six wickets and Bradman unbeaten on a score of 102. Arthur's bowling figures in the Australian's second innings were one wicket for 30 runs off 9 overs. He opened the bowling with Farnes and took the first wicket down, that of the Australian opener Jack Fingleton, caught in the slips by Hammond when eight runs were on the board.

It is not hard to imagine how elated Arthur must have been to be part of such a prestigious and thrilling match. The official number of paying spectators for the match was 100,933, a record for Lord's, and gate receipts amounted to £28,164.11*s*.9*d*. It had also been the first ever appearance of the television cameras at Lord's and, to top it all, the teams had been presented to King George V1 by Stanley Baldwin during the lunch interval on the first day's play. It was one of Arthur's most proudest moments and the framed photograph of the England team waiting in line to shake the King's hand would take pride of place on the Wellard mantlepiece from this day onwards.

The Test ended on the Tuesday and the following morning, Arthur caught an early train to join his Somerset colleagues at Trent Bridge. There had not been much time for reflection but the journey to Nottingham would have provided a quiet moment to evaluate his Test match contribution. He would conclude, with some satisfaction, that he had acquitted himself well. His partnership with Compton had enabled England to reach a safe target and his match bowling of three wickets for 126 runs was reasonable in the circumstance. He had bowled mainly from the Nursery End and his figures did not look out of place when compared with his opening partner Ken Farnes who had been given the more favourable Pavilion End. Farnes had match figures of three wickets for 186 runs. Pelham Warner, in his book *Cricket between two wars*, described Farnes as being 'not in his best form' and Arthur, rather disparagingly, as being 'useful but not convincing.'

Arthur arrived at the ground to find his side in buoyant mood after beating Middlesex at Bath by nine wickets. Bill Andrews could not resist seeking out Arthur to tell him that, given the rare chance to bowl with the wind at his back, he had taken thirteen wickets for 141 runs. Bill admits in his biography to thinking to himself, 'this'll show Arthur Wellard that we can win a game without him.' Bill had his fleeting moment of triumph but was soon put in his place. Arthur took eight wickets at Trent Bridge and scored crucial last-minute runs to secure a Somerset victory by one wicket. He hit Voce to the boundary three times and despatched a long-hop from Gunn for six.

The next day they played Northamptonshire at Kettering but the match ended in a draw. Somerset put up some stubborn resistance against Reg Partridge and John Timms who were getting assistance from the pitch towards the end of the match. Only Harold Gimblett had the class and the skill to stay for any length of time, scoring 105 out of Somerset's second innings total of 181 runs. Trevor Jones remembers waiting his turn to bat and receiving the only advice Arthur ever gave him. Arthur, in laconic mood, turned to Trevor and muttered 'get forward.' It did not do the trick as Trevor was soon bowled by a Partridge off-break. Arthur had an indifferent game; he was not in the right frame of mind after learning that he had been dropped for the third Test match at Manchester.

In the light of Pelham Warner's comments about Arthur's bowling it is perhaps not surprising that Arthur was left out of the squad of thirteen players. Farnes was also excluded from that number, which amongst several potential changes, would have seen Goddard and Hardstaff in contention. The final X1 was never announced because it rained through Thursday to Tuesday and the match was abandoned without a ball being bowled. Meanwhile Somerset travelled from Kettering to Yeovil, where rain appears not to have affected Somerset's match against Hampshire. After a few overs of fast-medium, Arthur changed to off-breaks with great success. He had a deadly spell of six wickets for 32 runs during the middle of Hampshire's first innings but could not prevent Somerset from losing the match.

This timely reminder of Arthur's current form with the ball was followed by a fine all-round performance at Cardiff against Glamorgan. On the first day, he scored 18 runs out of Somerset's meagre total of 150 runs and with a sustained spell of fast bowling he took five wickets for 59 runs by the close of play. The following morning he took a further wicket to finish with six wickets for 62 runs, which kept Glamorgan down to a score of 156. The Somerset batting was immediately in trouble and when Arthur went in, his side were 84 for six wickets with the Glamorgan attack of Wooller and Mercer, well on top. He scored a brilliant 73 not out which accounted for all but seven of his side's remaining runs and his innings including six sixes, four of which came in two overs off Emrys Davies. He also hit Wooller for a mighty six then drove another ball from the same bowler out of the ground. Arthur's innings gave Somerset a chance of winning the game but, with the wicket easing, Glamorgan registered a comfortable six-wickets victory. These performances were not sufficient to attract the selectors' attention. Farnes, unaccountably back in favour, and the now fully-fit Bill Bowes were chosen as the strike bowlers for the fourth Test at Leeds starting on the 22nd July 1938.

In a low scoring match at Leeds, Australia won the Test by five wickets thanks mainly to the bowling of Fleetwood-Smith and O'Reilly who took seventeen wickets between them. Bradman also scored a brilliant century. Australia went one up in the series and thereby retained the Ashes. The game was completed on the Monday and on the Wednesday the Australians were facing Somerset at Taunton with six of the players who had played at Headingley. The pitch at Taunton was so docile that none of the star batsmen wanted to stand down. Jack Fingleton always said that playing at Taunton used to ensure that they would be in good form for the next Test. Somerset were soundly beaten by an innings and 218 runs after scoring 110 and 136 runs in their two innings. Arthur still managed to entertain the crowd with some spirited batting. His 20 runs in the first innings came from four scoring strokes; the first six hit the far bank of the river, the second dropped in it. Australia's first innings total of 464 runs was achieved for the loss of six wickets. Badcock scored 110 and Bradman scored his third double-century of the tour before being bowled by Bill Andrews.

The Bradman wicket was to give rise to Andrew's much repeated greeting, 'shake the hand that bowled Don Bradman', which he used as the title of his autobiography. He would quickly add, in a self-effacing tone, that Bradman was on 202 at the time! Arthur's bowling analysis was two wickets for 146 runs and Bill took two wickets for 108 runs. The Australians must have loved playing at Taunton. They had won by an innings and 158 runs in 1930, an innings and 77 runs in 1934 and would return after the war to plunder the Somerset bowling, winning on this occasion by an innings and 374 runs!

Somerset moved on to Bristol where Arthur took seven wickets for 80 runs off 32 overs in Gloucestershire's first innings. On a gorgeous Bank Holiday Monday, in front of 14,000 spectators, he had Charlie Barnett leg-before-wicket with the first ball of the innings. This wicket was very special; it was his thousandth wicket in first-class cricket. The Gloucestershire match was followed by the Weston festival, which was badly affected by the weather.

Arthur did manage to take five wickets for 32 runs against Glamorgan and he also had an excellent game in the final match of the festival. Somerset beat Lancashire by ten wickets and Arthur had a match analysis of ten wickets for 149 runs. Most of his success came in Lancashire's second innings when, in fifty minutes of play, they collapsed in spectacular fashion to 59 for five wickets. Arthur took four of these wickets with his off-breaks.

Arthur again bowled exceptionally well in the very next match, against a full-strength Middlesex at Lord's. Somerset always faced a visit to Lord's with trepidation. The championship high-flyers, having a typically good season, would win fifteen of their twenty-two matches in 1938. Middlesex batted first and Arthur, bowling 31 overs in the innings and taking seven wickets, was mainly responsible for restricting Middlesex to 267 all out. Somerset replied with a poor batting display and were all out for 125. Arthur was one of the four batsmen to reach double figures, thanks mainly to a huge six off Ian Peebles. This six was a colossal straight drive that landed halfway up the upper terrace on top of the pavilion. It had always been his ambition to clear the Lord's pavilion and this would be the closest Arthur ever came to emulating Albert Trott who is still the only cricketer to hit a ball right over the structure. Trott just managed to do it in 1899 and few cricketers since have got as close as Arthur did with the six off Peebles.

Edrich, Compton and Human all batted well for Middlesex in their second innings and Somerset were set a target of 418 runs to win the match. Never believing for one moment that the target was achievable, the Somerset top-order batting collapsed. By lunchtime on the last day of the match, the young Trevor Jones and Arthur faced an impossible task. To enliven the afternoon session and provide some entertainment for the MCC members, Judge Wilfred Dell sent word that he would pay Arthur five shillings for every six he hit after lunch. Wilfred Dell, an eminent London judge, had more than a passing interest in the game for he had originated from Wells and was a Somerset member. Arthur had some success, dumping a full toss from R.W.V.Robins over the square-leg boundary but didn't seem to be timing the ball properly. To make matters worse, Trevor Jones, who was not noted for his hitting, hit the old scoreboard with a six off Ian Peebles. Arthur was furious and came down the pitch muttering, 'What the hell do you think you're doing? That's my bleedin' job, you stick to the fancy stuff.' Both were out shortly afterwards; Somerset lost by 263 runs but Arthur collected his 'five bob'!

Arthur's bowling continued to go from strength to strength and he had another ten-wickets haul in the following game at Worcester. In a lively opening spell lasting 100 minutes, he kept a fine length and swung the ball appreciably, taking the first six wickets that fell for 50 runs. Worcestershire never recovered and Arthur finished the innings with figures of seven wickets for 59 runs. His wickets included the wicket of the Nawab of Pataudi. Coming in with two wickets down, the prolific run scorer was dropped first ball off Arthur's bowling by Horace Hazell. Arthur, perhaps not trusting his slip fielders, bowled the Nawab of Pataudi the next ball. Worcestershire performed better in their second innings and just won a close-fought match.

It was about this time that the squad for the final Test was announced. Arthur was not among the names despite having an extremely impressive run with the ball throughout the whole period since the end of the second Test. Farnes and Bowes were retained as the strike bowlers although neither had done a great deal in the previous Test. Bowes, in particular had been disappointing. England won the last Test at the Oval by an innings and 579 runs. The Test will be remembered for Len Hutton's score of 364 and England's first innings of 903 for seven wickets declared. Farnes and Bowes took twelve of the 16 Australian wickets to fall in the match and perhaps justified their selection. There was, however, no doubt that Australia had been demoralised by the enormous England total and by the absence [hurt] of Bradman and Fingleton in both innings.

Somerset were playing Surrey at Taunton in a match affected by rain. It gave the Somerset players a chance to listen to the Test match on the radio and indulge their usual wet afternoon pursuit of playing cards. Trevor Jones remembered this particular school because he was listening to Hutton's innings:

It was raining cats and dogs and there was a poker school in the dressing room with Arthur, Alf Gover, Garland-Wells and a couple of others - Bill Andrews was walking around the table in hysterics - as usual! - because of the large sums of money changing hands (large for those days that is).

Arthur is likely to have profited from the card school as he rarely lost at poker. He was in his element when playing the game; a Grand Master of poker. His face would be expressionless, never revealing the strength of his hand and when it came to bluffing he had no equal. In 1936, he took £50 *[£1,200 at today's prices]* off two bookmakers in a Sheffield hotel before they saw the light and cut their losses. He would chuckle about this game, which would usually draw the rueful comment, 'bookies have had enough out of me over the years!' When the card schools were in full-swing, Bill Andrews would fret and show such concern for his friend who would be prepared to risk everything on the turn of a card. There were few Somerset players willing to risk playing with Arthur and those that did were usually left to rue the consequences. Arthur was, however, a champion of fair play and would never have taken advantage of his colleagues. Horace Hazell used to tell the story of his first experience of playing with Arthur in 1929. He lost £5 in the card game, which was considerably more than a week's wages, and went to bed in something of a sulk. Arthur later came into Horace's bedroom, threw a £5 note on the bed and said, 'never play cards with me again, son.' Horace heeded the advice.

The Test series had ended in a 1-1 draw and Arthur's modest contribution to the series was now history. Arthur had been at the peak of his game for the past four years and despite his advancing years seemed to be improving with each season. He could not have foreseen that the Lord's Test match would be the last time he would play for his Country. His two Test appearances were an extremely modest reward for his efforts and appear mediocre by comparison with Test cricketers from the present era. Such a comparison would be an irrelevance given the greater number of Tests now played and the plethora of genuine fast bowlers available in Arthur's days. There is little doubt that he would have walked into many a recent England Test team.

The second Test at Lord's would remain a treasured memory for the rest of his life. The season was still far from over for Arthur and as so often before, he reserved one of his best performances in the championship for his native county of Kent. He repeated his 1936 record of five sixes in an over, again at the small ground of Wells. His victim this time was the great England all-rounder, Frank Woolley. It is hard to understand what Woolley was doing bowling to Arthur. He was in his last season of a long career that began in 1906 and included over seven hundred appearances for Kent. Woolley was fifty-one years old and for the past ten seasons had been rarely used as a bowler. There was never any suggestion that the bowling was contrived. Woolley, a fierce competitor, would not have been party to such a thing and Arthur's record occurred in the first innings when considerations of 'gifting' runs would not have applied. The most likely explanation is that Kent were prepared to 'buy' Arthur's wicket but were clearly not prepared for the eventual cost.

Arthur began his innings by twice hitting Lewis out of the ground and into the villa gardens. Woolley then came into the attack, presumably in an attempt to draw him into an error of judgement. Arthur swept Woolley's first five balls for six. Four of them went out of the ground and the other just cleared the boundary ropes where it was caught by Archie Jones. Arthur did not quite time the last ball of the over despite, according to Arthur's suspicion, Woolley pitching it up on purpose. Valentine, fielding near the sight screen, leapt into the air and just got the tips of his fingers to the ball. It fell inside the boundary rope enabling Arthur to take a single. If Valentine had not got a hand to the ball it would have carried the boundary and would have pre-dated Gary Sobers' achievement of six sixes in an over by thirty-seven years.

Three of the balls that left the ground were lost forever, which caused the umpire, Alec Skelding, to plead with Arthur to go easy since they only had one ball left. Arthur duly restrained himself and was out soon after, having scored 57 runs in just thirty-seven minutes. Forty-two of these runs came in sixes! Woolley's figures for the innings were none for 40 runs off two overs.

Arthur hit a further four sixes in his second innings score of 37, which including two consecutive sixes off Watt. A further six off Watt and one off Harding completed the tally. The one off Harding was driven high over the pavilion and into a neighbouring garden. Frank Woolley, wisely declined to bowl. Arthur's 94 runs for the two innings did much to turn the match in Somerset's favour. They would still not have won, however, were it not for an exceptional bowling performance from Arthur which accounted for thirteen wickets in the match. In Kent's first innings, he took seven wickets for 65 runs with a mixture of pace and spin. In their second innings, Arthur and Bill Andrews opened the bowling attack without any success so Arthur persuaded his skipper, Bunty Longrigg, that the wicket would take spin. Bill was replaced by Horace Hazell after only four overs and Arthur signalled his intention to bowl his off-breaks.

Arthur took the new ball and very deliberately rubbed it in the dirt until the shine had been completely removed! This action did not contravene the rules of fair play as there was no precise equivalent to the modern Law 42.5. Altering the condition of the ball in this way would certainly not have attracted the controversy, debate and litigation that now surrounds this Law. The extravagant 'ball-tampering' was designed to impart the right amount of doubt in the minds of the opening pair, Woolley and F.G.H.Chalk. It certainly appears to have had the desired effect as from then onwards, the Kent batsmen struggled to come to terms with the Somerset spin partnership. Arthur bowled 27 overs unchanged and ended with figures of seven maidens, six wickets for 50 runs. Horace Hazell took the remaining four wickets for 60 runs. Kent were all out for 160 and Somerset scraped home by 27 runs to record a memorable victory. Not for the first time, Kent would have cause to regret not signing Arthur when they had the opportunity. His wickets, rather uncharitably, included the double dismissal of the unfortunate Woolley, in both cases leg-before-wicket. He was out for a duck in the first innings, which moved Frank Woolley to enquire, 'have you got something against me, Arthur?'

Arthur capped a tremendous season by helping Somerset to win their last match against Leicestershire at Taunton. On the first day, Leicestershire were all out for 113 runs after excellent bowling by Bill Andrews who took six wickets. Somerset, in reply, were 265 for three wickets at close of play. Arthur had been advanced up the order in a tactical move to score quick runs. They could not have come more quickly and in the last twenty minutes of play, Arthur scored 52 runs. He hit 18 runs in an over from Thursting, including four consecutive fours, 20 runs in an over from Lester, which included two sixes and in the final over of the day he drove a ball from Prentice over the shilling stand and into the car park. Arthur survived only two overs the next morning and was out for 56 runs; Somerset were all out for 432 runs. Arthur then took five wickets at just over 7 runs apiece in the second innings to enable Somerset to win by an innings.

By winning their final match, Somerset recorded their biggest number of victories in a championship season and climbed to seventh place in the table. R.C.N.Palairet, the Somerset President, made special mention of the greatly improved fielding when summarising the reasons for the County's success in 1938. Palairet also announced in his annual report that 1939 would be Arthur's benefit year with the match against Glamorgan at Weston as his club benefit match. He wrote:

Wellard's cricket for Somerset has been simply invaluable. Gifted with a big heart, courage and determination, he puts his soul into the game and goes 'all out' whether fortune is kind or the reverse. At the present he is one of the most popular cricketers in England. It is hoped that Members of the Club and the general public will subscribe to this most deserving player.

Arthur was also singled out in the *Wisden* account of Somerset's 1938 season:

Far from being tired after a tour of India with Lord Tennyson's X1 Wellard remained a glutton for work. His arm showed no signs of getting lower and the usual energy and determination characterised his run up to the wicket. Nearly every day Wellard accomplished something of note and he well merited his inclusion in the England X1 which met Australia at Lord's. Wellard's versatility in changing from fast medium to off-breaks around the wicket without losing command of length and direction deserved more notice than it generally received. The late Albert Trott of Middlesex and Voce of Nottingham are the two other bowlers to alter their style in a similar way. Owing to numerous long spells with the ball, the reputation of Arthur Wellard as an aggressive batsman suffered to an appreciable extent but he hit 50 sixes.

Arthur took 169 wickets for Somerset at 19.24 runs apiece and topped the bowling averages. It is a Somerset record for the most wickets taken in a season, one that is never likely to be beaten. He had bowled almost 1,200 overs in the season and it is therefore not surprising that his batting suffered at times. He still managed 779 runs at an average of 19 runs per innings.

Arthur had one final game to play in the 1938 season, which was his last appearance for the Players against the Gentlemen, this time at Scarborough. The wicket, described as perfect, was clearly not to Arthur's liking and he bowled 33 overs in the match without taking a wicket. His batting, however, proved the brightest point in a dull match and he scored 42 in the Player's first innings and 21 in the second, driving fiercely. Freddie Brown who had been his partner in some memorable batting stands for Leveson Gower's X1, came in for some harsh treatment. As if to show his friend who was the most dominant hitter, Arthur scored 37 runs off the twelve balls that Brown bowled him in the first innings. Arthur pulled him for two huge sixes in one over and then in his next over scored 24 runs, including two sixes hit out of the ground. He was eventually caught at deep mid-on trying a similar stroke. The Players won the match by five wickets.

It had been a glorious year! In all first-class matches during the 1938 season, he took 172 wickets at

20.30 runs apiece. No other bowler in England took more first-class wickets than Arthur during this season. It was still not enough to convince the selectors that he was worth a place in the MCC party that toured South Africa during the winter of 1938. The selectors preferred Tom Goddard and Ken Farnes, supported by Reg Perks, a bowler of similar pace to Arthur but almost ten years his junior. With the benefit of hindsight, Arthur was probably glad to have missed the tour as the wickets in South Africa were so placid that even the timeless Test had to be abandoned, after ten days of play, so the MCC tourists could catch the *Athlone Castle* for home!

Arthur's Test career may have floundered but his future in county cricket looked secure. It had been the fifth consecutive season that he had taken more than 100 wickets. The only worry on the horizon was the disturbing news from Europe where the possibilities of war loomed large. The Munich Crisis talks at the end of September 1938 offered some hopes and Neville Chamberlain's famous declaration of 'peace for our time' gave certain reassurances. The declaration would prove worthless and Hitler's aggressive designs on Europe would soon become the subject of great public concern.

Arthur returned to New Eltham for the winter and settled into his usual routine. He would help out at the shop whenever pressed and spend the rest of his time in pursuit of the dog or horse which would make his fortune. Arthur's sister-in-law, Betty, used to accompany him on his trips to the nearby Catford dog track where he would invest considerable sums of money. She christened him 'Mustafa' because he would always say of some animal or other that it 'must 'ave a chance!' Arthur would curse his luck when the animal failed to live up to his prediction but it never got him down. They would have a drink on the way home and plan the next trip to recoup his losses. The rest of his winter was spent in contemplation of the coming summer and his eagerness to return to the West Country was as strong as ever.

8

The war years

AFTER THE TRIUMPHS OF 1938, the last season before the
Second World War was something of an anticlimax for Arthur
and for Somerset cricket. The 1939 season was played out
amid constant worry over events in Europe. Germany now
occupied Czechoslovakia and an escalation of hostilities
was likely at any time. Arthur did not have a good start to
the season and he played most of the early matches
handicapped by injury. He also missed five championship
matches in August with severely strained knee ligaments
and, deprived of his services, Somerset managed to lose
four of these matches.

The highlight of Somerset's season was their victory
over the West Indies at Taunton in August. The West Indies
lost by an innings and 72 runs, their only innings defeat
of the tour. They never recovered from being skittled out
for 84 runs in their first innings, their lowest score of
the tour. The West Indies were disturbed by the pace and
swing obtained by Arthur and Bill Andrews bowling 16 overs
apiece. Arthur returned figures of four wickets for 43 runs
and Bill Andrews took six wickets for 40 runs. Eight of the
ten wickets were bowled or leg-before-wicket.

J.H.Cameron, the leg-spin bowler who played for
Somerset between 1932 and 1947, was one of only two West
Indian players to get into double figures. He skippered the
side against Somerset in the absence of R.S.Grant, the West
Indian captain. Cameron won the toss and, despite the
conditions, decided to bat. He remembers the events quite
clearly despite the passing of almost sixty years:

It was not a green wicket; our undoing was the heavy atmosphere which helped Arthur and Bill Andrews. Incidentally, Bunty Longrigg, the Somerset captain, told me that he would have batted first, had he won the toss. Our bowlers were below standard and we batted poorly in the second innings.

Arthur produced the usual match-winning performances during the 1939 season. Against Sussex at Hove in May, he scored 42 runs and took ten wickets for 130 runs to set up a nine-wickets victory. Later in June at Bath, in a low scoring game, he took five wickets for 46 runs, bowling his off-breaks, to reduced Leicestershire to 119 all out in their first innings and set up another nine-wickets victory for Somerset. The Bath festival proved very successful for Arthur as he took ten wickets against Oxford University and he saved Somerset from certain defeat against Kent. Kent had established a valuable first innings lead of 31 runs on a turning wicket and Somerset's batting folded in the second innings when facing the bowling of Doug Wright. When Arthur came in, Somerset had lost eight wickets and were less than twenty runs ahead. Arthur was missed four times in the course of five balls from Wright but he stayed doggedly at the wicket. He was last man out for 48 runs when Wright eventually took his wicket, his sixteenth of the match. It left Kent to score 99 runs for victory. Arthur and Bill Andrews bowled tightly, taking three wickets apiece, and Kent were still 27 runs short of their target when stumps were drawn.

Arthur bowled exceptionally well throughout July, taking fifty-five cheap wickets during this period. This included match figures of eight wickets for 107 runs against Worcestershire, eight wickets for 96 runs against Kent, twelve wickets for 132 runs against Northamptonshire and twelve wickets for 103 runs against Essex.

The Worcestershire match at Kidderminster ended rather unusually in a tie. Arthur, bowling off-breaks in Worcestershire's first innings, took seven wickets for 45 runs off 16 overs, including a glorious spell of six wickets for 15 runs. Worcestershire were all out for 130 runs and Somerset just managed first innings points. Horace Hazell kept Worcestershire quiet in their second innings, which left Somerset needing 142 runs to win. The batsmen continued to struggle but hopes were raised when Arthur hit a ball from Jenkins out of the ground. His dismissal in the next over ended Somerset's chances of victory.

In the match against Kent played at Maidstone, his eight wickets were out of twelve to fall. He also hit boldly in Somerset's second innings in an attempt to provide Kent with a challenging target. His brief innings of 21 runs contained three consecutive sixes off the bowling of Doug Wright. Arthur also played his best innings of the season in July when he hit 87 runs against Hampshire at Taunton in the space of seventy-five minutes. His innings included seven sixes, a five and three fours.

As previously mentioned, Arthur had his benefit year in 1939 and expected a good response. The County's fixture list for 1939, which also listed the benefit matches, included the following exhortation:

SUPPORT THE GATE BY YOUR PRESENCE AND GIVE ARTHUR A CHEER

Nineteen fixtures had been arranged mainly against local clubs and invitation X1s. Unfortunately, some benefit matches were affected by the uncommonly wet weather, other matches were cancelled towards the end of the season because of the imminence of war. Those matches that did get played were well attended and Arthur was generally expected to entertain the crowds with his hitting. He rarely disappointed when presented with some 'friendly' bowling from the opposition. The matches were also not without ceremony as illustrated by the match against Bridgewater in the Parks on the 25th May 1939. Lord Somerset, the President of the Bath and West Show and a Vice-President of the Somerset County Cricket Club, was one of the honoured guests. The mayor of Bridgewater and Vernon Bartlett, the local member of parliament were also present. The Bridgewater Club Secretary spoke a few words in praise of the beneficiary and there were vociferous calls for Arthur to respond. Arthur may have been an entertainer on the field of play but the prospect of speaking in public would fill him with abject terror. Arthur politely declined and Brigadier Lancaster had to step into the breach.

As if the weather and the War were not enough to contend with, Arthur had the bad luck to be sidelined with a knee injury at the time of the Club's benefit match. Arthur had chosen the Glamorgan match at his beloved Weston-Super-Mare. This traditional match was chosen because it was always well attended. The normal holiday crowds would be swelled by the Glamorgan supporters who came in their hoards across the Bristol Channel on the Campbell's Steamer. The weather stayed fine throughout and his absence from the field at least provided the opportunity to mingle with the crowds. The County's benefit match helped compensate for the rest of the season and, despite all the adverse circumstances he had to endure, Arthur received £1,413 from his benefit year. This was a club record at the time, *[worth in the region of £38,000 at today's prices]*.

Arthur had not been considered for the three-match summer Test series against the West Indies, which was won by England. The selectors were aware of Arthur's injuries, which prevented him from bowling at full pace for most of the season. He was also injured and missing from the Somerset team when the last Test was played. It was therefore a pleasant surprise to receive an invitation to go on the MCC tour of India during the winter. Arthur readily accepted the invitation but did not build up his hopes of touring because there were talks of cancelling the tour, even before the touring party announcement in early August.

The 1939 county season was played out in bizarre and surreal circumstances as if unaffected by what was happening in Europe. At the end of the day's play, the evening newspapers were scanned for news of Hitler's latest exploits rather than for news of other counties. During the evenings the latest news replaced cricket as the main topic of conversation and the players, especially Arthur, would be worrying about the Luftwaffe bombing their families while they were away from home.

The last match of the season, which was played at Taunton against Northamptonshire, ended in a comfortable innings victory for Somerset. As on many previous occasions, the opening bowling partnership was too much for the visitors with Arthur and Bill Andrews each taking seven wickets. At dawn on the 1st September 1939, the last day of the match, the German Panzer tanks rumbled across the Polish border. It was just two days before the declaration of War with Germany and the players who could scarcely concentrate on the cricket, were thankful of an early end to the match and the season. Some players had already joined the reserve forces so they had precious little time to prepare for what was about to happen. The players could not have predicted on this day that the Second World War would have such a catastrophic effect on their lives and careers. The war put an end to county cricket for six years, curtailed many promising cricket careers and tragically ended the lives of others.

R.P.Nelson, the Northamptonshire captain, would be killed in just over a year's time while serving with the Marines. His opening bat, E.J.H.Dixon, a fine young prospect and an Oxford blue in 1939, would die in 1941 presumed killed in action. F.M.McRae who had shown such promise during this season, finishing second in the Somerset batting averages, would be another casualty of the War. He died at sea in 1944, serving on *HMS Mahratta* in the Barents Sea. Six players who played that day would never play first-class cricket again. Those that did return after the war would have cause to reflect on the damage done to their cricketing careers. Arthur, on the brink of further recognition by his country, would have more reason than most to consider himself unlucky but never showed any signs of resentment.

At the close of the season, Arthur's bowling figures were not far short of the previous year's record. They would have been closer still had it not been for the injuries that kept him out of the game in August and prevented him from playing at Weston, one of his most profitable bowling grounds. Arthur topped the Somerset County Averages in 1939 with 114 championship wickets and in all first-class matches he took 130 wickets at a little over 21 runs apiece. He also scored 652 runs, including 31 sixes, at an average of 20 runs per innings.

Arthur received final confirmation that the MCC winter tour of India was being cancelled while playing in the Northamptonshire match. It was a great disappointment to him as he had been looking forward to experiencing the delights of India for a second time. However, he was encouraged in the knowledge that he had not been completely overlooked as a England player. The tour was not the only thing to be cancelled. The Folkestone and the Scarborough Festivals were also casualties of the War. Arthur had been asked to play in both. He had also received an invitation to play for Sir Pelham Warner's X1 against an England Past and Present X1 at Folkestone. This invitation had been declined because of his benefit commitments but he would have played in the later stages of the festival.

Arthur left Somerset for New Eltham immediately after the end of the Northamptonshire match. The public transport systems were chaotically stretched to the limit. Apart from coping with the general mobilisation, people were cutting short their summer holidays or evacuating London for places of safety. There was an eerie sense of disquiet about Arthur's homeward journey to the South East with the towns and cities already blacked-out in readiness for War.

At the age of thirty-seven years and at this stage of the War, Arthur would not have been expected to volunteer for the armed forces. It would be some time before he would be obliged to register for active service in accordance with the conscription regulations. Meanwhile, Arthur was reported to have volunteered for the Civil Defence Corp although there are no records to confirm his involvement with this service.

The War may have stopped county cricket but it did not end organised cricket entirely. The armed forces played competitive cricket throughout the War and the representative sides, like those of other organisations such as the Civil Defence Corp, included many of England's top cricketers. Several new teams were also created as a result of the War and Arthur was involved with one of the best-known, the London Counties Cricket Team. London Counties was formed in the spring of 1940 following an earlier meeting in February at Sandham's Cricket School in

Wandsworth. The objective was to augment the professional cricketers' depleted income. It was agreed that most of the gate receipts would go to the players, although for their part, it was insisted that a percentage should go to charity.

London Counties seldom played their matches on first-class grounds as it was agreed that the team should take cricket into the surrounding areas of London. In any event, many first-class grounds, Taunton included, had been commandeered by the armed forces for military purposes such as billeting and training. London Counties did, however, play the British Empire X1, another newly created team, which played its fixtures at Lord's. The first encounter with the British Empire X1 was on the 13th July 1940 and it was the first time that the click of turnstiles had been heard since the start of the War. There were 8,000 spectators and 6,425 of them had paid the entrance fee of 6d (2.5p). A Red Cross collection during the match netted £120. London Counties played the British Empire X1 later in the year and on this occasion the game was watched by over 13,000 people.

London Counties had a nucleus of fifteen players in their first year of existence. They played twenty-six one-day matches during the 1940 season, the hottest summer for many years. Eight players played in twenty or more matches. Apart from Arthur, who played twenty-one matches, they were A.E.Fagg (Kent), J.Hulme (Middlesex), F.S. and J.W.Lee (Somerset), A.Sandham (Surrey), F.Woolley (Kent) and W.F.Price (Middlesex). Not surprisingly with such an array of first-class cricketing experience, the team won twenty-three of their matches and attracted great crowds with their cavalier play. Arthur had few opportunities to bat because London Counties usually had so many runs on the board by the time his turn came that a score from him was rarely needed.

On the one occasion a big score was required - at Hoddesdon on the 24th August 1940 - Arthur did not disappoint. London Counties had lost five wickets for 52 runs when Arthur went out to bat and in the space of fifty-two minutes he scored 102 out of 130 runs. Some of his hits carried far out of the ground and his century included eight sixes and seven fours. Arthur also took six wickets for 45 runs in this game. His bowling for London Counties was consistently good throughout the summer. *Wisden* records that 'Wellard mixed his pace cleverly though he rarely resorted to bowling round the wicket like he used to do for Somerset.' In all, he took 70 wickets at under 12 runs apiece.

The extra money received from London Counties was appreciated since the Somerset professionals were only paid a retainer of £3 per week in 1940. This represented about a third of what they could have expected from their contracts with match fees and bonuses added. Arthur had the additional cushion of the recent benefit monies but his wife was quite anxious about their long term financial future. Jack resolved to find some means of supplementing their income and eventually settled for buying a sweet and tobacconist lockup shop, situated in Wellhall Road, Eltham, which was a short bus ride from their home. The shop was purchased for around £600 using part of the proceeds from Arthur's benefit year. Jack reasoned, quite correctly, that the money was safer in bricks and mortar than on the horses and dogs. Small sweet shops in these days, without the competition and degree of choice that exists today, were regarded as providing a secure, if modest, source of income.

The added responsibility for the shop did not change Arthur's lifestyle a great deal. He did help out at the shop, particularly in dealing with the early morning library and cigarette trade, but Jack mostly organised and ran the business. While Jack could be found serving behind the counter, Arthur was more likely to be found at the top of the Eltham High Street in the ex-servicemen's snooker and bowls club. The winter of 1940 passed uneventfully in New Eltham although it was occasionally affected by bombs aimed at neighbouring Woolwich. Slightly further afield the Blitz was having a devastating effect on London's civilian population. People grew accustomed to the sound of air raid sirens and to living and sleeping in the discomfort of an air raid shelter. The Wellards were more fortunate than most as Jack had a substantial and comfortable brick-built shelter constructed in the garden of the house. The family would spend their nights in the shelter and would invariably while away the time playing cards.

Arthur's knee troubles meant that he rarely played top-class cricket in 1941. He did play in a one-day match for a Lord's X1 against the Anti-Aircraft Brigade at Lord's. The Lord's X1 was captained by Major G.O.Allen and also included F.M.McRae of Somerset. The Anti-Aircraft Brigade could also turn out a strong representative side, which on this day included Sgt J.Hardstaff, Sgt M.Leyland, Major E.R.T.Holmes and Lieut. D.V.P.Wright. Arthur took one wicket for 25 runs in the match won by the Lord's X1 and was not required to bat.

London Counties, after the first successful season extended their fixture list in 1941 but Arthur only played in nine of the 38 engagements. In one of these matches he took eight wickets for 17 runs against Bexleyheath and in another, at Hayes in May, Arthur scored what was described by *Wisden* as probably the fastest fifty ever seen in any type of cricket. He reached the half-century in eight minutes and the accuracy of the timing was vouched for by both scorers. He hit seven sixes, all off the bowling of H.Schofield. The sixes were taken off nine deliveries, three in succession in one over and four off Schofield's next. The hapless bowler, who had been bowling with great success until Arthur appeared at the wicket, returned figures of five overs, three wickets for 66 runs. Arthur retired on reaching his fifty and then took a hat-trick with his off-breaks.

Allowing for the time taken to retrieve the ball from the far corners of the ground, it is extremely unlikely that the achievement of scoring 50 runs in eight minutes could be improved upon in any standard of cricket. The time was equalled in first-class cricket by Clive Inman when playing for Leicestershire in 1965 but this was achieved in 'contrived' circumstances.

When not playing competitive professional cricket Arthur could always be persuaded to play club cricket where the strain on his knees and joints was less severe. He had played occasionally as a 'guest player' for Blackheath Wanderers Cricket Club, which was not far from Arthur's house in Footscray Road. He continued to play for the club until he was called-up for the Army. He usually bowled his off-breaks on such occasions but it was his batting for which he was remembered. Mr G. Jessop of Sidcup lived at the time in a house overlooking the ground and remembered those times with great fondness:

We lived in a three-storey house in a line of similar properties all of which were a long back garden away from the boundary line, but Arthur cracked so many tiles on our roofs that we residents had a standing repair scheme operating with the club. The thing that impressed me most about his striking was that it appeared effortless, was never a slog, but a beautiful smooth unhurried action that remains outstanding with me in a lifetime of sporting memories. Arthur, of course, did not restrict his hitting to the mid-on direction of my house, but regularly peppered the neighbouring territories all round the ground. (Arthur also provided another bonus by occasionally bringing along as a second guest player his friend and county colleague-Mr Andrews).

Arthur continued to receive his £3 per week from Somerset until October 1941 when his contract expired, along with those of five of the other seven professionals. Informal arrangements were made to continue the payment of a retainer fee for a further twelve months but at a greatly reduced rate. Bertie Buse, whose contract did not expire until the end of December 1942 generously agreed to the same terms. With little income coming in and reduced member's subscriptions, the club simply did not have the money available to pay their professionals. The accounts for the year ended 31st December 1941 show that by the end of the year their accumulated balances had dwindled to £219. On the 13th July 1942, Arthur received a letter from Brigadier Lancaster, the Somerset Secretary. Ever mindful of cost and ignorant of feelings, the Brigadier had duplicated the letter leaving appropriate spaces for the inclusion of the professional's name and a reference to past service. The letter began by explaining the 'low position of the club's finances' and referred to a meeting of the Committee on the 9th April, which had decided not to renew the contracts from the 31st October 1942. The letter thanked Arthur for his service against which the Brigadier had inserted the words 'very valuable' and expressed the hope that they might 'renew old associations' and 'soon meet again in happier circumstances.' Lancaster's letter was not unexpected but the perfunctory manner in which it was written did not help to soften the blow. The Wellards resigned themselves to managing on the income provided by the shop although even this income was affected by shortages and rationing.

With the War expanding on all fronts, the need for fresh supplies of men and women for the armed forces increased. Conscription had been imposed in October 1939 and required all twenty and twenty-one-year-olds to apply to be registered for active service. It was soon apparent that the Country's needs could not be met from the Register or from volunteers so the registration requirements were gradually widened. By the end of 1941, seven million people between the ages of nineteen and forty were required to be registered and processed. Arthur, at the upper extreme of the age range and being married, would have some wait before the next step in the process that required his attendance at a medical board. Arthur, at almost forty, was not a young man but apart from continuing to suffer with knee problems he was in good health and unlikely to be pronounced medically unfit.

Arthur did have an ally in Doctor Trimmer, who was the Wellard family doctor. He had sympathetically provided Arthur with a medical condition, a bad back, which until the middle of 1942, forestalled any searching medical examination. However, for someone with a bad back he was a little too active on the cricket field and he had the misfortune to play against a team fielding a representative from the local medical board. After a particularly athletic and successful stint of bowling, the board member formed the opinion that if he was fit enough to play cricket he was fit enough to go into the armed forces. He was added to the register of men available for posting and shortly afterwards, in the late summer of 1942, received his enlistment papers. Arthur was instructed to report for basic military training.

Arthur was assigned to the Royal Army Ordinance Corp and was posted for training to Maryhill Barracks near Glasgow. It was not long before news of his posting reached the organisers of a cricket match in aid of The British Sailors Society. The match, on the 19th September 1942 at Hamilton Crescent, was between the Western Union of Scotland and a Services X1 captained by Major Mike White, the Cambridge University and Northamptonshire player. The organisers, scarcely believing their good fortune, arranged for him to be drafted into the Services X1 team and the publicity in the local paper ensured a bumper attendance. The crowd were not disappointed as Arthur hit two sixes in his brief innings of 19 runs and took three wickets for 20 runs.

There were no further opportunities to play cricket as he was posted overseas before the start of the 1943 season. His posting took him to the Italian war theatre, via North Africa, which was where he would spend the next two years of his life. His regiment supported the advancing troops and Arthur played his small part in this operation. He was never in the front-line of any action despite being a fine shot and the only time he had to use his weapon was for a spot of poaching. Arthur was, as would be expected, an artful poacher. After the war, he was asked whether he had ever tickled trout in his fishing days. 'Yes cock, tickled 'em out with hand grenades, when I was in Italy,' was his reply!

Italy, though ravaged by war, was a considerably more comfortable posting at this stage of the Second World War than many others. Arthur never spoke to his family about his war exploits except to recall that one of his less demanding duties was to make the regular trips to the Islands. Here, on Islands such as Elba and Sicily, he would requisition whatever the Army needed, including donkeys for the troops and goats for the Gurkhas. Arthur had a natural aptitude for this line of work and soon earned a reputation for wheeling and dealing. Alec Bedser recalls that his unit needed a half shaft for a Dodge truck but official sources had drawn a blank. They drove sixty miles to find Arthur and were astounded when he came up with the part.

There was no chance to play cricket during the offensive in Italy because the troops were constantly on the move. However, with the ending of hostilities in sight, the senior brass returning from the north began to turn their thoughts and attention to the summer game. It was known that many famous cricketers were in Italy and arranging cricket matches could be justified as providing recreation and entertainment for the thousands of restless servicemen. There were major difficulties when it was first considered in the spring of 1945, not least the difficulty of finding suitable flat surfaces. However, with considerable effort from a few dedicated officers, wickets were prepared at such places as Bari, Eboli, Caserta, Capua, Rome, Naples and Civitavecchia. With typical British ingenuity, wickets were produced using bulldozers and matting. Sightscreens, score boxes, seating and refreshment areas were hastily constructed with loudspeakers and score cards to complement the action.

The first big game in Italy took place on the 10th June 1945 in the Royal Palace Grounds at Caserta. Arthur, and Alec Bedser among others, took the opportunity to visit the grave of Captain Hedley Verity who is buried nearby. He died of wounds received when leading an infantry attack in Sicily on a July night in 1943 - a grievous loss to Yorkshire and English cricket. The match at Caserta was organised by Lt.-Col. A.L.Gracie who had been instrumental in securing the wicket at Caserta. His team challenged a Lt.-Col. Sugden's X1 that included the impressive opening bowling combination of Corporal Arthur Wellard (Somerset) and Flight Sgt. A.V.Bedser (Surrey). Lt.-Col. Gracie's team were shot out for 72 runs in their first innings. Arthur took four wickets for 24 runs and Alec Bedser - who a year later would begin his test career at Lord's - took five wickets for 42 runs. Not surprisingly, Arthur's team won the match by six wickets in accomplished style.

Soon after this match, on the 24th June, Arthur played in a one-day fixture at Eboli for Major Emery's X1 against Lt. R.E.Henty's X1. On this occasion the Bedser twins were in opposition. Alec Bedser and W.E. (Bill) Merritt, the New Zealand test player, each got five wickets and Major

Emery's side were dismissed for 132 runs. In reply, Arthur took three quick wickets but a fine 72 from Mike White, now a Lt.-Col., won the match for Major Henty.

By this stage of the war, Arthur was permanently attached to the base ordinance depot at Pontecagnano, near Solerno in Southern Italy. It was an excellent base from which to play cricket and Arthur was much in demand for the many matches that were played during the rest of the summer. It was an idyllic lifestyle and the standard of hospitality was always first-class as the host officers attempted to surpass each other. Meanwhile back at Lord's, a Lord's X1 got together by Sir Pelham Warner played a team representing the Second Army. Field-Marshall Alexander - a keen cricketer who had played for Harrow in the Eton versus Harrow match at Lord's in 1910 - found out about the match. The Field-Marshall, whose conquest of Sicily had led to the deposition of Mussolini and the taking of Rome, was anxious not to be outdone by the Second Army. He challenged the MCC on behalf of his Central Mediterranean Forces and a match was arranged for late August at Lord's. The CMF places were hotly contested. For some, they offered the chance to see England for the first time in many years, for others it was the chance of an 'early boat home'.

Just before leaving for England, a match was played in the Sports Stadium at Rome on the 17th and 18th August. Arthur played for the CMF X1 against a Middle Eastern Forces X1, flown in specially from Cairo, which included Sgt. Jim Laker and Captain Norman Yardley. Arthur took five wickets for 31 runs in a fine bowling spell that helped dismiss the MEF X1 for 139 runs. Their total would have been considerably lower but for an impressive innings of 88 runs from the twenty-two-year-old Bert Sutcliffe, soon to become an outstanding Test cricketer for New Zealand. The CMF X1 won easily by an innings and 13 runs. The art of wicket-taking had clearly not deserted Arthur despite his long absence from the game and it was a fine ending to his stay in Italy. On Arthur's penultimate night in Italy he was presented with an even finer memory of the country as the two teams dined together and then went on to the open-air opera house in Rome to listen to Gigli. It was a beautiful balmy evening and even Arthur, a man not given to great emotion and no lover of opera, could not have failed to be moved by such a cultural experience.

The day after the Rome match, thanks to the patronage of Field-Marshall Alexander, fourteen players flew to England to represent the Central Mediterranean Forces X1. Nine of the fourteen players, were or would become Test players including Tom Pritchard and Bill Merritt of New Zealand, Tom Dollery, Frank Smailes and Arthur McIntyre. The RAF had not been interested in providing an aircraft so the team flew home in an American Dakota. It touched down at St. Albans Airport in the early evening of Monday the 20th August and the party travelled to London by coach. The team arrived in England during cold and wet weather vastly different from the conditions they had left behind. In a match at Civitavecchia, the temperature had been recorded as 110 degrees in the shade! They stayed privately overnight and for some it provided the opportunity to return to their families. The team spent the next day having nets at Lord's and generally getting as much practice as possible. On the Wednesday there was a practice game against the Forty Club but Arthur did not play in this game.

The first proper game, a two-day match starting on Thursday the 23rd August, was against a strong Lord's X1. The Lord's X1 included Freddie Brown, R.J.O.Meyer, Trevor Bailey, Donald Carr and Martin Donnelly. The CMF X1 were not disgraced losing a closely fought game by one wicket. Arthur took two wickets for 21 runs in the first innings but bowled few overs in the second. He was feeling the effects of the travel and the change of climate did nothing for his aching knee joints. *Wisden* described the team as 'composed of county cricketers who had been away from England for years' and their performance as 'a gallant display although short of match practice.'

The CMF X1 also lost their second match on the Saturday against the Buccaneers at Southgate by a narrow margin in a game that was continually interrupted by heavy showers. Again Arthur managed to avoid playing and did not attend the match. Most of the team were scheduled to return to Italy on the Sunday but thanks to the poor weather and the cooperation of the American pilot they were delayed by three days. A few of the team spent their time watching England play the Dominions at Lords where 1,241 runs were scored in the match including a breathtaking innings of 185 from Keith Miller. Others looked for more distracting entertainment. Some, like Frank Smailes and Arthur, had been informed that they were not needed to return to Italy and had made themselves scarce after the Lord's match had ended.

In the week since landing in England, Arthur had spent the time with his wife, looking up friends and relatives in New Eltham and securing his demobilisation. Jack had received only a few days notice of Arthur's trip to London and she clearly had not prepared herself for what she had to say on his return. Their reunion was not a happy experience and Arthur remained baffled by the cool reception he received. It took several days before Jack could bring herself to tell Arthur that her feelings towards him had changed.

While Arthur had been abroad, Jack had become involved in a wartime romance with a man she met while visiting Agnes Lee. Agnes and Jack Lee were living at Mill Hill School where Jack Lee had taken a coaching job after finishing at Somerset. Jack Wellard and Agnes remained in contact while their husbands were away and regularly stayed at each other's houses.

On this occasion, Jack Wellard was introduced to an Australian named Jimmy, who was a distant relative of the Lees, serving with the RAAF and based in London. There was an instant attraction and after further clandestine meetings, Jack became infatuated with the young airman. He was extremely attentive and provided the warmth and companionship that had been missing in her marriage for such a long time. Jack, flattered by all this attention, fell in love with Jimmy and was determined to spend the rest of her life with him.

Jimmy, who was married, had already returned to Australia but, before leaving, had promised to come back for her after settling his affairs in Australia. Jack was confident that Jimmy would keep his promise and she eventually found the courage to tell Arthur about the relationship. Arthur was devastated by Jack's revelation and for a long time refused to accept or confront the issue, believing that she would 'come to her senses'.

Arthur was deeply hurt by Jack's infidelity but would not have allowed it to jeopardise their marriage. The physical side of their relationship had never been of great importance and he could have forgiven and forgotten the affair if Jack had shown the slightest signs of interest in a reconciliation. Jack's immediately family, tried to build the necessary bridges but it soon became clear that Jack was not interested. It would be several years before Jack finally accepted that Jimmy was not coming back for her and before she would entertain thoughts of renewing her relationship with Arthur.

Arthur remained in the South East for a while. His Mother had died in May 1945 and there were still matters to resolve that kept him busy. He was also hoping that Jack would have a change of heart but by Christmas, with no improvement in the situation, he decided to return to the West Country earlier than anticipated. Arthur was never short of friends who readily found him places to stay and he kept himself amused by following his favourite pastimes and sporting pursuits. He immersed himself in the local club and pub scene playing skittles and billiards, he rarely missed a national hunt race meeting at Wincanton, Newton Abbot, Devon and Exeter or Taunton and there were frequent trips to the greyhound track at Eastville. Arthur also had many farming friends and never turned down the opportunity for a spot of shooting. It was, in many ways, a thoroughly agreeable bachelor existence and he enjoyed his pre-season freedom. It was a good time to be alive with the nation still revelling in the euphoria that followed the ending of hostilities.

Nobody sought to question Arthur's premature return to Somerset. His private life was rarely discussed with others and if drawn, he would usually provide an evasive or flippant response. Arthur would certainly not have confided in anyone about his troubles at home. These were kept to himself because he was an immensely proud man and his strong, masculine image allowed no room for sentiment or emotional weaknesses. If Arthur was affected by his separation from Jack, his feelings were cleverly disguised. For the moment, his problems were blocked from his mind as the start of the first-class cricket season approached. Like most of the professionals who returned to Somerset in the spring of 1946, he had no hesitation about resuming his career and no thought of his long term future beyond the coming season.

9

1946-49: Post-war with Somerset

WHILE ARTHUR WAS IN ITALY he was asked if he would be returning to Somerset after the War. He is quoted as saying 'I doubt it, the old buggers are going and I'm forty-one.' However when the time came to report for duty in April 1946, his age, the niggling fitness problems and the troubles at home were all forgotten and he was as enthusiastic as ever about playing. He was forty-four years of age, a time when most cricketers have retired or at least given it serious consideration.

The thought did not enter Arthur's head and he was to tell Ron Roberts, the Somerset historian and writer, that he intended playing until he was sixty-five. At this point in his life, county cricket was his only security and he was keen to make up for the six years of lost cricket. His bachelor winter in Taunton had not done much for his waistline but the pre-season training routines helped to get him in shape and dismiss a local rumour that Arthur now weighed over eighteen stone!

Somerset were fortunate to be able to call on the seven professionals - Gimblett, Lee, Buse, Luckes, Wellard, Andrews and Hazell - who had been the backbone of the side in 1939. They were all present for the opening game at Taunton although Bertie Buse only just made it back from RAF service. An eighth professional, Johnny Lawrence, a leg-break bowler from Yorkshire had also been engaged for the 1946 season.

The senior professionals were very unhappy with the contract terms offered them but the Somerset secretary, Brigadier Lancaster, was in no mood for negotiating. Bill

Andrews was blamed by the others because, without thinking about contacting his fellow professionals, he had signed and returned his contract. The Brigadier insisted that if it was good enough for Andrews it was good enough for the rest. In the end, all the professionals signed the contracts as offered. They were not in a position to demand better terms. The War had sapped their confidence and created a general feeling of insecurity. The senior professionals were also acutely aware that they had a great deal to lose if their bluff was called. Most of them were due a benefit or testimonial during the next few seasons and this was the prime motivation for returning in some cases. As the season unfolded, with record crowds attending, there would be mounting discontent over wages but for the moment they were just glad to be back on the field of play.

They spent the month of April coaching the schoolboys, practising in the nets and playing warm-up games. The eight professionals, together with R.J.O.Meyer, E.F.Longrigg and N.S.Mitchell-Innes, played their opening first-class match against Essex at Taunton starting on the 11th May 1946. Ron Roberts described the scene in his book *Sixty years of Somerset cricket*:

When play began on the May morning, the Taunton ground, with a new coat of paint and the playing area, freshly mown, smelling as good as it looked, was fit for the finest match.

The first match was appropriate for the occasion being an exciting and tightly fought game. Essex snatched victory with two wickets to spare after Somerset had been in a good position to win the match by the end of the first day. They scored 287 in their first innings and had Essex in serious trouble at 32 for five wickets before the visitors recovered to 130 for six wickets by close of play. Arthur and Bill Andrews bowled with all their old vigour and produced a fine opening spell of aggressive bowling. It was as if the pair were trying to dispel any suggestion that they had lost their effectiveness after such a long absence from the first-class game. Arthur took three wickets for 32 runs and Bill Andrews took three wickets for 67 runs in the Essex first innings. However, on the last day a fine innings of 166 not out from the Essex skipper, Tom Pearce, was the difference between the two sides.

Somerset's next match was at Lord's where they began in fine form with most of the side contributing to their score of 364. The real excitement began after tea when Arthur joined Bill Andrews at the wicket. They added 51 runs in 18 minutes with Arthur dominating the partnership. Arthur scored 35 of these runs before being caught in the deep field. His brief innings included two huge sixes into the Grand Stand at square leg. Five wickets from Arthur ensured a first innings lead of over 100 runs but Somerset's batting in their second innings let them down on an awkward pitch. They were all out for 55 runs and Middlesex, although made to struggle, won the game with four wickets to spare.

Somerset had lost their first two matches after having the upper hand in both. The next two matches, at the Oval and at Birmingham, were also lost thanks to some further indifferent batting. It had not been an encouraging start and there was no improvement during the next few matches. To make matters worse, Arthur's knee problems were already causing concern and no amount of strapping seemed to ease the pain. He had started the season a little too vigorously and with scant respect for his age. By the end of May, the problem could not be ignored and as May turned to June he was forced to rest the knee for two matches.

While Arthur was out of action, Somerset recorded their first victory of the season, against Leicestershire at Melton Mowbray. Arthur recovered sufficiently to play in the traditional Whitsun match against Gloucestershire at Taunton. The match was spoiled by rain but Arthur scored an aggressive fifty in Somerset's innings of 313 runs. He also took four wickets in Gloucestershire's reply but he had the misfortune to be bowling to Hammond at his very best. He hit Arthur for two sixes to bring up his century, taking 20 runs off the over. When Hammond was in this mood - as he frequently was against Somerset with a career average of 73 runs in his 43 innings against them - there was no way of containing the great batsman. The rain had the last word after Hammond's efforts secured first innings points.

Somerset's season changed for the better at the Bath festival in Mid-June when they won all three matches against Kent, Cambridge University and Hampshire. Arthur played his usual part in the victory over Kent. He took three wickets for 29 runs and two wickets for 52 runs in Kent's two innings. In the next game the undergraduates were completely baffled by Arthur's slow off-breaks and he took thirteen wickets in the match at just over 7.5 runs apiece. Somerset achieved a comfortable innings victory in under two days of play. The University batsmen were unlucky to have faced Arthur at all. He usually managed to get himself rested during this fixture when it was the middle game of the Bath festival. The middle game coincided with Bath Races on the Thursday and Arthur hated to miss this meeting. Arthur's exceptional bowling performance was inspired by the desire to bowl the 'bleedin' college boys' out in time to make the first race!

In the final game of the Bath festival, Arthur made his highest score of the season against Hampshire. He scored 74 in just fifty-three minutes to help Somerset reach a first innings total of 293. This was enough to secure an innings victory for Somerset after Arthur did most of the damage with the ball. He had match bowling figures of nine wickets for 97 runs. In the three matches at Bath this year, he had taken twenty-seven wickets at 10 runs apiece!

Soon after the Bath festival, Somerset beat Northamptonshire at Taunton. Arthur had a fine game with match bowling figures of ten wickets for 151 runs. The next match against Middlesex, also at Taunton, produced Somerset's best and most spectacular victory of the season. They were not expected to win. Middlesex had finished championship runners-up in the four seasons before the war, would finish runners-up to Yorkshire this season and become champions in the famous Compton/Edrich year of 1947. Their team in this match included five England players - Robins, Sims, Price, Edrich and Compton - and two future Test players in Robertson and Young.

On the first day, the Middlesex bowlers were treated to a merciless onslaught as Somerset reached 472 for eight wickets by close of play. Harold Gimblett produced a masterful innings of 231 - his first double century - and Arthur chipped in with 56 quick runs late in the day. Arthur's innings included four sixes and the tired Middlesex attack must have yearned for the stumps to be drawn. On the second day, Somerset declared at 523 for nine wickets. In the Middlesex reply, the openers, Robertson and Brown, appeared to have little trouble with the bowling. The partnership put on over 100 runs by lunch of the second day and the easy-paced pitch looked full of runs.

Arthur must have had a very good lunch because in the post-lunch spell he bowled both openers. Denis Compton was then caught at short leg when playing an uncharacteristic defensive prod. Arthur's three wickets had cost 9 runs and with Bertie Buse bowling well at the other end, Middlesex collapsed to 205 all out. Arthur and Bertie Buse with three wickets apiece in the second Middlesex innings ensured a memorable innings victory.

This notable victory marked the beginning of a fine run for Somerset who, suitably inspired, won five of their next seven games. They did it mostly without Arthur's assistance as his knee problems forced him to miss five of these matches, including the innings victory against the Indian tourists. He also missed the championship match against Gloucestershire at Bristol that followed but this was probably a mixed blessing since Wally Hammond scored an immaculate double-century and destroyed the Somerset bowling. It was said that he did not hit a shot in the air until he had passed 200 runs.

Arthur celebrated his return after this five-match absence by scoring 70 against Glamorgan in the first festival match at Weston. His 70 runs were out of a Somerset first innings total of 167 runs. He shared a significant partnership of 52 runs for the last wicket with Horace Hazell to restore respectability to the innings. Horace contributed just three of these runs, which gives a indication of Arthur's dominance within the partnership. Arthur also took three wickets in the first Glamorgan innings but the bad weather intervened before either side had a chance to take control of the match.

Arthur played a crucial role in the following match at Weston against Worcestershire, which Somerset eventually won by the narrow margin of 35 runs. He took five wickets for 85 runs in Worcestershire's second innings but it was Arthur's blistering catch that turned the game. Worcestershire, needing 269 runs for victory, were cruising at 159 for three wickets when Arthur held a one-handed catch off a full-blooded drive from Howorth. Howorth had been well set on 65 and was beginning to go for his shots. Ron Roberts described Arthur's catching position as 'within almost touching distance of the bat.' The catch turned the game in Somerset's favour and the last six wickets fell for just 85 runs.

Somerset won their last festival match against Surrey by a huge margin with Arthur taking eight wickets in the match. A further victory, in their penultimate game of the season against Worcestershire, ensured a high position in the championship table. The County had achieved a record of twelve championship victories as well as registering impressive wins against India and Cambridge University. They were eventually fourth in the table, the County's highest finish since their third position in 1892. Somerset's lofty position owed much to the batting of Harold Gimblett who just failed to reach 2,000 runs. This target would have been achieved if appendicitis problems had not ruled him out of the last three championship matches.

Arthur had also played a considerable part in Somerset's successful season despite missing seven games through injury. The knee strains had been a problem for much of the season yet he still finished second to Horace Hazell in the County bowling averages. He took 119 wickets for Somerset at under 19 runs apiece and was the only Somerset bowler to take more than a hundred wickets. His batting had been subdued by his pre-war standards but his 531 runs still included twenty-seven sixes.

Somerset's fortunes had also improved off the field. The club had made a substantial profit of £4,785 thanks to

the record crowds, which deprived of first-class cricket
for so long had flocked to the grounds. The senior
professionals argued that the profit was largely due to
their efforts on the field. It also had not escaped their
notice that these record profits were more than the cost of
the club's combined annual wage bill. The dispute over
their wages had festered all season with Bill Andrews
getting most of the blame for the professionals
predicament. When it came to negotiating their terms and
conditions for 1947, Bill was 'volunteered' as their
'agent' and told to convey their demands to the committee.
Bill wrote in his best copperplate handwriting but the
letter was not well received by the Somerset secretary and
he was incorrectly identified as the instigator of these
demands.

The War may have changed certain attitudes but little
had changed in the relationship between the professionals
and the administrators. The committee still clung to the
old amateur ways and treated the professionals little
better than servants. Bill Andrews would have cause to
regret his part in the wage revolt as it got him on the
wrong side of John Daniell, now club president. Bill's
position with the club was not very secure and he could
ill-afford to upset either Daniell or Lancaster. Apart from
a match-winning performance at Portsmouth when he took
eight wickets for 25 runs, he had a poor season with the
ball. This was one of the matches that Arthur missed
through injury and, as before, Bill took full advantage of
the rare opportunity to choose the most favourable bowling
end. He would need more performances like this in 1947 if
he was to keep his place in the side.

Arthur still had one first-class game to play before
the end of the 1946 season. He was asked to play in the
North v South match, which was the middle game of the
Scarborough festival. The selection came as a surprise to
Arthur who had assumed his representative days were over.
With memories of happier times at this resort, he readily
accepted the invitation. This fixture was being revived but
it had been a regular and popular feature of the Festival
for many years. The North won the match but Arthur bowled

well throughout, taking one wicket for 44 runs in North's first innings and four top-order wickets for 58 runs in the second. His five wickets brought his season's first-class tally to 124 at 18.69 runs apiece.

Arthur returned to Somerset to continue his bachelor existence during the winter of 1946. He stayed with Bill Andrews and other friends who were more than happy to find him a bed. The friend that gave him most support during this time was Len Creed, the man that would later bring Vivian Richards to Somerset. Len Creed had first met Arthur at the Winter Gardens Pavilion in 1937. During the festival, the Winter Gardens held 'Special County Nights' to which the teams were invited. On this occasion, Len was introduced to Arthur and Bill Andrews while the pair were earnestly chatting to two local young women. Len and Arthur hit it off right away as they had many similar interests, not least their love of sport, drinking and gambling.

Len Creed had a large farm at Evercreech, near Shepton Mallet and although farming was very much in his blood, he preferred town to country. Arthur was made most welcome at the farm and it was here that he spent most of the winter. It was an idyllic lifestyle for Arthur who was basically a countryman at heart. He used to relish the unlimited opportunities for fishing and hunting. It was said that Arthur liked nothing better than to have a gun in one hand and a fishing rod in the other. At Len Creed's farm, he could indulge both field sports to his heart's content. Arthur did exactly what he wanted and there was never any pressure to 'earn his keep'. As far as Len Creed was concerned, he could have stayed as a friend at the farm for the rest of his days.

It was about this time that Len Creed decided his future lay in turf accounting. Arthur would help Len with his new interest, taking bets for him at the farm and accompanying him to horse race meetings and the Eastville greyhound stadium. Arthur's almost encyclopedic knowledge of horses and dogs was finally put to good purpose! From these small beginnings, Len Creed developed a very successful bookmaking business and Arthur and Len became great friends.

There was little contact between Arthur and his wife, Jack, and there was no concerted effort from either side to bring about a reconciliation. On the odd occasion that Jack's name entered the conversation, Arthur would refer to her as the 'trouble and strife' and change the subject as quickly as possible. If Arthur had been honest with himself, he would have acknowledged that life was far too enjoyable to think about repairing their relationship. In their eighteen years of marriage, he had spent the greater part of his time away from the matrimonial home so another winter was hardly to make much difference!

Arthur enjoyed his winter. It was the first time, since joining the County in 1927, that he could be truly counted a Somerset man. Ron Roberts would say that Arthur was as much Somerset as a glass of farmhouse cider but in reality he had never thought of the West Country as his home. His South East London accent softened under the influence of the local dialect and by remaining in the area, joining in the social activities, it was easier for the Somerset public to claim him as their own. As the 1947 season approached, the County looked forward excitedly to the prospect of building on Somerset's fine start to post-war cricket. There was much that augured well for 1947 and with the eighth professional, Johnny Lawrence, now well established the signs were very encouraging.

Somerset had a sensational start to the season when they beat the eventual champions, Middlesex at Lord's. Middlesex only lost five championship matches, which to everyone's surprise included a further defeat by Somerset later in the season. Somerset won the match at Lord's by one wicket after bowling Middlesex out for 78 in their second innings. Arthur, who was not fully fit, got the early wickets of Brown and Edrich and ended with three wickets for 20 runs. However, it was the young Maurice Tremlett, in his first match for Somerset, who did most damage with five wickets for 39 runs. Tremlett's brilliant debut was almost too good to be true for he was also to hit the winning runs in a tense last-wicket stand. For good measure the winning runs included a six. On this occasion Arthur Wellard had been well and truly upstaged!

The victory over Middlesex was a case of flattering to deceive and the loyal Somerset supporters were soon brought down to earth. Their confident and optimistic predictions for the season too easily ignored the weaknesses in the side and the fact that Somerset's prospects rested on the fortunes of its fading senior professionals. John Daniell summed up the disappointing season in the Annual Report, even if he did not quite put his finger on the cause of the problem. He stated that:

It was caused by hopes set too high, as a result of the very successful season of 1946, a certain amount of wishful thinking and bombastic talk during the winter and before the start of the season, capped by a magnificent opening victory at Lord's against a Middlesex X1 at full strength. Unfortunately Somerset had to wait a long time for the second victory - eight matches in succession being lost.

Arthur, carrying the injuries and strains that would be expected of a forty-five-year-old, still managed to bowl consistently well throughout the season. He took five or more wickets in an innings on eight occasions and despite missing five of the last six championship matches through injury, including most of the Weston festival, he narrowly missed taking 100 wickets for the seventh consecutive season. Arthur took 93 wickets - the most of any Somerset bowler - at under 24 runs apiece. He was second in the County averages and bowled by far the most number of overs during a hot and dry season that offered almost perfect run getting conditions.

His best performances of the year were reserved for the Bath festival, towards the end of June 1947. In the first match against Leicestershire he took eight wickets for 68 to secure a comfortable win for Somerset. He was rested for the middle match against Cambridge University, much to the relief of the undergraduates, so he did not have to grumble about missing Bath Races. He returned to the side with a vengeance in the final match of the festival, against Worcestershire. They were all out for 131 runs in their first innings and Arthur, bowling unchanged, took eight wickets for 52 runs off 27.4 overs. He followed this with seven wickets for 49 runs in their second innings to record his career best bowling figures. These were achieved by employing the now familiar mixture of pace and off-break bowling. In the first Worcestershire innings he took five wickets with fast-medium swing bowling and the other three with slow off-breaks, bowling round the wicket. *Wisden* described his bowling performance as 'reminiscent of his best pre-war form.'

Arthur had an indifferent season with the bat and although he scored 521 first-class runs he failed to get above 50 during the whole of the season. There was still some excitement for the crowds, however, as 150 of these runs came in sixes!

Bill Andrews was unable to secure a regular place in the side and played few games in 1947. He took just 24 wickets at around 30 runs apiece and was promptly released at the end of the season. Bill had been out of favour since his letter to the committee and was rarely given the chance to play. He was unhappy at being regularly selected as twelfth man, which he felt was demeaning for a professional of his standing. Arthur, thanks to the dearth of genuine pace bowling in the Somerset ranks, was given a two-year contract starting on the 1st October 1947. As a grade A player - ten years a contract professional - Arthur would receive about £600 a year for his services. It was as much as he could hope for; the strains and injuries were getting difficult to ignore. He would be forty-seven before the contract expired and age, which had seemed an irrelevance in his case, was beginning to catch up with Arthur.

R.J.O.Meyer, the eccentric founder of Millfield School, was Somerset's amateur skipper in 1947. This fine all-rounder was a popular choice among the professionals and he had a reasonable season with bat and ball. In this year, his only full season for the Club, he played 25 of the 28 games, scored 853 runs and took 43 wickets. He was, however, plagued by lumbago - an affliction that beset his predecessor Bunty Longrigg - and though he carried on courageously, it might at times have been better if he had stepped down. He was a liability in the field because he could not bend down and this did not help a side that already had to hide too many fielders.

Bill Andrews told a poignant story about Jack Meyer's fielding. Playing at Bristol that year, he was in the slips when Charlie Barnett, the Gloucestershire opener, was facing Arthur. Barnett flashed at the ball in the very first over and gave what should have been an easy slip catch. Meyer dropped it and Arthur stood rooted to the spot, cursing his bad luck. At the end of the over, R.J.O. came down the wicket and pressed a pound note into Arthur's hand. R.J.O. was immediately forgiven!

Arthur took advantage of Len Creed's winter hospitality for a second year. He was as always a frequent visitor to the West Country racetracks and it was nothing for him to go off with £200 in his pocket. If anything, his gambling had become more intense and he would throw all caution to the wind when betting on a dog or horse. His Mother, who had died in 1945, left Arthur a small legacy and this money was used to feed his passion for gambling. His aunt Ada died soon afterwards and her money plus most of his summer earnings probably went the same way. Ennyd Andrews remembers that Arthur would return after a good day at the races with a beaming smile and telling everyone that he had given the bookies a 'good hiding'. Bill Andrews would remark - with Arthur safely out of earshot - that he never told them when he had a bad day!

It was now two years since Arthur came home from the War, by which time Jack Wellard had finally accepted that her Australian airman was not about to return. Jack's sister Betty had moved to Mottingham, which left Jack and her mother alone in the family home at New Eltham. Jack looked after the shop while her mother did the household chores and kept the shop accounts. Jack was lonely and finding the business a strain. She was also missing Arthur and was determined to end their estrangement. Her new-found determination may have been prompted by hearing rumours of Arthur's fondness for Betty Andrews, Bill's younger sister. Bill felt that they might one day marry, which would have pleased him very much. It is doubtful whether Arthur was as keen as Jack to get back together but throughout their married life Jack held a strong and persuasive hold over Arthur. Len Creed remembers there were quite a few phone calls from Jack while Arthur was at the farm. She wanted him back for a family Christmas and Len had a job to persuade him that he should go. Eventually it was agreed that he would go home and the Christmas of 1947 marked the beginning of the couple's gradual reconciliation.

Arthur returned for the 1948 season to find Somerset struggling to appoint a captain. It was unthinkable that they should appoint a professional even though this was now the norm for many counties. R.J.O.Meyer's back problems ruled him out of contention and there was no other amateur available for the full season. In the end, N.S.Mitchell-Innes, J.W.Seamer and G.E.S.Woodhouse shared the task. Fred Castle and Hugh Watts also led the side on occasions and the consequences are not difficult to imagine. Somerset ended the season in twelfth position, losing fourteen games out of twenty-six, which was more than any other county. Captaincy was not the only problem in this season. Except for Gimblett who scored all the Somerset centuries, the batting consistently failed. At the end of the season, the club adopted the desperate measure of offering their professionals a £5 'win bonus' for every victory.

Conditions in 1948 were generally unsuitable for seam bowling. All too often, Arthur found himself bowling on perfect batting wickets. On one occasion in May at Lord's, Middlesex gained revenge for the defeats of the previous two seasons with a resounding ten-wickets victory. The match was memorable for a stand of 424 runs between Compton and Edrich who recaptured their marvellous form of the previous season. It is still the record stand for a third-wicket partnership in the county championship. Arthur, bowled 39 overs in less than a day's play with no wickets for 158 runs to show for his efforts or 'nowt for plenty' to borrow one of Arthur's favourite expressions! He would remember this day with good reason; they were easily the worst bowling figures of his career. In due time, he would recall this day with great amusement as he did with Harold Pinter some thirty years later:

Compton and Edrich? On a hiding to nothing, son. Never known anything like it. What year was it, after the war, at Lord's, we got rid of Robertson, we got rid of Brown and then those two buggers came together and they must have made something like a thousand. I'd been bowling all bloody day and the skipper comes up to me and he says, Go on, Arthur, have one more go. One more go? I said. I haven't got any legs left. One more go, says the skip, go on, Arthur, just one more go. Well, I had one more go and then I dropped dead.

Arthur would also take 'nowt for plenty' against the 1948 Australians, before a record Taunton crowd of 10,000 spectators. Three Somerset bowlers failed to take a wicket for over a century of runs each. The Australians made 560 runs for five wickets on the first day and then bowled Somerset out twice before tea on the second day! The Australian leg-spinner, Colin McCool, who later proved a very successful signing for Somerset, took the wickets.

Arthur did better at Worcester in mid-June when a match analysis of seven wickets for 72 runs helped Somerset to win by three wickets. His best bowling performance of the season was against Sussex at Weston where he took six wickets for 80 runs in the first innings bowling slow off-breaks. Somerset's return fixture at Eastbourne was a match that featured Harold Gimblett's highest first-class innings of 310 runs. On returning to Taunton for their next match against Yorkshire, Arthur went to see Brigadier Lancaster to request a ground collection for Harold. The players were in buoyant mood and Arthur's request had been made on the spur of the moment. Had he given some thought to the secretary's likely reaction he would have known that permission would be refused. Arthur was told, in no uncertain terms, that Harold was paid to score triple-centuries. It was another lingering example of how professional cricketers were treated by this archaic county administration; Arthur slammed the door on his way out of the secretary's office.

It had been an average season for Arthur. He took 62 wickets at 28.5 runs apiece but this included just 50 championship wickets. Arthur would have taken more if it had not been for the troublesome knee problems that limited his ability to bowl at full pace. The injury also kept him out of the side for over a month - from the 3rd July to the 4th August - missing eight games in total. His batting was rarely spectacular although he still managed twenty-three sixes. He scored a total of 530 runs at an average of 16.56 and only exceeded fifty runs on one occasion. This was against the eventual county champions, Glamorgan, at Swansea in late May. He hit 60 runs with some bold batting that just failed to secure first innings points.

Somerset used much the same side in 1949 but it was more settled under the captaincy of George Woodhouse. They had a disastrous start in what turned out to be a peculiar up and down season. They lost their opening five matches and had to wait until the end of May before securing their first £5 win bonus, against Hampshire at Taunton. They won the next game against Leicestershire, beat Gloucestershire in the bank holiday fixture and then Hampshire for the second time in a fortnight. This victory was achieved thanks to Arthur's second innings bowling return of six wickets for 81 runs. Arthur produced a devastating spell in this innings to take three wickets for 2 runs in 4 overs. These victories were followed by a period, between mid-June and the end of July, when Somerset lost ten matches in succession. Their fluctuating fortunes changed yet again at the Weston festival with the arrival of the schoolmasters, M.M.Walford and Hugh Watts. Thereafter, Somerset stayed unbeaten until the last match of the season and finished a creditable ninth in the championship.

Arthur's bowling during the early part of the season was as good as ever. He had one memorable game against Middlesex at Bath in June where, as *Wisden* prophetically recalls, Arthur showed 'one last flash of brilliance.' He had figures of five wickets for 71 runs and six wickets for 61 runs in Middlesex's two innings. This left Somerset to score 230 runs for victory and the tail-end batting of Angell and Stephenson, with a contribution of 27 runs from Arthur, gave Middlesex some anxious moments. Middlesex eventually won the match by 36 runs inside two days. This match was exactly half-way through the season and Arthur, having already taken sixty-two wickets, was well on course to take a hundred wickets.

There were also some flashes of brilliance with the bat although they were becoming fewer in number. There was one spectacular hit in the game against Northants at Taunton when his six went soaring over the press box into the enclosure at the rear where it hit the wife of the caterer busy preparing tea. The match against Warwickshire at Birmingham in early July also produced some impressive hitting. Arthur and Harold Gimblett were the only batsmen to show any sort of resolve. They hit 79 of Somerset's first innings total of 144 runs and in the second innings, Gimblett scored 68 and Arthur made the next highest score. His 41 runs were hit during a brief, explosive innings, which included three successive sixes off the bowling of Eric Hollies. It was the fourth time in his career that he had achieved the feat of hitting three or more consecutive sixes, a record that has never been equalled.

The match-winning performances, once commonplace, were all but over and Arthur was beginning to lose the battle against injury and advancing years. There were many that sensed his declining enthusiasm for the gruelling county cricket circuit. Jim Sewter, the Worcestershire scorer, certainly gained that impression during the match that followed the game at Edgbaston. It was against Worcestershire at Kidderminster and Jim, who was playing for Kidderminster in the Birmingham and District League at the time, was asked to field for an injured Worcestershire player. Arthur had taken three wickets in the first innings and Somerset looked favourites to win the match until Don Kenyon changed the course of the game. He scored a brilliant 182 in the second Worcestershire innings to earn his side a two-wickets victory. Kenyon was particular severe on Arthur who tried every type of ball in his armoury. He finished with figures of one wicket for 120 runs but the worst of it was that Arthur was given the last over of the day. Worcestershire needed seven runs to win with two wickets in hand and in such a situation the smart money would have been on Arthur. Jenkins hit a four and a single. Yarnold took a single off the third ball and Jenkins drove the next ball to the mid-off boundary bringing a roar of approval from the crowd. Arthur stormed off the pitch in disgust. His reaction was out of character and had nothing to do with losing the match. It was the ease with which the pair had reached their winning target that upset him and forced him to confront the evidence of his declining powers.

Arthur was in a sombre mood later that evening and there was none of his customary cheerful exuberance. Jim Sewter recalls having a drink with Arthur after the match and remembers that he seemed disillusioned with the county game. Gerald Humphries, who had played for Worcestershire and was Kidderminster's captain, was also party to the conversation. The Birmingham League side were seeking to recruit a new professional so it was suggested to Arthur that he should consider a contract with Kidderminster for the next season. Arthur was beginning to doubt whether he would get his contract with Somerset renewed so he said he would bear the offer in mind.

Arthur had very little joy with either bat or ball during the next few matches and when it came to the Weston festival he had to play second fiddle to Horace Hazell and Johnny Lawrence. They took 25 and 21 wickets respectively in the three championship games. Arthur bowled well when given the opportunity but, with the pair in such good form, he was given very few overs. During the three festival matches, he bowled eighteen overs against Worcestershire, twenty-four against Glamorgan and twenty-seven against Kent. It was a frustrating time for a man conditioned to bowling all day. What he found hardest to accept was that Somerset achieved three comfortable wins without him needing to make any sort of a contribution. Arthur was a proud man, used to being a key member of the side and playing in a subservient role did not suit him at all.

Arthur had been desperate to do well because he was well aware of the importance of the festival, which the players would call 'hiring and firing time'. The most influential committee members met as an unofficial cricket committee to discuss the player's contracts. Although decisions on contracts and player retention were not made public until approved by the Executive Committee at the end of the season, the news would trickle out of the bars as tongues gradually loosened. It was no fun for the professionals trying to concentrate on the game knowing that their future livelihoods were being debated by all and sundry. Arthur was more tense than most and knew that the Committee would show no mercy when it came to sacking players.

The committee members would have had doubts about Arthur's fitness uppermost in their minds. His fitness problems were hardly likely to improve and in addition to contending with the knee weaknesses he was now plagued by backache. He referred to this condition as his 'little bit o' grit' but his usual remedy, which was a large gin and tonic, was not the panacea it had once been! The Committee were also mindful of the parlous state of their finances so taking all these factors into consideration, it was decided that Arthur Wellard should be released.

His release could have been managed in a more sensitive way, in view of his long and valued service. However, the Somerset administration were not renown for their sensitivity in these matters and Arthur should have known better than to expect any other treatment. Like most senior professionals nearing the end of their careers, he felt there was at least another season in him and there were many people who would have supported this view. The Committee, on the other hand, needed only to point to the improvement shown in some of the younger players as evidence of Arthur's expendability.

They could have reasonably expected the young Maurice Tremlett to replace Arthur in the opening pace attack, although this would prove to be an ill-judged expectation. The committee also had a high opinion of Jim Redman, an honest seamer from Bath, as a replacement bowler but their hopes for Redman also proved over-optimistic. They should have asked for Arthur's opinion of Redman or, for that matter, any of his team-mates. Jim Redman's reputation was based mainly on his celebrated performance against the 1948 Australians when he took three of the four wickets that fell to a Somerset bowler. This performance did nothing to impress Arthur who said to Eric Hill, 'I'm bowling an impeachable *(sic)* line for bugger all, while that bugger bowls bleedin' rubbish at t'other end and takes all the wickets going!'

In normal circumstances, Arthur would have been expected to take the news of his impending release philosophically but he reacted quite badly. According to Bill Andrews, he took to the curious habit of walking around Clarence Park with his bootlaces undone as a means of showing his displeasure. As Arthur always took pride in his appearance, his lack of attention to dress suggests that he was not in his normal state of mind. This was not an intentional act of dissent, merely an unconscious reaction to his deep-rooted sense of rejection. Arthur was completely devastated; Somerset cricket had been his life for twenty-two years and at times its only stable influence. Arthur may have known this moment was coming but it did not make him any better prepared. He was not qualified to do anything other than play cricket and his immediate future looked bleak.

With the benefit of hindsight, the Somerset Committee should have retained Arthur as a player/coach. It would have provided the playing cover as well as the coaching required to bring on the next generation of Somerset cricketers. Arthur was a natural and very able coach, which was apparent to all those close to the game. He had demonstrated throughout his years with the Club his interest in coaching youngsters. In Arthur's days, the professionals had a clause in their contracts, which required them to provide pre-season coaching for the sons of members. It was a member's privilege, providing the professional with an extra source of income, but not every player warmed to the task. Arthur, however, would undertake these duties with diligence and enthusiasm. He was always very willing to put himself out whenever he felt his advice and guidance was being appreciated. Eric Hill, the Somerset opening batsman, remembers with gratitude his coaching sessions with Arthur:

Usually, we started school a bit earlier than the other schools in Taunton, and Arthur enquired where I was when I was absent. So it was arranged that I would go and be coached by him after school, with only Arthur, my dad and me there. I think dad used to slip him a tip for this.

Arthur continued to take a keen interest in Eric Hill's development and helped him a great deal as a young Somerset professional after the war. Arthur also helped other Somerset youngsters such as Harold Stephenson and Maurice Tremlett and he used to call the three of them his 'colts'. Eric Hill reckoned that Arthur was the fount of most of their cricketing knowledge although they tried to pretend otherwise! Harold Stephenson also confirms this view, remembering Arthur [referred to as 'his idol'] with fondness and as a great influence during his formative years with Somerset. There were many others that could confirm his ability as a coach. Ray Clavey of Watchet, who was briefly on the ground staff in 1949, also has fond memories of Arthur coaching the young hopefuls. Ray remembers a particular one-to-one session with Arthur:

I was lucky, one afternoon there was Arthur and myself, he gave me two hours of coaching, both bowling and batting, he even picked out the stumps he would hit when I was batting. Of course, he was always right.

Somerset were considering the appointment of a coach in 1949 and there was much local press speculation that Arthur or Wally Luckes might be asked to stay on in this capacity. The committee, which was hopelessly out of touch with the players, would not have been aware of Arthur's potential as a coach and made no sort of approach. Arthur decided to apply for the job after some encouragement from his team-mates. Bill Alley, writing in his book *My incredible innings*, recalls Arthur's version of the event that unfolded:

They told me I would never make a coach. Then, at the end of the season, they told me they would not want me next year. That hurt a lot. I could, I think, have been given more notice. Some time later they came to London and asked me to take the coaching job but I was not prepared to risk the same treatment again.

In the end, Somerset did not make an appointment in 1949, financial expediency probably got the better of any long-term development considerations. It would be another year before the County finally appointed their first coach.

The decision to release Arthur was made public following an Executive Committee meeting held on the 22nd September 1949. Arthur did receive the sweetener of a testimonial year in 1951, which would follow the testimonial year of Wally Luckes, another senior professional to be given his marching orders. Miles Coope was the third player not retained.

Meanwhile, Somerset had four championship matches left to play after the Weston festival. Arthur played in three of the matches but his combined bowling analysis of five wickets for 339 runs suggests that he was just going through the motions. His lack of motivation was the reason for his absence in the other match. Somerset had beaten Essex at Clacton and Arthur had toiled unsuccessfully while Maurice Tremlett hit a brilliant century and took nine wickets in the match. The young pretender had won the match for Somerset in true Wellardian style and although they were great friends [*Arthur was godfather to Maurice's daughter*], Arthur was in no mood to be reminded that he was surplus to Somerset's requirements. He was 'rested' for the game at Trent Bridge and went home to New Eltham to recharge the batteries for the final match of the season at Taunton against Warwickshire. Arthur probably regretted coming back as there was no fairy-tale ending. He took one wicket in the match for 143 runs and, in what appeared at that stage to be his last innings for Somerset, was bowled by the medium-pacer, Cannings, before getting off the mark. Few people in the crowd were aware of his impending release so there were no plaudits. Arthur left Taunton quietly and without ceremony, contemplating his future.

Once he had overcome the shock of rejection, it did not take him long to agree a contract to play for Kidderminster the following summer. Kidderminster were delighted with their acquisition. They had finished seventh out of ten teams in the Birmingham and District League and their professional Jack Holroyd, who had held the side together, was not available for the 1950 season. Signing Arthur would boost attendance at the Chester Road ground and would also bolster the bowling, which had been Kidderminster's major weakness. Even at the age of forty-eight, Arthur still had plenty to offer the League in terms of his bowling ability. It was not as if his bowling had deteriorated in the 1949 season to any great extent. In fact, the *Playfair Cricket Annual* of 1950 was moved to comment that 'Wellard's pace at so advanced an age remained one of the wonders of cricket.'

Despite having little opportunity at Weston and the miserable end to the season, he had still taken 87 wickets. They may have been achieved at a cost of over 31 runs apiece but Arthur had been seriously overbowled for a man of his age and should have received more sympathetic treatment. The old workhorse had bowled over 1,000 overs in the season, the most he had bowled since 1938. It is an incredible number for a man approaching his fiftieth year, which would test even the fittest of modern fast bowlers. In contrast, Maurice Tremlett had bowled 490 overs and the worry for Somerset would be whether they could fill the substantial void created by Arthur's departure. Arthur was still the best new-ball bowler in the side and Tremlett was never likely to take on this mantle.

It is not clear when the penny dropped that they might struggle without Arthur but, in less than a month, the committee turned volte-face and approached him to play for Somerset in 1950. Arthur had already signed for Kidderminster by this time so it was agreed that Arthur would make himself available for matches that did not clash with his weekend league commitments. An announcement was made on the 3rd November that Arthur would play 'on a match basis' and would appear for the County in 1950 as and when required.

10.

1950-52: New beginnings

THE CONTRACT WITH SOMERSET FOR 1950 was arranged for the Club's convenience. It was not a particularly generous offer; he was paid only when selected to play. Arthur was not too concerned as he had nothing to occupy his weekdays and would rather have played cricket than do anything else. Arthur still felt he had something to offer Somerset so the opportunity to remain on the staff had not been one to pass up lightly. He was not worried about the money as the proceeds from his testimonial the following summer would more than compensate for the club's playing terms in 1950. Arthur was quick to appreciate that staying with the club would improve his chances of a good testimonial. He spent a lot of time spectating at the County Ground where his loyal supporters could usually cheer him up with the offer of a drink or a curse on the Committee for not picking him to play. Arthur was also in evidence at Bath and would have loved to have been given a game. He did not get the opportunity but it did give him the chance to prepare the ground for his testimonial year.

Kidderminster's terms had been much more attractive than anything Somerset could have offered. They played in Division One of the Birmingham and District League, which included ten of the top sides in the Midlands. Matches were played at weekends and each team played the others on a home and away basis. Arthur was paid eighteen pounds per match plus expenses, which was not significantly short of what Somerset were paying their professionals for a full week's work. He was not required to undertake any other duties as professional although Ron Sewter remembers that

Arthur took his responsibilities seriously. Arthur was unavailable for practice nights but at the weekend he would put himself at the young cricketers' disposal and advice was always freely given.

As Kidderminster's professional, Arthur had the chance to renew many old acquaintances. Each club employed a professional, most of whom had recently left the first-class game. His friend, Bill Andrews, had been with Stourbridge since leaving Somerset in 1947. Another old acquaintance of twenty years, Alf Gover, played for West Bromwich Dartmouth. Bill Merritt, the New Zealander who had played cricket with Arthur in Italy was the Dudley professional and the others included such contemporaries as Frank Smailes (Walsall), Alf Pope (Mitchells and Butlers) and Morris Nichols (Aston Unity).

Kidderminster paid for Arthur's match fees from their gate receipts obtained by charging sixpence *[2.5p]* admission. It was not unusual to get 3,000 paying spectators for a Saturday match. This was a considerable increase over previous seasons and it was due mainly to Arthur's engagement. The crowd would feel cheated if Arthur did not bat but he was not normally required until late in the innings because Kidderminster had a strong batting line-up. When he did bat, he rarely wasted his energy running between the wickets. Jim Sewter, who used to open the bowling with Arthur, had good cause to remember Arthur's batting:

When he was required to bat, he could be counted upon for some big hitting. When I played for the RAF in South Africa I bought a bat. Not being much of a batsman I considered it out of balance, but Arthur used to love to get his hands on it, because he was convinced it had an engine in it. Playing in a friendly at Stratford-on-Avon he scattered picnickers and broke a car window in a flurry of sixes. I still have that bat. He was particularly effective on Old Hill's small ground and the black country spectators couldn't wait to see him out in the middle.

Even if his batting was not always needed, he still managed an average of over 28 per innings. Kidderminster had higher expectations of Arthur's bowling and again he did not disappoint the Club. He finished third in the league bowling averages with 52 wickets taken at 12.9 runs apiece. He bowled mostly fast-medium and his outswinger was very effective, producing many chances of a catch in the slips, not always taken. His all-round performance made a great difference to Kidderminster's fortunes and they won nine of their eighteen matches, which enabled them to win the league by a clear margin. Kidderminster wasted no time in engaging him for the 1951 season.

Arthur produced several match-winning performances for Kidderminster in 1950. During the Whitsun bank holiday weekend, he made up for the Saturday game being spoilt by rain when he took nine wickets for 43 runs against Old Hill on the Whit Monday. It enabled Kidderminster to win a very exciting game by one wicket. This was not Arthur's best bowling performance of the season, however, for he went one better against Stourbridge. It is no coincidence that his best was reserved for Stourbridge where Bill Andrews was plying his trade. In what became a personal battle between the two, Arthur was determined not to be outdone by his friend. It was a matter of pride, an instinctive urge that compelled him to assert his supremacy. Kidderminster batted first and made a useful total although Arthur did not trouble the scorer. He was out for a duck, caught off a full toss, but at least Bill had not been the fortunate bowler. Bill, bowling from the other end, was disappointed at not taking Arthur's wicket but pronounced himself well pleased with his figures of seven wickets for 57 runs.

Stourbridge started their innings with Bill Andrews opening the batting as usual and not relishing the thought of facing Arthur. Bill survived a turbulent first over as nothing was held back but was out in Arthur's next over, caught at leg-slip for a single. None of the Stourbridge batsmen withstood the onslaught for long. Arthur made use of his full bowling repertoire, a combination of fast inswingers, some medium pace off-breaks and even a few slow leg-breaks round the wicket. Stourbridge were never allowed to settle and lost the game by 60 runs.

Arthur's analysis was ten wickets for 33 runs taken off 18 overs. It was the only occasion in his life that he took ten wickets in an innings. Bill Andrews got £4 from a collection taken at the ground and Arthur was presented with the ball, which the club generously paid to be mounted and inscribed. The pair had a good session in the bar after the game. They returned to Somerset in the small hours, a little more gingerly than usual! Arthur is bound to have slept soundly through the journey with poor Bill drowsily fighting the effects of the day's labour and alcoholic consumption. Arthur took full advantage of his devoted friend's 'taxi service' but Bill never really minded as is evident from the comments in his autobiography *The hand that bowled Bradman*:

It's difficult to keep that man Wellard out of the book. When he signed for Kidderminster he again stayed with me in Somerset and we travelled up to the Midlands in my car every Saturday. He'd been my travelling companion before and I should have known what to expect. As soon as we left Weston-Super-Mare, he'd fall asleep and I'd have to wake him at Kidderminster. The same thing would happen on the return, only perhaps he would sleep more deeply after several pints of beer and a few of his favourite pink gins. I was always flaked out, too, on the way home after bowling so many overs. Just once Arthur did wake me at about 2 am. It was just as well that he did-I was also nearly asleep, at the wheel.

While the 'terrible twins' earned their living and thoroughly enjoyed themselves in the Midlands, Somerset were managing surprisingly well under the guidance of their new captain, Stuart Rogers. They had to wait for their first win of the season until the 13th June and they suffered from the poor weather throughout August but still achieved a creditable seventh equal position in the championship. Somerset's achievement is all the more remarkable considering they were without bowling of penetrable pace. Maurice Tremlett, a reluctant bowler, had lost confidence and had a miserable season with the ball. There were no seam bowling reserves so Somerset had to rely on the spinners, Lawrence, Hazell and the new recruit from Yorkshire, Ellis Robinson. Lawrence and Hazell, in particular, had exceptional seasons but Somerset were fortunate that the wet and damp conditions throughout the season helped to nullify their deficiencies in pace bowling. It meant that the absence of a new ball specialist in the team was not as critical as it might have been.

At the end of May, Arthur was asked to play at Taunton against the West Indian touring side. The West Indies struggled in their first innings after Arthur opened the bowling and, reminding the Somerset public of what they were missing, sent down some extremely lively deliveries. He bowled splendidly, finishing with figures of four wickets for 60 runs. Arthur took another two wickets in the West Indian second innings, which was notable for a stand of 213 runs between Worrell and Walcott. Arthur ended the partnership when Frank Worrell was caught by Harold Stephenson, the second time in the match he fell to this combination. The partnership laid the foundation for a West Indian victory, which was achieved with thirty minutes of play to spare. A bright young prospect by the name of Ramadhin also played his part in the victory, taking eleven wickets in the match. Later in the season, he and his partner Valentine would create all sorts of problems for the English Test batsmen. Their contribution of 59 wickets in the four Tests, played a significant part in the West Indies 3-1 victory, which secured their first rubber in England. Few batsmen were confident of 'reading' Ramadhin who could spin the ball either way without any noticeable change of action. Arthur was bowled by him for a single run in the first Somerset innings. He decided a change of tactics was called for in the second innings and started to 'get after' Ramadhin. Arthur had some initial success but was soon back in the pavilion, caught on the boundary off the same bowler.

Arthur's services were not required again until the Weston festival in August when he was chosen to replace Jim Redman. Jim Redman had a wretched season, having singularly failed to establish himself in the team. In the first festival game against Nottinghamshire, Arthur was immediately in action. He bowled forty-four overs in the first day's play, which for a man of his age must have taken some considerable effort. He started well, trapping William Keeton leg-before-wicket for a single run, but otherwise had no luck. He did not bowl at all in the second innings. Arthur watched with uncomfortable memories of the previous season as Lawrence and Hazell bowled Somerset to a nine-wickets victory. Arthur did not play in the middle festival game because of his weekend commitment to Kidderminster but returned for the last festival game against Middlesex.

Arthur bowled just three of the 31 overs that were possible on the first day and the match was abandoned without play on the last two days. The festival cricket had been miserable and frustrating and had done nothing to obliterate the bad memories of the previous season. It was a pity that his Weston festival cricket should come to such an ignominious end as it had been his special favourite. Arthur would retain many happy memories of Weston-Super-Mare both on and off the pitch. He had been made to feel welcome during his early days as the Weston C.C. professional and he valued the friendships he had made. Above all else, he would miss the companionship and the end-of-day socialising that would take place at the various Weston watering-holes, like the Winter Gardens Pavilion or the Cavendish Hotel kept by the old Somerset player, Jim Bridges.

The Weston supporters would retain their own memories of Arthur and they had many spectacular incidents from which to choose. They might remember any number of steepling sixes hit out of the ground. His huge six, which hit the roof of St. Paul's Church in 1933 would be high on the list or perhaps the sight of him hooking Harold Larwood into the adjoining park in 1935. Others would remember his bowling and the times when in the space of a few overs he would completely alter the course of a match, like the one against Sussex in 1936.

The younger supporters would have very different memories of Arthur. They would remember bowling to him in the nets before the amateurs turned up for the day's play and they would remember his kindness. Arthur was never too busy to spare the youngsters some time or give them his autograph, despite the ridiculous clause in his contract that forbade such practice. Arthur always seemed happiest when at Weston. It brought out the best in him and complemented his approach to cricket, which is manifested in the figures his festival cricket produced. He played in fifteen Weston festivals during his career, scored 1232 runs and took 165 wickets. He and J.C.White, who played in twenty festivals, are the only Somerset cricketers to have achieved the 'Weston double'.

From Weston, Arthur travelled with the team to Trent Bridge but there was no improvement in his fortune. The game was spoiled by the rain and he took just one wicket for 76 runs in the only innings that was possible. All in all, it had been a dismal return for Arthur and the elements seemed intent on making Arthur's swansong as difficult and unpleasant as possible.

Arthur's last first-class match was the final game of the season against Worcestershire at Taunton. The match was also ruined by rain, which prevented play on the second day and restricted playing time to six hours in total. Worcestershire declared at 149 for nine wickets and Arthur took two wickets for 20 runs. Somerset struggled on the rain-affected pitch and with further rain likely, settled for the limited objective of first innings points. When Arthur went in, they were still well short of their goal so he immediately started hitting out in fine style with Leslie Angell standing firm at the other end. Just when it seemed they might overhaul their target, the elements played their final card. A huge storm broke out over the ground finishing the day's play and bringing the curtain down on Arthur's first-class cricket career.

These last few matches provided a sad ending to a long and distinguished career, which had brought him 1,614 wickets and 12,485 runs. His figures for Somerset were 1,517 wickets and 11,432 runs from 391 matches. Although Arthur never cared for statistics, except when needed to secure a further contract, he was immensely proud of the fact that only J.C.White took more wickets for Somerset in his 409 appearances for the County. His figures need also to be viewed in the light of the various limiting factors he had faced during his first-class career. He started late in life, missing the years regarded as the best for a fast bowler; he played for a county noted for its poor fielding; the war deprived him of cricket when still in his prime and he competed for honours at a time when England had a surfeit of pace bowlers with genuine class. Without these limitations, there is no doubt that Arthur would have challenged the select band of nine cricketers with 2,000 wickets and 20,000 runs to their name.

Arthur's cavalier approach to cricket was just as much to blame for limiting his impact. He did not fulfil his potential or receive the recognition he deserved because he never wanted it badly enough. He was content with his lot and the honours he received were looked upon as a bonus. As in life, he was basically lazy and just did what was required of him unless a seemingly hopeless challenge came along to extract his best cricket. He would have been the first to acknowledge that he would have received greater recognition in the game had he applied himself more diligently. However, diligence was not one of Arthur's strongpoints and more application may have stifled the flair and freedom of expression that was such a feature of his cricket. His achievements are greater than the sum of his statistics and will be remembered long after those of many celebrated accumulators of runs and wickets.

Arthur had expected more from his arrangement with Somerset and was disappointed to have played in only four matches. He returned to the South East but remained in close contact with Bill Andrews who had offered to organise his testimonial. Somerset, meanwhile, were reconsidering their coaching appointment. It had taken courage for Arthur to apply for the job the previous year. It was the first time in his life that he had ever applied for a job and he had felt uncomfortable with the need to go 'cap in hand' to the Somerset administration. Their initial rejection of his application had caused Arthur much embarrassment and some delicate negotiation was now required to secure Arthur's services. He was a proud man and Somerset should have made the right noises to assure him that he was still needed at the club. Arthur could have been easily persuaded had this been done but it was too much to expect that they would have the slightest understanding of Arthur's needs. The committee, on hearing that the old Sussex player Harry Parks was available, offered him the job as County Coach instead. Parks, who had a distinguished county career stretching back to 1926 and was coaching at Taunton School, accepted the appointment. Somerset missed their chance of employing a first-rate coach and further alienated a player who had given twenty-five years service to Somerset. Arthur would have cheerfully had nothing more to do with the County were it not for his testimonial year.

Arthur was content to leave most of the arranging to Bill including the production of a brochure, priced at one shilling *[5p]*. The brochure was extremely well produced by the standards of that time and included many of the original photographs reproduced in this biography. Bill Andrews had set himself the task of making his friend's testimonial year a great success. There is no question that without Bill's drive and enthusiasm, Arthur's testimonial would not have produced anything like the return that was achieved. The brochure contains an expansive tribute from Bill, which betrays the great affection he had for Arthur. He wrote this of him:

Arthur made one big mistake in his career, but it was one he, like myself, had no opportunity to avoid. He was not born in Somerset! But the county for which he has performed such countless deeds of derring-do could not have produced a more typical Somerset player. His lusty, zestful, plucky spirit added tonic to the most listless game, and in an hour of crisis his personality, imperturbable, unshakable, stood out like a rock. He challenged fate blithely, even recklessly, and whether his gambles came off or not, the crowd loved him.

Arthur still had his Kidderminster commitment to consider for the 1951 season. Bill Andrews did not return to Stourbridge, being replaced by Tony Riddington of Leicestershire, so Arthur had to rely on the trains to get him to and from the Midlands. There were other new faces among the professional contingent of the Birmingham league. The great West Indian test player, George Headley, who took over from Bill Merritt at Dudley, was the most notable replacement. Headley would score 922 runs during the season and finish with an average of 76 runs per innings. It was always going to be unlikely that Arthur could match the success of his first season with Kidderminster but he still managed to take 52 wickets at an average of 16.7 runs. He bowled 365 overs, of which 90 were maidens. As a result of his consistent bowling, Kidderminster had another good season and narrowly missed retaining the league title. They eventually finished runners-up in the league.

Meanwhile, back in the West Country, Arthur and Bill were doing their best to generate support for the testimonial year. Bill was the driving force. He was resourceful, enterprising and had countless contacts, which made him the ideal man for the job. Bill had no trouble in enlisting the support of the local cricket teams within the County and the Somerset players readily gave up their weekends and spare time to support the testimonial year. The fixture arrangements got off to a fine start on the first weekend of May with games against Webbington and Long Ashton. The Somerset X1s amassed large scores in both games before dismissing the opposition cheaply. Long Ashton's match, arranged as part of the festival of Britain celebrations, was a grand affair and over a thousand people squeezed into the small ground. Arthur's contribution with the bat was short and sweet; hitting three fours before giving a hard return catch to the bowler.

The match arranged for the following weekend proved to be something of a sensation when the Burnham C.C. team comfortably beat a strong Somerset X1. Arthur, who was due to captain the Somerset side, was not present and sent his regrets but the side included Gimblett, Andrews, Luckes, Tremlett, Stephenson, Buttle and Hill plus a mystery man who turned out to be the coach driver, press-ganged into taking Arthur's place. After Bill and Harold Gimblett put on 42 runs for the first wicket the side were all out for 98, which Burnham passed with four wickets to spare. There were several red faces that day and the Burnham crowd were far too excited by the result to make a fuss about Arthur's non-appearance.

The match against Watchet was typical of the spirit in which these games were played. The Watchet skipper told his team that there would be no appeals and no catches taken while Arthur was batting. They were told in no uncertain terms that the crowd had come to see Arthur Wellard not them! Arthur duly obliged the delighted crowd with a knock of 49 runs that included 42 runs in sixes! Arthur's testimonial fund benefitted by £40 and a bat signed by the West Indies, Middlesex, Sussex, Hampshire and Sussex realised £9.3s. Typically, Arthur raided the day's takings after the match to buy both teams a drink.

There were many fine knocks that year, even if they were aided by a sympathetic field. At the Imperial Ground, Knowle, Arthur thrilled a crowd of about a thousand with a hurricane score of 102, which included ten sixes and nine fours, a remarkable 96 in boundaries! One of the sixes went out of the ground - not an easy task at the Imperial Ground - carried the embankment and landed on the railway track. At Clevedon, he cracked 68 runs in 30 minutes, which included nine sixes and a total of 66 runs in boundaries. The next day at Ilminster, he hit 46 runs, all in boundaries, including several huge sixes.

Arthur's testimonial sides roamed the County throughout the summer and occasionally farther afield to places such as Chippenham. Wherever they went, they attracted good crowds anxious to pay their respects. Arthur made his last appearance at the County Ground in a limited-overs match against Taunton C.C. It was played under Baker Cup rules, which allowed each side twenty eight-ball overs. When Arthur went out to bat, the crowd clapped and cheered him all the way to the wicket. As is often the case on such occasions, he was out first ball - it was the middle wicket of a hat-trick for the Taunton bowler Norman Ogden - and the crowd promptly cheered Arthur all the way back to the pavilion. Arthur would have dearly loved to have deposited the ball in the river for one last time but he made up for the disappointment with a fine bowling display. He opened the bowling and removed Taunton's top-order batsmen. He tactfully took himself off with half the side out for 51 and a personal tally of four wickets for 24 runs.

He received a similar reception when his side played Bath on the Sunday of the Bath festival week but this time he left the Bath supporters with a vivid memory of his batting at its very best. It would also revive memories for some older supporters who, twenty years earlier, had watched him hit 147 runs in a similar match. He hit 121 runs in 38 minutes and 104 of these runs came from boundaries. He hit twelve sixes and eight fours no doubt trying to avoid the effort of running between the wickets. Arthur was particularly severe on Bath's K.Sydee, and he collected 24 runs off one of his overs. Arthur's batting helped the Somerset side to 345 runs, scored in just two and a half hours but Bath held out for a draw, being 216 for eight wickets when stumps were drawn. The gate realised £50 for the testimonial, a collection raised a further £20 and Bill sold tickets for an autographed bat that realised another £20. Everyone present went home happy with the day's events.

Not all the games proved such a success. Arthur was unlucky with the weather, which was poor for most of the summer and ruined quite a few of the games. A total of £2,345.11s.9d was raised during the testimonial year. Arthur was pleased with the results although it was less than might have been expected when compared with Frank Lee's record benefit year total of over £4,000 in 1947 and Bill Andrew's testimonial total of £3,000 in 1948. There would, however, be equally modest totals for some other long serving professionals including Horace Hazell (£2,300) in 1949, Wally Luckes (£1,776) in 1950 and Bertie Buse - whose county benefit match was a disaster, being all over in a day - (£2,814) in 1953.

He left Taunton vowing never to return. He was still resentful about the manner in which he had been discarded and the way Somerset had appointed Harry Parks as coach. Arthur stayed away from the West Country for seventeen years and when he did come back it was reported that he had stayed away because of a disagreement with the County. In truth, there had not been a convenient opportunity to visit the West Country; he could never have harboured a grudge for so long. He referred to his 'disagreement' as 'water under the bridge' and offered no further elaboration.

Arthur returned to New Eltham and to settle in the South East after twenty-five years of constant travel and living out of a suitcase. He did not have the first idea about how he was to earn a living from now on so the testimonial money was a tremendous help. It gave him financial security and the time to consider his options for the future. He was not required by Kidderminster in 1952; they decided they could not afford him nor did they feel sufficiently confident to take a risk on his fitness to play. Arthur and Jack, now fully reconciled, were able to make a modest living from the lock-up shop but it was insufficient to keep them in a reasonable standard of comfort. It was clear that Arthur would have to find some means of employment but he was in no particular hurry. He helped out at the shop and whenever he sensed he was getting under Jack's feet he would find the excuse to wander up the Eltham High Street for a bet, a pint and a fag.

Jack could see Arthur settling into this cosy routine and concluded that a change of scenery was required. She had always needed the close support of her family and she was missing the company of her sister, Betty, who had moved from nearby Mottingham to Sutton. Jack decided to follow her sister to Sutton and Arthur, always one for the quiet life, went along with her plans. Jack started to look for a suitable property but in the meantime a chance meeting with Jack Higginson gave Arthur the opportunity of further league cricket. Jack Higginson was from Lancaster Cricket Club, which played in the Ribblesdale League, one of the oldest and most respected of the Lancashire leagues. Higginson had played for Lancaster since 1921 and had been captain since 1932. He had ambitious plans for the club and was the driving force behind the club's migration to the newly formed Northern League. On finding that Arthur was not intending to play professional cricket in 1952, he immediately offered Arthur a contract as the Lancaster professional. Arthur accepted the offer without hesitation or thought for the consequences. With the benefit of hindsight, it was one appointment too many and not a very fitting end to his professional career. The main difficulty was the travelling distance and he surely had many opportunities to regret his decision on those long journeys to Lancaster. Arthur was also not fit enough to perform at this level. In spite of all these difficulties, he did not let the club down but his contribution was less than the

Lancastrians had expected. Tom Alderson's book *Cricket by the Lune* describes Arthur's contribution to the history of Lancaster Cricket Club:

[The weekend travelling] certainly had its tiring effect, and if he had been confidently expected to match the terrific hitting of his first-class career there was disappointment to come. No club could have had a more courteous newcomer, but the sharp eye was no longer there, and though he did not at the time realise it, Arthur Wellard was not in the best of health. His highest innings, in fact, was only 22, and it was through his bowling, if these days rather reduced in pace, that his strength was to be sought. In the event he neutralised his batting failures with 51 wickets at 11.56 apiece and headed the bowling.

The Lancashire crowds were clearly difficult to please. Arthur's reputation as a hitter had preceded him but as a bowler, first and foremost, he had acquitted himself well. While Arthur continued to fulfil his commitment to Lancaster, Jack Wellard found the property she had been seeking. Later in the year, they sold the house and the shop in Eltham and moved to Sutton. She had found a much larger property in Sutton Common Road, which included a shop on the ground floor with accommodation above. It also had a decent garden, which had been Arthur's one and only requirement of the move. They would be happy living in Sutton for the next twenty-five years and the move would provide a fresh start for the couple. It was the beginning of a new chapter in Arthur's life.

11.

Settled in Sutton

SOON AFTER THE MOVE TO SUTTON had been completed, Arthur found himself a new job. He could not have settled as a shopkeeper; cricket was his consuming interest, his raison d'être. 'I prefer something a little more active,' he would say of shopkeeping and it did not take him long to find what he wanted. It was another of those chance meetings that secured most of his offers of employment. One evening Arthur was persuaded to go to the indoor cricket school in East Hill, Wandsworth for a net with friends from Blackheath Wanderers Cricket Club. The indoor school was run by Alf Gover but still known as the Sandham, Strudwick and Gover School, taking the other parts of its name from the two famous cricketers who founded the school in 1928. It would later be known as the Gover School. After the net, Arthur and his friends retired to the bar where Arthur spent the rest of the evening reminiscing with Alf Gover. There was much to talk about since they had shared many experiences during their cricket careers. As the evening wore on and the conversation became more animated, Alf offered Arthur a job helping out at the school. Arthur accepted Alf Gover's offer without a moments hesitation and a deal was worked out across the bar. The arrangement would secure Arthur's services for the next sixteen years and neither of them would have cause to regret the decision made that evening.

The Wellards were soon settled in Sutton. Jack had her sister and family nearby plus the shop to occupy her time. Arthur was employed at the Gover School on a full-time basis so he would set off every morning at 8.30am for the bus journey from Sutton to Wandsworth. He worked from about 9.30am until 6.00pm and had a ninety minute break for lunch, which gave him enough time to study *The Sporting Life* and sort out his bets for the day. He had the stamina to bowl for hour after hour without seeming to need a break and he carried out his duties conscientiously and with tremendous enthusiasm. He was well-liked by the pupils and Alf Gover rated him as a first-class coach. At the end of the day he would make his weary way to the bar where he would replenish the day's labours with a few pints. There was never any shortage of people wanting to buy him a drink in exchange for some advice or cricketing tale. When he felt it was time to go, he would make his way down East Hill to catch his bus. He never seemed to be in any hurry to get home and he would seldom leave the school before 9.00pm.

Arthur was kept busy playing or coaching cricket for most of the week. He had wanted to carry on playing so soon found his way to the Sutton Cricket Club ground about a mile from his home. A number of the first team players, including Doug Sayers, Ron Taylor and Peter Thwaites were in the nets when Arthur walked into the ground. Peter Thwaites had been stationed in Southern Italy with Arthur. As Arthur approached them, Peter enquired, 'what on earth are you doing here?' They could not believe their luck when Arthur asked to join the Club. Peter Thwaites produced a membership form immediately and proposed him as a member. Arthur played for them during the 1953 cricket season on most sundays and as many saturdays as his Gover School commitments would allow. The only inducement he needed was that someone had to be nominated to act as his chauffeur. Ken Ohlson, the club's president, remembers the first game Arthur played for Sutton; a 2nd X1 match versus Epsom:

Arthur was bowling off about four paces and I was the only slip. The batsman got an edge, I dived forward and thought I had caught it cleanly, I felt it smack into my hand. As the batsman stood there I appealed, the umpire said not out and the wicketkeeper told me I had taken it after it had bounced. At the end of the over Arthur said, 'I think you'd better leave the appealing to me. I've got me reputation to think of!'

For twenty-five years, Sutton Cricket Club finished the
season with a match against a team organised by Sir Harry
Secombe. The Harry Secombe X1 consisted of radio and
television celebrities like Eric Sykes and Peter Sellers
strengthened by the inclusion of a professional cricketer
or two. Tom Graveney, Peter May and Jim Laker all played
regularly for Sir Harry. Arthur played in the 1953 match
and remained a popular choice for this fixture. The Harry
Secombe match was one of the few matches in which he could
be persuaded to bat for Sutton - unless they had a big
crisis - and he would always protest that he could not see
the ball to bat properly. Nevertheless his walk to the
wicket was awaited with keen anticipation. Sir Harry has
fond memories of those days:

When I lived in Cheam opposite the Cricket Ground, I used to bring a team
down every year to play a charity match against the Sutton Side.
Arthur Wellard always played in the local eleven, and no game was complete
without him clobbering a couple of sixes over the pavilion. He continued
to do this even when his sight was none too good.
he was a much loved figure and a most wonderful character.

Doug Sayers was another regular Sunday player who
captained the team for many years. He counted Arthur as a
good friend and took every opportunity to seek his advice
on cricketing matters. Arthur taught Doug, who was an off-
spin bowler, how to bowl the floater and it would gain him
a lot of wickets over the years. Other members of the team
were not so quick to take advantage of Arthur's knowledge
of the game and it used to annoy Doug when the younger
players thought they knew better and did not need to learn
from Arthur. Arthur was always ready to provide advice for
anyone willing to listen. During his Sutton days there were
plenty of opportunities during and after the match until
the obligatory card school monopolised his attention.
Arthur played for Sutton Cricket Club First X1
throughout the fifties and early sixties and was very much
part of the club's centenary year celebrations in 1957. The
highlight of the year was a match against a strong
E.W.Swanton's X1. Tom Graveney, Alan Oakman, Colin Cowdrey,
Jim Simms and S.C.Griffith were among those playing in the

match, which was spoilt by rain but not before Arthur had finished his spell of 25 overs taking four wickets for 77 runs. Although approaching his sixtieth year, Arthur would open the bowling and often bowled through the opposition's innings. Few skippers had the temerity to take him off, especially as he would threaten not to return for a second spell. 'For Gods sake, don't take me off 'cause I'll stiffen up,' he would exclaim. Apart from playing, Arthur would also lend a hand with the coaching. When Sutton introduced a new coaching scheme for promising young cricketers, it was Arthur they turned to and the Tuesday evening session became a popular event, held under his watchful eye.

Meanwhile, he continued to work at the Gover School and had become a valuable member of the coaching team. He was capable of producing any type of ball that was required to test the customers so was usually sought out by those seeking to eliminate a particular batting weakness. During the forty years that Alf Gover ran the school his customers would come from all walks of life. They would include the aristocracy, the highest ranks of the church and the sons of celebrities and politicians including the son of the first female prime minister. John Major was another pupil who travelled the two miles from Clapham Common, pocket money in hand, to receive a lesson at the school. The school catered for all ages and all cricketing abilities. It taught schoolchildren, club cricketers and helped develop the careers of countless numbers of first-class cricketers. Colin Cowdrey and Ken Barrington were two of the more famous England players who owed a great deal to the Gover School. There were also many overseas cricketers such as Vivian Richards, Andy Roberts, Ian Bishop, Phil Simmons and, most recently, Brian Lara who spent their formative years at the school.

Arthur was involved in coaching many of the famous names that came through the School but he was most at home with the schoolchildren. He loved teaching the youngsters, imparting his passion for the game and seeing them benefit from his knowledge and experience. He had boundless patience so that nothing was too much trouble for any boy

who genuinely wanted to improve his cricketing skills. He
also had an uncanny knack of being able to quickly identify
a bowling or batting fault and his diagnostic skills were
often called into play. It is doubtful whether Arthur would
have considered his coaching at the school to be a job of
work, such was his enjoyment of the task.

The best testimony to his coaching ability must come
from David Sydenham who played 142 matches and took 487
wickets for Surrey as a left-hand fast medium bowler.
David's coaching when he first joined Surrey as a young
professional had been a disaster and he was making little
progress until Arthur took him under his wing. David
supplemented his meagre professional earnings by taking a
saturday coaching job at the school and this was how he
came to receive coaching from Arthur. Alf Gover admits in
his autobiography *The long run* that he could not help David
but Arthur managed to sort him out. David Sydenham recalls
the extent of his debt to Arthur:

On reflection the coaching appointment proved to be, without a doubt, the
salvation of my cricket career as Arthur Wellard was a member of Alf's
coaching staff.
I can recall during this period, towards the end of the season I made my
county debut [in 1957]. All my expectations were dashed during the second
innings against Warwickshire when my mediocre bowling was smashed to all
parts of the Edgbaston ground – four overs, no maidens, fifty-four runs,
no wicket. I was fortunate to be offered terms for another year.
During the following winter I discussed my poor performance with Arthur.
He suggested another 'trick' should be added to my bowling armoury if I
was to trouble first-class batsmen. He suggested an outswinger would be
the perfect foil to my natural inswinger.
'Artie' offered to give me the necessary coaching to obtain such skills –
an offer I could not refuse. A change of grip, release, line and a
modification of action had to be co-ordinated if this particular delivery
was to be mastered.
In real terms instead of taking the rest period between each hour's
coaching, this time was spent in Arthur's net bowling at his pupils whilst
he taught me how to deliver an accurate outswinger. I have lost count of
the total hours we spent together. he was so supportive, full of
encouragement and had the ability to diagnose any fault.
I can recall, during the height of my cricket career, Arthur would study
my action during televised matches and subsequently relate any faults back
to me by telephone.
All the hard work paid rich dividends in the years to come. Arthur should
take all the credit for transforming my capabilities.

At around the same time, in 1958, Arthur's connections with the Gover School led to an offer to become coach at Epsom College. The job required him to coach the boys in the nets during the summer term on the Wednesday games afternoon and on other normal school days between the hours of 4.00pm and 6.00pm. In addition he had to be present at all the 1st X1 matches. His salary for the summer term was according to Alf Gover between £400 and £500, substantially more than he was earning for the comparative period at the Gover School. The hours and the travelling were also less onerous so with Alf Gover's blessing, he accepted the appointment. He continued to coach at the Gover School for the remainder of the year, between October and May. The headmaster of the College at that time had hired Arthur partly in the expectation that the College might obtain a full show of his old expertise. He was disappointed because Arthur used a shoulder injury to excuse him bowling outside of the nets. The headmaster, however, was not disappointed in him as a coach and Arthur was hugely popular with the boys. D.C.'Charlie'Moore, an Epsom College pupil at the time, remembers Arthur well:

When Arthur came to Epsom he could no longer bowl fast but he could still 'bowl'. The pace was slow to medium, his arm so obviously bent that he could only use it in the nets.
We would go out for net practice and Arthur would watch from the bowlers end. He would watch and advise. Bowlers and batsmen would benefit from his considerable, first-class experience until Arthur felt that he had to illustrate a point to the batsmen.
'See what you can do with this one, Charlie,' he would say to me, as he trundled off a few paces, arm like a dog's hind leg. The ball would swing in to me from outside the off stump, pitch on a length and then rear upwards and away from the edge of my bat to the slips.
'I bet you couldn't do that again Arthur,' I would say, but he could. Time after time he could. The control he had with a cricket ball! You could only cringe at the thought of facing Arthur at full speed, thirty years earlier.

His popularity and success as coach was sufficient to secure his appointment at Epsom College for the next fourteen years. It ensured that the Wellards had financial security with Arthur's income from the College and the Gover School. They continued to run the shop although they had less need to rely on the income it generated. Jack, however, was finding it increasingly hard to look after both the shop and her mother who had become extremely dependant since breaking her hip in 1959. Jack eventually persuaded her sister Betty to care for the old lady during the last ten years of her life.

Arthur and Jack continued to manage the shop until about 1967, by which time it was becoming too much for them both. They rented out the shop and the living accommodation above and bought a retirement bungalow at 20 Benhilton Gardens, which was a short distance away, just off Sutton High Street.

One of the first things that Arthur and Jack did after their move to the bungalow was to take a holiday, their first since moving to Sutton. There could have been only one destination. Their busman's holiday was spent with Bill and Ennyd Andrews at Weston and, not surprisingly, their stay spanned the Weston festival week in July 1968. Arthur and Bill spent a good deal of their time at Clarence Park, sat in the deckchairs outside the beer tent, reminiscing with old friends and colleagues. Bill Andrews, never one to miss an opportunity for self-publicity, made sure that his journalist friends were informed of Arthur's return to the West Country after an absence of seventeen years. One of the local papers covered the occasion under the headline 'TERRIBLE TWINS TOGETHER AGAIN' and the photograph of the two remains a perfect testament to the warmth of their friendship. Arthur even managed an appearance at the County Ground, Taunton as a guest of the BBC for a televised match featuring Somerset against a Cavaliers X1.

The move to the bungalow was not a complete retirement for Arthur because he continued to coach at the Gover School and also had his job at Epsom College during the summer. Even at pension age, Arthur was still capable of bowling all day if required. This was no easy task as it would have been a long day for someone half his age. Alf Gover who had made Arthur a senior coach in 1962, knew better than most the effort required. He had no intention of dispensing with Arthur's services and always said that Arthur would know when it was time to quit.

David Frith, the cricket writer, has a poignant memory of Arthur in his final years at the school:

Arthur was then close to seventy but wheeled down roundarm off-cutters for hours on end, smiling somewhat painfully whenever some young pup belted one of his rare long-hops. He was kindly and down-to-earth, and the saddest recollection of all that I have of him is a rear view of him as he walked slowly up East Hill, raincoat draped from rounded, weary shoulders, having had his pub lunch, now gearing himself to transmit further cricket wisdom to the paying pupils. This was the tired old man who had once taken wickets and thumped runs against Bradman's 1938 Australians at Lord's. People passing took no more notice of him than if he was a retired shopkeeper.

The liquid lunch at *The Royal Oak* just about kept him going but Arthur was finding the long days at the school increasingly hard to manage. The travelling across London was also becoming tiresome. Arthur had near enough decided to call it a day but it was the declining activity at the school that left him with little alternative. In 1968, the Gover School was going through a lean period and the lessons were drying up, particularly during the day. Even at this stage, Alf Gover had not considered the possibility of ending his good friend's services. It was Arthur who saved any embarrassment and said to Alf, 'I've nothing left on at the moment, it's time we called it a day.'

Most men in their late sixties and after a lifetime of cricket would have confined their cricket kit to the loft and put their feet up, but not Arthur. He was asked to coach at the Middlesex indoor cricket school in East End Road, Finchley and readily accepted the job. The offer came from the Middlesex coach, Don Bennett, who knew Arthur from the days when, as an Arsenal apprentice in the mid-fifties, he would spend his afternoons at the Gover School. Don finished playing cricket in 1968 and was appointed County Coach in January 1969. Shortly afterwards, he recruited Arthur for the Middlesex Indoor School. With some respect for his age and the travelling distance it was agreed that he would work an average of 24 hours a week. Getting to Finchley meant a ninety-minute journey by tube and bus even on a good day. He would endure this punishing routine until he and Jack moved to Eastbourne. Arthur actually spent his seventieth birthday on Saturday, 8th April 1972, at the Middlesex Indoor School. In an interview which appeared in *The Cricketer* he was surprised that anyone should expect him to celebrate his birthday in any other way. 'It won't be different from any other day,' he said.

Arthur fully intended to coach the boys at Epsom College in 1972 but some quiet words from the College administration persuaded him that it would be in everyone's interest to retire. At seventy years old, the College had become anxious about his reliability and his general demeanour was thought to be setting a bad example to the boys. The College set up an appeal fund for his retirement and also presented him with a tankard inscribed:

'To Arthur Wellard from Epsom College Cricketers 1972. Many Thanks'

Quite a number of ex-pupils made the effort to attend his presentation party and it was a great occasion for swapping Arthur Wellard anecdotes. They would remember how supportive he had been, his tips for the horses, his wicked sense of humour and the way he would playfully throw a ball in such a devious way that it would curve in the air and could not be caught. They would remember as well the encouragement he gave them whilst umpiring the 1st X1 fixtures. He was not adverse to whispering 'corner of the mouth' assessments of the opposing batsman's weakness although he was never biased in his umpiring. There were always friendly words of encouragement for the opposition as Huw George remembers when playing for Dulwich College against Epsom. Arthur quietly said 'Well bowled, son' after a particularly useful dismissal; it was something the opponent's umpire usually did not say. Gerry Wells-Cole who was a pupil at Epsom College in the early sixties, has one splendid memory of Arthur in the nets. It provides an excellent illustration of his bowling skills and captures a little of his sense of humour:

Our school captain was a young man called Maurice Manasseh. *[Oxford University Blue 1964 and Middlesex 1964-7]* He had been in particular fine form and had scored, I think, three centuries in a row for the school. He was in the nets and treating the school's main bowlers with disdain.

Arthur was running the nets and decided to bowl a few off-breaks to Maurice. He bowled three or four balls which Maurice smashed through the cover/extra-cover area. Maurice was full of himself and shouted to Arthur, 'Honeymoon stuff!' Arthur then said to us, 'watch this.' He bowled another off-break, slightly slower than the previous balls which pitched three or four inches shorter. Maurice's eyes lit up as he attempted another cover drive. He failed to anticipate the length and was bowled 'neck and crop' between bat and pad. Arthur just burst out laughing along with the rest of us and this brought Maurice down to earth with a bump!

Derek Fenner, who was cricket master at the College remembers that they managed to get Arthur to the wicket at least once. He was protesting that he would not be able to see the ball yet immediately hit a vast six, which soared way over the trees that surround the ground. To coincide with Arthur's retirement, Derek wrote this of him in the College magazine:

All Epsom cricketers of the last fifteen years will be sad to hear that Arthur Wellard has retired from the post of cricket coach at the College. He took over from Larry D'Arcy in 1958 and immediately established himself as a perceptive coach, a stern critic of the idle and the rash, as knowledgeable about the game as any cricketer I have ever met and a confident but possibly less knowledgeable racing tipster.
It is no co-incidence that the success of Epsom sides in recent years has been based on good fast bowling and fluent batting. At the age of 68, though less active than formerly, Arthur was still wobbling the ball both ways in the air and off the ground, bamboozling in the nets another generation of 1st eleven cricketers. He was at his best with the senior boys and many will remember his penetrating analysis of opposition batsmen – he could usually spot a weakness within two overs – and will remember with feeling the fielding practice in which he demonstrated his unbelievable powerful underarm flick which many an aspiring slip fieldsman has narrowly avoided taking straight between the eyes.
But the joy was, and is, to listen to him talking about the game, usually over a modicum of ale; on a personal note I shall always have pleasant memories of the quiet half hours spent with him and a pint regaining strength after an exhausting afternoon in the nets.

Arthur was not unduly upset to be leaving Epsom College. He was well aware that his contribution in recent years had diminished but as in most things concerning his life, Arthur needed someone else to make the decision for him. He carried on at the Middlesex school despite the travelling which would have been exhausting for a much younger man.

Arthur's release by Epsom College did make it easier to consider another holiday in 1973. Bill Andrews had been pestering Arthur ever since their last visit in 1968 and so the Wellards returned to Weston-Super-Mare. The timing of the visit had, of course, to coincide with festival week at the beginning of August. As with Arthur's previous visit, there was plenty of interest in his return. Arthur and Bill were at the festival every day; Bill took the opportunity to publicise his new autobiography, Arthur spent the time renewing old acquaintances.

For the Somerset public it was a chance to pay their respects and many a middle-aged man persuaded his offspring to ask for the autograph of the 'old man sitting in the deckchair'; Arthur would always oblige. Despite Arthur's age he was easy to recognise. His hair may have thinned but it had retained its colour and characteristic centre-parting. He may have acquired some extra weight, particularly around the middle, but his bearing was much the same and his back as straight as ever. He was also the same snappy dresser. His ties were just as loud and his well-cut sports jacket, immaculately creased trousers and highly polished shoes set him apart from the holiday crowds. There was never any chance of mistaking Arthur Wellard. One of the highlights of the visit was a reunion at Clarence Park, which Bill had organised with Bertie Buse, Harold Gimblett and Horace Hazell. A few pints were supped that day!

Arthur was now in his seventy-first year but still continued to play social cricket. The players were glad to have him play and were always tolerant of his increasingly bent arm and fielding limitations. He could still take spectacular catches but his success was based on experience and instinct as opposed to being able to see the ball. He never needed any persuasion to play cricket and continued to play for anyone who was short of a player, just as long as transport was provided and he was not asked to pay for his tea. It was said that if you played cricket in the home counties you would usually come across Arthur in the ranks of the opposition at some stage of the season. As far as can be made out from the Sutton Cricket Club records,

Arthur played his last game for Sutton in cricket week, 1973 but he continued with the odd charity or celebrity match.

Arthur even turned out for an Old England X1 as late as August 1973. The limited-overs match, which was sponsored by the *Evening Standard,* was played at the Oval on a hot summer's day. The match was against the victorious England Ladies X1 who had just triumphed in the first World Cup. The Old England X1 included Len Hutton, Denis Compton, Godfrey Evans and Harold Gimblett. The men just managed to beat the ladies with one ball to spare although it has to be recorded that the men had a ten-over handicap. Arthur was not required to bat, which no doubt disappointed the crowd of about five thousand but he did bowl four overs for just seven runs.

It was through his cricket with Sutton Cricket Club that Arthur first became involved with the Gaieties Cricket Club, a wandering band of cricketers with theatrical leanings and captained by Laurie Lupino Lane. The Gaieties had a regular fixture with Sutton Cricket Club and Arthur played against them on several occasions. Arthur first started to play for the Gaieties on a regular basis in the late sixties and continued playing until 1975 when he took to umpiring their games. Arthur's contribution to Gaieties cricket was valued for the advice and guidance that was freely given, both on and off the field. Arthur had seen and done everything in cricket and won every honour so for many of the team, mixing in his company was sufficient reason for his inclusion in the side. Arthur was always fine company, always ready with a story to tell and the sessions in the bar after the match were highly prized except possibly for when the cards came out. The Gaieties team quickly learnt, like their Somerset and Sutton predecessors, that it did not make sense to play poker with Arthur. In fact, at one Gaieties AGM, a whole hour was devoted to discussing a ban on Arthur bringing his cards to matches!

One of the key members of the Gaieties team was the actor, Robert East. He was a key member in the sense of his playing ability but also performed the essential function of 'official chauffeur'. Robert East remembers Arthur with great affection:

I first met Arthur when I was still at school and playing for Surrey Club and Ground against a team somewhere in South London. He was over sixty and still a fine figure of a man, built like a village blacksmith and with the de rigeuer centre parting of a pre-war professional sportsman.

I went out to bat and Arthur ran up to bowl, or perhaps ambled is a better word. I thought I'll soon see this old boy off; poor old sod, he'd be better off with his feet up in the pavilion. I think I faced five balls and I managed to lay a bat on only the last one. Not much of a bat, though, as I was caught at slip. Even at sixty, off a five yard run, Arthur could still make the ball move both ways in the air and off the seam.

Five years later I played my first match for the Gaieties. Actually I didn't play; nobody played because we were rained off, so a card school was formed and I was introduced to another of Arthur's talents. Three hours later and with half my week's wages in his pocket he said, 'Well, who's going to give me a lift home, then?' Who else, of course, but Muggins. I dropped him off in Sutton and he weaved his way up the garden path. 'See you next week, son.' He was well pleased; a nice bit of pocket money and he'd found his chauffeur for the season.

So I'd drop him off every Sunday night and help him out of the car and point him towards his door. His path was long, crazily paved and on a steady incline up the garden he loved and cared for. Sometimes the beer had taken its toll and he'd need my shoulder to lean on. One night after a particular heavy session I said did he want a hand and he loftily waved me away. 'I'm all right, son. See you next week.' I drove away as he lurched up the path.

There was something about that lurch that made me ask him next Sunday when I picked him up if he'd been all right the previous week. 'Bit of a crisis half way up the path, son. Lost my bearings. Must have fallen in the hedge. God knows how long I was there. Woke up soaking wet and the missus standing there in her nighty. She wasn't best pleased. I'll have to go a bit easy tonight.' I don't recall him going easy. The same several buckets of booze he always had!

Harold Pinter, the playwright, was another active member of the Gaieties side and became good friends with Arthur. He wrote a moving tribute to him, full of stories and conversations, variously described in this book, which bring this colourful old cricketer to life. Arthur played his last game for the Gaieties in 1975, Harold Pinter records:

By this time his arm was low and discernably crooked and his bowling was accompanied by a remarkable range of grunts. He was also naturally, slow, but his variation in length still asked questions of the batsman and he could still move one away, late. But he could now be hit and he could no longer see the ball quickly enough to catch it. He retired from the field at the age of seventy-three and became our umpire. He had been playing cricket for some fifty years.

Arthur continued to coach at the Middlesex School until about 1975. Peter Atkins, a coaching contemporary, remembers that towards the end of his time at the school, Arthur needed a chair to sit on while taking a lesson because he could not stand for too long. Peter has a vivid memory of Arthur having to hang on to the side netting, such was the effort of bowling. He had been a great influence with the schoolchildren and the young Middlesex professionals, like Keith Jones who was successfully taught to swing the ball both ways. There was also one particular Thursday afternoon group of club cricketers that would regularly persuade Arthur to carry on the lessons in the bar afterwards. Arthur was usually the last to leave on such occasions. However, by 1975, he had slowed to the extent that Don Bennett advised him it was time to pack it in. Arthur replied, 'I know Don, I've been thinking that for some time.'

Despite giving up coaching, Arthur still led an active life by the standards of a septuagenarian. He had not finished with cricket entirely as he continued his links with Sutton Cricket Club. During the week he had his garden, which was his pride and joy. He grew all manner of vegetables which Jack, ever careful with the pennies, would bottle or freeze and he also had a great passion for growing chrysanthemums. His day followed a set routine and when not gardening, he would walk the short distance to Sutton High Street where the newsagents, the bookmakers and the *Cricketers Arms* were conveniently sited. Mr Jim Beard, a near neighbour, remembers sharing cricket conversations and nicely laced coffees in Arthur's garden. He could also set his clock by the times Arthur walked up and down Benhilton Gardens on his several daily trips to the High Street. At weekends he would wait for the designated 'chauffeur' that would arrive to take him to the cricket club.

There was still at least one cricket match left in him for which he needed no persuasion to play. The match was appropriately held at Clarence Park, the scene of his many triumphs. It was played in August 1975 and the trip to Weston-Super-Mare would be his third and final return to the West Country since his days with Somerset had ended. He had been invited to play for Old Somerset versus a Celebrities X1 in a match which was part of Somerset County Cricket Club's centenary celebrations. Den Smith was the Area County Cricket Chairman at the time and was designated to act as Arthur's chauffeur:

I collected Arthur from the station with Bill Andrews in the car. En route, I had to call at the turf accountants so that Arthur could place his bets for the day! I was also warned to be careful of his 'luggage' which was precious and breakable - it was certainly heavy!!

The baggage probably included Arthur's sustenance for the day. The after-match drinks were supplied by Harold Stephenson's brewery interests and a buffet was held in the adjoining Church Hall, with the vicar's enthusiastic agreement. The match was a great success and a large crowd turned out to welcome their old heroes. David Foot was privileged to share the field with Arthur and remembers that Arthur opened the bowling with Bill Andrews amid moist eyes and laughter. The arms were no longer quite at 12 o'clock! Trevor Jones who was also playing for Old Somerset, remembers that Harold Stephenson was standing up to Arthur's bowling when the inevitable happened. Harold dropped a catch. Arthur stood motionless, hands on hips, a disbelieving frown on his face. For a split second, the years rolled back to the bright August festival days of some five decades past. Arthur on his way back to his mark, turned to Harold Gimblett, who was fielding at mid-off and said, 'things haven't changed much down here have they cock!'

Arthur returned to Sutton with many fine memories and acquaintances renewed. There were promises of a further return but as he made the familiar journey back to London, he must have realised that this would be his last visit to Somerset. There were no further trips to the County which had adopted him as one of their own. Sadly, it would also be the last time he would see Bill Andrews and his other Somerset colleagues. Arthur returned to Sutton, to his garden, to the *Cricketers Arms*, to his bookies and to his cricket. He had everything he needed, within close proximity, to make his life happy and would have lived contentedly in Sutton for the rest of his days. However, within a year, Arthur and Jack made their final move to Eastbourne; it was hardly a move of Arthur's choosing.

12.

All at sea

JACK WELLARD MADE UP HER MIND TO LEAVE SUTTON the minute
she was told about her sister's retirement plans. Betty and
her family realised an ambition by acquiring *The Smuggler's
Wheel*, a restaurant in the village of Boreham Street, near
Herstmonceux, East Sussex. They moved to East Sussex in
February 1977 while Jack started looking for property in
the same area. It would not have been necessary to move had
Arthur or Jack been able to drive but the journey by public
transport would have been too much for them. Arthur was
reluctant to move but knew that resistance was pointless
since Jack always got her way in the end. Arthur explained
his dilemma to Robert East, his Gaieties Cricket Club
chauffeur, over an after-match pint:

The missus wants to be near her sister, son. She's read me the riot act.
She's going whether I like it or not. I'm not keen but I owe it to her
after all those summers on her own.

Jack would have gone without Arthur; this was no idle
threat. Arthur prudently went along with Jack's wishes, his
conscience eased and his duty done. He was also missing
Betty and her family more than he would care to admit. He
had always been very close to his sister-in-law and doted
on his three nieces who were substitutes for the children
he never had. Arthur loved children and had joked about
wanting enough children to field a cricket team. Jack,
however, had not been keen on the idea. She was very
fastidious and extremely house-proud; children would have
interfered with her well-ordered life. The Wellards had
also spent so much of their married life apart that the

time had never been quite right. They would both live to regret not having a family of their own and therefore the contact with Jack's sister and her family was all the more important.

Jack set about finding a new home. She took a bus to Eastbourne on her own and, such was the desire to move at all cost, settled for virtually the first property on view. It was a small bungalow at 113 Gainsborough Crescent in Langney, which is on the outskirts of Eastbourne. The bungalow was ten miles away from Boreham Street and still not easily accessible by public transport but it was close enough to guarantee regular contact with her family. The Wellards completed their move later in the year severing their twenty-five-year link with Sutton.

Once the move had been completed, the first item on Arthur's agenda was to locate a new watering hole. As this was a modern housing estate, the choice was limited and he settled on *The Martello*, a short distance from the bungalow in Langney Rise. Few lunchtimes went by without Arthur making an appearance at the public house. He seemed contented enough with the new surroundings and his garden but he missed his cricket. Arthur decided not to get involved with a local cricket club and if the Wellards left the confines of their bungalow for any length of time, it was usually to visit or stay with Jack's sister at *The Smuggler's Wheel*. They were frequent visitors to the restaurant and Arthur spent many a pleasant hour in the restaurant bar or in *The Bull's Head* nearby, where he could usually be persuaded to reminisce about his old cricketing days.

Arthur would still have a modest flutter on the horses and as an avid reader of westerns was a regular customer at the local library. Apart from these interests there was nothing else to occupy his mind. He was not well-read and rarely glanced beyond the back pages of the tabloid newspapers. He had also never taken an interest in television, except occasionally when there was horse racing or cricket to watch. Arthur was not impressed with what he saw of the modern game but was a keen supporter of one-day cricket and regretted not having the opportunity to play it in his professional days. There is absolutely no doubt that he would have excelled in this type of cricket. He was a great admirer of Vivian Richards, although he would quickly add that Bradman took some beating and that Jack Hobbs was the best of the lot. Once, while watching a televised cricket match, he was greatly amused to be described as a hard-drinking gambler during an interval discussion. Jack did not see the funny side of the remark and was most indignant when a viewer sent Arthur a temperance leaflet to 'save his soul'. The television interview had given quite the wrong impression of Arthur but he didn't mind one bit and actually took it as a compliment.

The days and months passed quietly for the Wellards, the opportunities for socialising being mainly limited to the times spent at *The Smuggler's Wheel*. Arthur and Jack had their Golden Wedding Anniversary celebrations here in September 1978 and had a small party for family and friends. It seems almost a miracle that this oddly suited couple managed to reach such a milestone but then, they had spent as much time apart as together!

Arthur did not suffer any serious illness in his lifetime and he remained in extremely good health for a man in his late seventies. However, as time went by, he appeared to lose interest in life. He stopped reading altogether and became more and more withdrawn. Everything was too much effort for him and even an invitation to attend the Anglo-Australia Centenary Test celebrations in late August 1980 failed to arouse any interest. There were invitations to the Lord's Taverners Dinner and the TCCB pre-match banquet. He was also invited to attend the Test match on the Saturday where 163 English and Australian Test and former Test players gathered for the group photograph. There were seventy-seven surviving former Test players who did not make the picture but most of these took some part in the celebrations. Arthur, along with thirteen other English players, missed the whole event.

His family encouraged him to attend and he had many offers of transportation but no amount of pleading could persuade him to take up the invitation. Arthur would not have been attracted by the official functions, which were never his forte but turning down the opportunity to meet team-mates and old adversaries was out of character. His steadfast refusal served only to confirm the family's worst fears that he had given up on life.

The Wellard visits to Boreham Street had become less frequent but they always stayed for public holidays, especially Christmas and New Year when the whole family, including Arthur's great nephews and nieces, would gather. The Christmas of 1980 was typical of these gatherings. They had a quiet and enjoyable Christmas and were staying on at the restaurant to see in the New Year. The restaurant was busy and in the throes of preparing for a New Year's Eve dinner dance.

On Monday the 29th December, Arthur was in good form. He consumed a generously proportioned lunch and had his customary afternoon siesta. Later in the evening, Arthur seemed his old self as he nonchalantly dominated a family game of snooker. The adults finished the evening with a game of solo before they retired to bed around 2.00am. Several hours later, Jack woke the rest of the family to say that Arthur was not well. He was cold and appeared disorientated. The doctor suspected that he had suffered a heart attack so arranged for an ambulance to take him to hospital. As Arthur left in the ambulance he whispered to his brother-in-law, 'I'm no good for anyone now Fred, do what you can for Jack.'

Arthur was taken to St. Mary's Hospital in Eastbourne where he showed no signs of likely recovery. He was barely conscious throughout and died from heart and renal failure in the early hours of the morning of the 31st December 1980. It was too late to cancel the New Year's Eve celebrations at *The Smuggler's Wheel*. Jack was enlisted to help with the preparations in order to keep her mind occupied; she even managed a dance later that evening!

Bill Andrews was one of the first people to be told of Arthur's death. He was deeply upset by the news and set about trying to organise a proper tribute for his great friend. Bill was shocked by the indifference he encountered, particularly from the Somerset County Cricket Club, which showed little interest in honouring one of their most famous and popular cricketers. Bill Andrews, Horace Hazell and the Somerset scorer, Tom Tout attended the funeral as friends and at least gave some semblance of representation from the club that Arthur served so well.

The funeral was held in the Chapel at Langney Cemetery, just a short distance, across Langney Rise, from Arthur's bungalow. Kent County Cricket Club sent a representative - whom Bill Andrews disdainfully referred to as their 'Pools Organiser' - but the cricketing authorities were otherwise conspicuous by their absence. The small Chapel was nevertheless full of friends and representatives from various bodies such as Sutton Cricket Club and Epsom College. Arthur was buried in Langney Cemetery and the mourners adjourned to *The Smuggler's Wheel*. It was a send-off that would have brought a smile to Arthur's face.

Bill Andrews still felt aggrieved by Somerset's lack of interest and talked expansively about arranging a memorial service on his return. Arthur would not have cared in the slightest but it seemed to matter a great deal to Bill. He got quite drunk at *The Smuggler's Wheel* and was moved to apologise when he wrote to Jack later. Nothing went right for Bill that day and his party had a disastrous return journey. They lost their way about three times and had a puncture in the early hours of the morning, still some sixty miles from Weston-Super-Mare.

Bill redoubled his efforts to obtain some appropriate recognition of Arthur's contribution to Somerset cricket. He was hopeful of a big write-up in *The Somerset County Gazette* and lobbied for the memorial service. He wrote to Jack that 'they had one for Gimblett so they must have one for Arthur.' Neither the write-up nor the service ever materialised and Bill had to accept that Arthur's death was of only passing interest to the present generation of Somerset supporters. He was still upset by the slight on Arthur's memory and wrote a depressing letter to Jack that included the following comments:

You know I would not have missed coming to Eastbourne on this sad occasion - I was ashamed of Somerset - but it is typical of them - that at least the President or Chairman should have been there too.

Bill never got over the indifference shown by Somerset County Cricket Club towards Arthur Wellard [*it is still not too late for Somerset to make amends!*]. It was an unpalatable reminder of his own mortality and the transient nature of sporting fame. It played on his mind and probably contributed to his own decline. Bill became increasingly depressed and reclusive during the remaining years of his life.

There were, of course, many fine tributes paid to Arthur in the obituary notices that appeared in local and national papers. The most moving and heartfelt tribute comes from the pen of his one-time team-mate and protégé, Eric Hill. It is appropriate that these should be the last words on Arthur Wellard:

He enjoyed a good joke as he enjoyed a good anything. Above all, he was a happy chap doing a job he loved. A real gentle-man, he came from a rarely-used mould into that happily large library of memorable Somerset cricket characters. Unforgettable Arthur Wellard - how I love the thought of him talking cricket through all eternity with the great ones, and perhaps occasionally offering his old greeting 'Wotcher, cock' as W.G. comes in to take the chair.

Jack Wellard survived her husband by thirteen years, relying on the support of her sister to the end. She died on the 10th August 1994 at the age of ninety-two and now lies with Arthur in Langney Cemetery.

Statistical Appendix

A.W.WELLARD - FIRST-CLASS BATTING STATISTICS (CAREER)

Season	Inns	N.O.	Runs	H.S.	Ave.	50s	100
1927 Som	2	–	32	29	16.00	–	–
1928 Som	1	–	1	1	1.00	–	–
1929 Som	44	6	515	75	13.55	3	–
1930 Som	39	5	775	75	22.79	4	–
1931 Som	46	–	756	83	}16.55	2	–
1931 Other	2	1	22	16	}	–	–
1932 Som	41	4	765	93*	20.68	3	–
1933 Som	43	3	1055	77	26.38	9	–
1934 Som	41	1	922	112	}23.60	2	1
1934 Other	3	–	93	91	}	1	–
1935 Som	40	2	1232	112	}31.32	9	1
1935 Other	6	1	115	37	}	–	–
1936 Som	45	1	815	86	}19.18	5	–
1936 Other	6	1	125	65	}	1	–
1937 Som	53	4	901	91*	}18.73	5	–
1937 Eng	2	–	5	5	}	–	–
1937 Other	5	–	143	66	}	1	–
1937/8 Ind	16	1	433	90	28.87	2	–
1938 Som	42	1	779	73*	}19.64	4	–
1938 Eng	2	–	42	38	}	–	–
1938 Other	2	–	63	42	}	–	–
1939 Som	35	3	652	87	20.37	2	–
1946 Som	32	2	531	74	}16.97	4	–
1946 Other	2	–	12	7	}	–	–
1947 Som	40	1	521	46	13.36	–	–
1948 Som	37	5	530	60	16.56	1	–
1949 Som	46	3	603	54	14.02	1	–
1950 Som	6	1	47	19*	9.40	–	–
TOTAL	679	46	12485	112	19.72	59	2

A.W.WELLARD - FIRST-CLASS BOWLING STATISTICS (CAREER)

Season	Overs	Mdns	Runs	Wkts	Ave.	five wkts/ inns	ten wkts/ match
1927 Som	23.0	4	39	1	39.00	–	–
1928 Som	38.0	11	65	4	16.25	–	–
1929 Som	1126.1	274	2802	131	21.39	9	3
1930 Som	655.2	143	1710	37	46.22	1	–
1931 Som	1022.3	254	2295	85	}26.03	5	–
1931 Other	26.4	3	74	6	}	1	–
1932 Som	666.2	141	1643	43	38.21	–	–
1933 Som	1005.2	223	2660	104	25.58	6	2
1934 Som	751.3	137	2386	54	}41.79	2	–
1934 Other	59.2	10	205	8	}	–	–
1935 Som	803.5	163	2166	105	}20.68	9	0
1935 Other	68.5	18	192	9	}	–	–
1936 Som	946.1	188	2606	143	}19.32	14	3
1936 Other	68.0	14	215	3	}	–	–
1937 Som	1158.5	203	3320	140	}23.56	9	3
1937 Eng	44.0	6	111	4	}	–	–
1937 Other	73.2	11	244	12	}	–	–
1937/8 Ind	321.2	40	1022	47	21.74	2	–
1938 Som	1170.4	232	3252	169	}20.30	17	5
1938 Eng	32.0	3	126	3	}	–	–
1938 Other	33.0	5	113	0	}	–	–
1939 Som	850.0	131	2748	130	21.14	10	4
1946 Som	941.0	230	2216	119	}18.69	10	2
1946 Other	42.0	9	102	5	}	–	–
1947 Som	856.4	181	2187	93	23.52	8	1
1948 Som	735.3	157	1767	62	28.50	1	–
1949 Som	1020.1	221	2725	87	31.32	4	1
1950 Som	145.2	31	311	10	31.10	–	–
TOTAL	14684.5	3043	39302	1614	24.35	108	24

A.W.WELLARD - FIRST-CLASS BATTING (1935 SEASON)

Opponents	Venue	Scores	6s	4s	5s
Surrey	Oval	99 & 37*	6	11	–
Northamptonshire	Taunton	38 & 2	–	5	–
Essex	Frome	21	–	3	–
Middlesex	Lord's	45 & 7	1	4	–
Nottinghamshire	Trent Bridge	68	4	7	–
Sussex	Hove	6*	–	–	–
Derbyshire	Derby	8 & 8	–	2	–
Kent	Taunton	1 & 75	5	5	–
Gloucestershire	Bath	3 & 10	–	1	–
South Africa	Bath	29 & 5	1	4	–
Worcestershire	Dudley	38 & 0	2	1	–
Glamorgan	Pontypridd	20 & 0	2	1	–
Worcestershire	Wells	0 & 50	4	4	–
Essex	Clacton	57 & 83	9	8	1
Kent	Maidstone	74 & 70	10	13	1
Middlesex	Taunton	10 & 14	2	–	–
Hampshire	Southampton	1	–	–	–
Lancashire	W-S-M	44 & 12	2	4	–
Glamorgan	W-S-M	21	–	3	–
Nottinghamshire	W-S-M	21 & 24	3	4	–
Surrey	Yeovil	41 & 8	3	3	–
Lancashire	Old Trafford	112	5	10	–
Derbyshire	Taunton	0 & 2	–	–	–
Sussex	Taunton	68	3	8	–
Total - Somerset		1232	62	101	2
Players v Gents	Folkestone	9 & 37	3		
Leveson Gower X1	Scarborough	35*& 16	1		
Rest v Yorkshire	Oval	16 & 2			
TOTAL		1347	66		

A.W.WELLARD - MISCELLANEOUS STATISTICS

Arthur Wellard played 417 first-class matches between 1927 and 1950

He took 375 catches in first-class cricket

He hit fifty sixes or more in a season on four occasions (1933, 1935, 1936 and 1938)

He hit three or more consecutive sixes in an over on four occasions. He hit five sixes in an over twice (1936 & 1938)

He achieved the "cricketers double" of 1,000 runs and 100 wickets in a season for Somerset on two occasions (1933 and 1935) and additionally achieved the double in all first-class cricket during the 1937 season

He took over 100 wickets in a season on eight occasions, including the six successive championship seasons, 1935 to 1946

His career best bowling figures were 8-52 in an innings and 15-101 in a match, obtained in the same match (Somerset v Worcestershire, Bath, 28 June - 1 July, 1947)

He was one of the five *Wisden* Cricketers of the Year in 1936

He played for the Players against the Gentlemen on six occasions between 1931 and 1938

He played for H.D.G.Leveson Gower's X1 on five occasions between 1935 and 1937

He played twice for England (1937 & 1938). He was chosen to tour India in 1939 but the series was cancelled because of the Second World War

Bibliography

Books

Tom Alderson *Cricket by the Lune* (Lancaster, The Club 1985)
W.E.(Bill)Alley *My incredible innings* (Pelham Books 1969)
Bill Andrews *The hand that bowled Bradman* (Macdonald 1973)
Brian Bearshaw *The big hitters* (Queen Anne Press 1986)
Alec and Eric Bedser *Our cricket story* (Evans 1951)
Mihir Bose *A history of Indian cricket* (Andre Deutch 1990)
Don Bradman *Farewell to cricket* (Hodder & Stoughton 1950)
Gerald Brodribb *Hit for six* (Heinemann 1960)
Denis Compton *Playing for England* (Sampson Low 1948)
W.J.(Bill)Edrich *Round the wicket* (Muller 1959)
W.J.Edrich *Cricket heritage* (Paul 1948)
David Foot *Sunshine, sixes and cider: The history of
     Somerset cricket* (David & Charles 1986)
Alf Gover *The long innings* (Pelham Books 1991)
Roger Hill *History of Bexley Cricket Club* (1990)
E.R.T.Holmes *Flannelled foolishness* (Hollis & Carter 1957)
Michael Marshall *Gentlemen & Players* (Grafton Books 1987)
Playfair Cricket Annual
Ron Roberts *Sixty years of Somerset cricket* (Westway 1952)
Peter Roebuck *From Sammy to Jimmy* (Partridge Press 1991)
Ben Travers *94 Declared* (Elm Tree Books 1981)
Sir Pelham Warner *Cricket between two wars* (Chatto & Windus
     1942)
Sir Pelham Warner *Gentlemen v Players 1806-1949* (Harrup
     1950)
Wisden Cricketers' Almanack
Norman Yardley *Cricket campaigns* (Stanley Paul 1950)

Periodicals and newspapers

The Cricketer
The Daily Telegraph
The Somerset County Gazette
The Times
Wisden Cricket Monthly

Index